Letters o

John Cal

Letters of John Calvin

Selected from the

Bonnet Edition

with an introductory
biographical sketch

THE BANNER OF TRUTH TRUST

THE BANNER OF TRUTH TRUST

3 Murrayfield Road, Edinburgh EH12 6EL
P.O. Box 621, Carlisle, Pennsylvania 17013, U.S.A.

First published in 1855-7
This selection first published by The Banner of Truth Trust 1980
© 1980 The Banner of Truth Trust
ISBN 0 85151 323 9

Typeset, printed and bound in Great Britain by
Hazell Watson & Viney Ltd, Aylesbury, Bucks

CONTENTS

INTRODUCTION

Few great Christian leaders have suffered quite so much misunderstanding as John Calvin. He has often been dismissed as a theologian without humanity. In fact the very reverse is much nearer the truth, as the pages which follow amply demonstrate. He was a man of deep and lasting affection, passionately concerned for the cause of Christ in the world; a man who burned himself out for the gospel.

But this picture of Calvin the man, and the pastor, is often unknown because of a lack of knowledge of his writings. The true picture shines through his commentaries and sermons, and appears frequently in his famous *Institutes of the Christian Religion*, when carefully read. Yet it nowhere appears quite so vividly as in his long-out-of-print letters. It is hoped that the selection of these now presented will introduce many Christians to a fellow-Christian whose teaching and example has much to say to the church of today.

The seventy letters included here have been chosen from the 19th-century edition of Calvin's Letters, published in four volumes, and edited by Jules Bonnet. Apart from a minimum of alteration the text and notes of that edition are here reprinted, although, of course, this represents only one tenth of Bonnet's edition. As is the case with the older translations of Calvin's *Institutes of the Christian Religion*, Bonnet's edition of Calvin's letters abounds in long sentences and sometimes heavy language. The only proper alternative to reproducing the letters as they stand would have been the enormous task of a new translation which the publishers could not have undertaken. Even in a century-old translation Calvin can be heard to speak!

The principles on which the selection has been made have

been very simple. Several series of letters have been included. The correspondence with Farel illustrates the power and spirit of their friendship in the work of the ministry; the letters to the Five Martyrs of Lyons shows Calvin's deep compassion; those to Melanchthon annotate his continuing concern that the famous Lutheran might stand more boldly in the truth. These, along with letters to comfort the bereaved, show something of his true pastoral spirit. To them, a number of other letters to friends are added, with a selection of the correspondence which demonstrates his deep interest in the Reformation in England, and the wide circle of his knowledge of the church throughout Europe. Together they show a man whose heart belonged to Christ.

The Early Years

John Calvin is the anglicised form of the Latin *Johannes Calvinus*, and the French *Jean Cauvin*. For although he spent half of his life in the city of Geneva, Switzerland, Calvin was born and bred in France, as he was later to write, 'unus de plebe' – one of the common people. His grandfather had been a boatman, and perhaps also a cooper, on the river Oise, near the town of Noyon, 50 miles North-East of Paris. About the year 1480, Gérard Calvin, John's father, had moved into Noyon itself, and had steadily worked his way up the ladder of employment in the bureaucracy of the local cathedral. He was already forty years old when he married the reputedly beautiful and religious Jeanne Le Franc. John was their second son and was born on July 10, 1509. Within a matter of five or six years his mother died. Calvin and his brothers were then left to the care of his father, and within a short space of time, to a step-mother, of whom little is known.

Being a relatively important figure in the machinery of the Noyon cathedral, Gerard Calvin was able to procure *two* educational benefits for his sons. One was that they were educated within the aristocratic circle of the children of the local Bishop's family. John consequently became familiar with the disciplines of a superior private education. The rigours of personal tuition, and the advantages of supervision were not wasted on him. He seems to have had such a hunger for learning that he was able to take full advantage of it, and, according to one source, 'outstripped the others, thanks to his quick intelligence and excellent memory'. The second advantage he gained from his father's influence was the gift of a benefice in the local cathedral, when he was about 11 or 12, which served as a University scholarship for the young man whose father intended him for the priesthood.

Shortly after receiving this benefice, Calvin set out for Paris. There is some doubt about what age he was. It is usually suggested he was 14, and the year was 1523, but bright pupils often went to University at 11 or 12. It therefore seems fairly unlikely that Calvin's matriculation was so long delayed, and he may well have gone to Paris in 1520 or 1521, first to prepare himself to read for the degree in Arts, which was largely if not entirely a study of philosophy. He entered the *Collège de la Marche* to pursue a foundation course in Latin grammar, reading, writing, and speech.

It was here that one of the early providences of his life can be seen. Calvin, who was to write so much in Latin, and whose Latin style therefore was a matter of great importance, was taught by Mathurin Cordier who was among the finest teachers of Latin then living. In fact his Latin Grammar book was still being used at the beginning of the 19th century! Calvin himself recognized how important this teaching was to him, and dedicated his commentary on 1 Thessalonians to Cordier in 1550:

> ... it was under your guidance that I entered on a course of studies, and made progress at least to the extent of being of some benefit to the Church of God. When my father sent me as a boy to Paris I had done only the rudiments of Latin. For a short time, however, you were an instructor sent to me by God to teach me the true method of learning, so that I might afterwards be a little more proficient ... for me it was a singular kindness of God that I happened to have a propitious beginning to my studies ... It was my desire to testify to posterity that, if they derive any profit from my writings, they should know that to some extent you are responsible for them.

Having completed this elementary course, he then moved to the *Collège de Montaigu*, which was renowned for two things: the strictness of the discipline, and the taste of the school dinners! Neither gave much pleasure to the students.

Again we find that a foundation for his future experience was being laid. Rising was at 4.00 a.m. each morning for the morning service. This was followed by a lecture until 6.00 a.m., and morning mass. After breakfast, the main class of the day came, from 8.00–10.00 a.m., and then an hour was devoted to discussion of the subject. Dinner was then taken, and was accompanied by public reading from Scripture, or the life of some saint, and then another hour was spent before 1.00 p.m. on questions to ensure that the morning work had been assimilated. A rest period was allowed from 1.00–2.00, but it was often accompanied again by public readings! At 3.00 the main class for the afternoon was held until 5.00 p.m. Prayers, discussion of the afternoon lessons, and supper with more readings followed. Then, before bed at 8.00 or 9.00 p.m. more time was devoted to questions and discussion.

It must have been a cruel life for many students: but for someone of Calvin's capacious intellect it seems to have been the kind of discipline which he relished as a challenge. Certainly it would have been physically, mentally, and psychologically impossible for him to have sustained the output which marked his life without these foundations being laid in early life. Few men or women who do not exercise discipline in the early years are able to introduce it in later life. But the really significant thing with Calvin was not that he spent so many hours at the desk, but that his mind was disciplined to use them profitably. Indeed he developed the habit of going over all he had learned during the day before he went to sleep, and then, when he awoke, recalling it to memory, lest he forget it.

Many writers on Calvin's life suggest that it was the poor diet and the physical rigours of those days which largely con-

tributed to his later ill-health. By the age of 30 he was a frequent sufferer from asthmatic attacks, from migraine head-
aches, and indigestion. By the age of 50, he was a chronic
victim of arthritis, haemorrhages, pleurisy and a form of
tuberculosis. When he died it is reckoned, from all he says in
his letters, and the details of his biography by his friend
Theodore Beza, that he was suffering from something like 40
different ailments or diseases. And the astonishing thing is
that, almost to the end, he was able to keep up an enormous
output of work. Calvin's life was considerably restricted in its
movements, and sedentary in its nature. But it was powerfully
marked by what Paul calls 'The energy which God mightily
inspires within me' (Colossians 1.29).

Throughout this whole period, as Calvin himself later ad-
mits, he was 'stubbornly addicted to the papacy'. His studies
in philosophy and later in theology were in the tradition of
the Roman Church, and along the lines of the Medieval
scholastic theologies which, for all their intellectual interest,
were ultimately unable to show salvation to the souls of men.
Besides this, the whole discipline of the College was that of
a monastery for teenagers. There were regular periods for
confession of sins, and sins that were not confessed one's
fellow-students were encouraged to denounce in a weekly
examination of behaviour. It may have been from these, and
his rectitude in them, that Calvin came to receive the nick-
name 'the accusative case'. Then, again, Calvin was probably
taught, for a time at least, by the eminent theologian John
Major. By this time Luther's teaching was spreading rapidly
across Europe, and John Major was in the van of those who
opposed it. He wrote a commentary on the Gospels in which
he attacked Luther along with Wyclif and Hus, for their
teaching, and it may well be that it was in the course of his
mentor's attacks that Calvin first encountered the weight of
the teaching of the Reformation.

In due course Calvin graduated. Again there is some debate

about when he did so, but it must have been when he was about 17. By this time, however, his father had fallen out of favour with the Bishop, and, apparently in the hope of inflicting some kind of revenge, ordered John to abandon the idea of becoming a priest, and begin training to become a lawyer. No doubt, as Calvin says, he had one eye also to the fact that the law 'commonly raised those who followed it to wealth', and it may be that he also had an eye to his own retirement in the process!

For the next period of his life, John Calvin went to Orleans and pursued his legal studies for several years, again with marked success, to such a degree that, on occasions, his teachers allowed him opportunities to lecture to the students. This period was interspersed with a period in Bourges, and it may have been here that he entered on the second great phase of his life, when he was converted.

Conversion and Vocation

So little is known about Calvin's conversion that it is dated as far apart as 1529, when he was 20, and 1534, when he was 25. Every dating is really an educated guess. There is only one place, for certain, where he speaks of his experience at any length at all. It is in his Preface to his *Commentary on the Psalms*:

When I was as yet a very little boy, my father had destined me for the study of theology. But afterwards, when he considered that the legal profession commonly raised those who followed it to wealth, this prospect suddenly induced him to change his mind. Thus it came to pass, that I was withdrawn from the study of philosophy, and was put to the study of law. To this pursuit I endeavoured to apply myself, in obedience to the will of my father; but God, by the secret guidance of his providence, at length gave a different direction to my course. And first, since I was too obstinately addicted to the superstitions of Popery to be easily extricated from so profound an abyss of mire, God by a sudden conversion subdued and brought my mind to a teachable frame, which was more hardened in such matters than might have been expected from one at my early period of life.

That is almost all we know about what happened. Theodore Beza says in his early biography that one of the great influences on Calvin was his relation, Pierre Robert, known as Olivetanus, or 'Midnight Oil', but of this Calvin says nothing himself, even in his preface to his friend's translation of the New Testament into French. But when he does describe his own conversion, he also mentions what happened afterwards:

I was immediately inflamed with so intense a desire to make progress, that although I did not altogether leave off my studies, I yet pursued them with less ardour. I was quite surprised that, before a year had elapsed, all who had a desire after purer doctrine were continually coming to me to learn, although I myself was as yet but a mere novice and tyro. Being of a disposition somewhat unpolished and bashful, which led me always to love the shade and retirement, I then began to seek some secluded corner where I might be withdrawn from the public view; but so far from being able to accomplish the object of my desire, all my retreats were like public schools. In short . . . God so led me through different turnings and changes, that he never permitted me to rest in any place, until, in spite of my natural disposition, he brought me forth to public notice.

He was on his way to Strassburg, and since the most direct road he could take was shut up by a war, he had to go through Geneva, and stay there overnight. A man, who was later to defect to Rome, recognized him, went to William Farel, the leader of the Reformation in Geneva, and said: 'John Calvin, the author of *The Institutes of the Christian Religion*, is here!' Calvin was looking for seclusion for study. Farel came and told him that if he did not stay in Geneva, God would curse his peace. Calvin says:

> By this imprecation I was so stricken with terror, that I desisted from the journey which I had undertaken. I felt as if God had laid his mighty hand on me to arrest me.

And so he came to share in the ministry which was then being exercised in Geneva.

Two things had clearly conspired to make Farel lay his hand on Calvin. One was the tremendous need in Geneva itself. The other was that this young man, still in his mid-twenties, was the author of a classic work on Christian doctrine, which at that time bore the title.:

The Institute of the Christian Religion, Containing almost the whole sum of piety and whatever it is necessary to know in the doctrine of salvation.

The title seems awe-inspiring to us today, and there is no doubt that it is one of the greatest single works of theology ever written. But it is essentially a simple book.

Calvin was just turned 26 when he wrote its concluding pages, and it was published in March 1536. At that time it contained only six chapters, on the Commandments, the Creed, the Lord's Prayer, True and False Sacraments, and the Church. It was about three-quarters of the length of the New Testament, and was written as a defence of the faith of reformed Christians, and particularly those who were being persecuted. The later editions developed into the form of studies in Christian doctrine, which, Calvin believed, would open up to students of Scripture the whole message of the

Bible. He wrote in his 'Letter to the Reader' in the final edition of the *Institutes*:

> It has been my purpose in this labour to prepare and instruct candidates in sacred theology for the reading of the divine word, in order that they may be able both to have easy access to it and to advance in it without stumbling. For I believe I have so embraced the sum of religion in all its parts, and have arranged it in such order, that if anyone rightly grasps it, it will not be difficult for him to determine what he ought especially to seek in Scripture, and to what end he ought to relate its contents.

When, in later life, he was trying to revise it and perfect it, he did so in a house with six children. The retirement which he sought, he never found. The rest of his life was 'tumults' and 'labours'. Indeed, he was not long in Geneva before he found his way back to Strassburg an unhappy man.

The First Geneva Period

It was in 1536 that Calvin had taken up residence in Geneva, and began to share in William Farel's ministry. The experience of the pastoral ministry must have been a tremendous shock to his system, with all the preaching, counselling, visiting and comforting that was involved. Furthermore, it was not long before his ministry was opposed in the city. The Reformers aimed at the reformation of the Church according to the Word of God. In 1536 therefore they had drawn up a Confession of Faith, to be subscribed by all members of the churches. But such measures as these had to pass the city fathers, and although they accepted the Confession, they did little to implement it. The crisis came when the ministers said that those who did not sign it could not come to the Lord's Table for Communion. The Council ordered Calvin and Farel to toe the line, and one of the other pastors was imprisoned. The Reformers protested, and were forbidden to preach. There was rioting in the streets outside Calvin's house. Muskets were fired, abuse was hurled.

On Easter day, 1538, they preached in the churches, but refused to administer the Communion. On April 23rd they were ordered by the Council, on a majority vote, to leave the city within three days, and Calvin separated from his good friend Farel, and made his way to Strassburg. He later opened his heart to him about his feelings in those first two years of ministry:

> Although Geneva was a very troublesome province to me, the thought of deserting it never entered my mind. For I considered myself placed in that position by God, like a sentry at his post from which it would be impiety on my part were I to move a single step. Yet I think you would hardly believe me were I to relate for you even a small part of those annoyances, nay miseries, which we had to endure for a whole year. This I can truly testify that not a day passed in which I did not long for death ten times over. But as for leaving that Church to remove elsewhere, such a thought never came into my mind.

If ever a man showed the consecration of the shepherd who is willing to lay down his life for the sheep, it was surely John Calvin.

Ministry in Strassburg

In one sense the next period of his life was one of the happiest he knew. His congregation grew to about 500, he enjoyed the fellowship of some of the other leading minds of the reformation, like Martin Bucer; he took part in various debates, and became a figure of international importance in the reformed churches of Europe. He there wrote his great commentary on Romans. It was also in Strassburg that he married! He was extremely happily married, but like others, he found the process of finding a wife was not without its pains! Earlier in his life he seems to have taken a rather matter-of-fact view of marriage, or rather, of the values of a wife:

> I whom you see so hostile to celibacy, have never taken a wife, and I know not if I shall ever marry. If I did so, it would be in order to devote my time to the Lord by being the more relieved from the worries of daily life.

Some time later, when the matter was raised by his friends, he wrote to Farel:

> Always keep in mind what I seek to find in her; for I am not one of those insane lovers who embrace even the vices of those they are in love with, when they are smitten at first sight with a fine figure. The only beauty which allures me is this – that she be chaste, not too nice or fastidious, economical, patient, and likely to take care of my health.

These quotations may seem to be rather bleak in their view of marriage; but when they are taken together, they present a more balanced and biblical view of marriage than it is sometimes suggested Calvin held. He was a man whose body constantly needed medical attention, whose means were scanty, and who recognized that the wife who could live happily with a man so burdened with labours would need to have more than her fair share of ordinary human virtues!

Calvin's various friends did their best to find him a suitable wife. Their first choice he refused because she knew no French – she was also from an aristocratic background, and he was concerned about the difficulty she might find in adjusting to his life-style. He seems to have become engaged to the second choice, through the good offices of his brother, but when the wedding arrangements were made, some blemish was found in the lady's character, and the wedding was called off. Calvin then wisely took the matter into his own hands, and was married within a couple of months, to Idelette de Bure, the widow of a former Anabaptist, who already had two children. They had only one child – a premature baby, who died in infancy. He wrote out of his grief to a friend:

> The Lord has certainly inflicted a severe and bitter wound in the death of our baby son. But he is himself a Father, and knows best what is good for his children.

They had no more children, and his wife died in the ninth year of their marriage. Again he wrote:

> You know well how tender, or rather, soft, my mind is. Had not a powerful self-control been given to me I could not have borne up so long. And truly mine is no common source of grief. I have been bereaved of the best companion of my life, of one who, had it been so ordained, would have willingly shared not only my poverty, but even my death. During her lifetime she was the faithful helper of my ministry. From her I never experienced the slightest hindrance. She was never troublesome to me throughout the whole course of her illness, but was more anxious about her children than about herself.

So much for some of the details of his married life. In 1540 he had been invited back to Geneva. One of his letters carries this confession:

> There is no place under heaven that I am more afraid of – I would submit to death a hundred times rather than to that cross on which I had to die daily a thousand deaths.

But it is the Christian's pathway to die daily; to take up his cross day by day to follow Christ, and no writer has given clearer expression to what is involved in such self-denial than Calvin does in chapters 6–8 of Book III of the *Institutes*. He had learned such obedience by the things he suffered—and so, in September 1541 he took up residence in Geneva once again, and remained there until he had finished his earthly course.

The Second Genevan Period

The supporters of Farel had returned to power in the city councils, and he in turn had contacted Calvin and frequently urged on him his duty to return. Eventually in the October of 1540, he replied:

> If I had any choice I would rather do anything than give in to you in this matter, but since I remember that I no longer belong to myself, I offer my heart to God as a sacrifice.

The Sunday after his arrival, he mounted the steps of the familiar pulpit, opened the Bible at the same page at which he had left off on Easter Day three and a half years before, took up the next passage as his text, and expounded it as though nothing had intervened. It was his own way of demonstrating his forgiveness for past wrongs, and his commitment to the preaching of the word in the twenty-five years which were to follow, in which the whole of Genevan society was to feel the weight of his ministry.

We cannot here consider in detail the character of Calvin's influence on the city of Geneva, and on the churches of Europe and elsewhere, but two things may be singled out for mention.

1. *His ministry continued almost to the end to be beset by opposition.* Calvin wanted to reform the city according to the

Word of God. It is sometimes suggested that his aim and weapons were political. But the fact is that he did not have the right to vote in Geneva until he was 50 years old! His influence was personal and moral rather than political. Calvin wanted to return to the New Testament pattern of elders who were themselves able to take a pastoral care for the flock of God – and so the minutes of their meetings record discipline on people for such a diversity of activities as: absence from sermons, criticism of ministers, the use of charms, gambling, dancing, family-quarrels, and wife-beating. But, again, it is striking that the church was not allowed the right of excommunication until 1544; and it says a great deal for the patience of Calvin's leadership, despite the personal impatience he must have felt, that he was willing to continue in his task with the long-term goal in view.

It was not long after excommunication was restored that the trial of *Michael Servetus* was held. It is impossible to consider the life of Calvin without drawing attention to or mentioning what is generally regarded as a dark blot upon his character. Michael Servetus was a highly intelligent correspondent of Calvin. He may have discovered the circulation of the blood before Harvey, to whom that discovery is usually credited. But Servetus was also a blasphemer. He was discovered in Geneva, despite Calvin's warnings of what would certainly befall him if he came. He was tried, and despite his confidence that Calvin's opponents would secure his release, he was found guilty and was publicly burned. The action cannot be justified. But Calvin was no more guilty than his fellow-citizens; and no more guilty than those Protestant Churches and Roman Catholic hierarchy who were demanding that Servetus be executed.[1]

2. *His influence was essentially exercised by preaching God's Word.*[2]

[1] For a helpful discussion of the Servetus incident, see P. E. Hughes ed., *The Register of the Company of Pastors of Geneva in the time of Calvin*, Grand Rapids, 1966, pp. 17ff.

[2] For a helpful introduction to Calvin's views on preaching, see *John Calvin's*

At first it seems he preached twice on Sunday and once on Monday, Wednesday and Friday, until in 1542 he was urged to preach more regularly by some of his enthusiastic listeners. He did so, but his health broke down after some time. In 1549, a scribe was employed to take down Calvin's sermons, and from that year on we have a remarkable record of what he was saying, and the passages of Scripture he expounded. It was now his custom to preach every week-day on alternate weeks, and twice on a Sunday, that is, ten times in every fourteen day period. During the week he preached on the Old Testament and on the New Testament on Sundays, sometimes expounding Psalms on a Sunday afternoon. On Sundays he preached from the Acts of the Apostles between 1549 and 1554, 189 sermons; on the Pauline Epistles from 1554 to 1558; 65 sermons on the Gospels from 1559 to 1564. During the week he was preaching a series on Jeremiah and Lamentations until 1550; the Minor Prophets and Daniel, 1550 to 1552; 174 sermons on Ezekiel 1552 to 1554; 150 on Job 1554 to 1555; 200 on Deuteronomy 1555 to 1556; 342 on Isaiah 1556 to 1559; 123 on Genesis 1559 to 1561; some on Judges in the same year; 107 on 1 Samuel and 87 on 2 Samuel 1561 to 1563; and on Kings in 1563 to 1564. And over and above that, there are the commentaries which he wrote, and the lectures which he gave in the Geneva Academy. The only book of Scripture on which he does not seem to have written or preached is Revelation, which he is supposed to have said he did not fully understand. Such a preaching programme seems staggering: but Calvin's preaching had a purpose. It was not to exhaust his hearers, but to present them mature in Christ. He realized that the great goal of apostolic ministry was to bring men and women to their full spiritual stature. He saw the need to preach what Paul called 'the whole counsel of God'. He therefore stuck closely to the Pauline pattern of daily exposition.

Sermons on Ephesians, The Banner of Truth Trust, 1973, pp. v–xvi. The sermons in this volume are of great value in their own right.

He is perhaps one of the few men in the history of the church who has so perfectly emulated the apostle's example. And there are many evidences that his ministry was sealed by the powerful testimony of the Holy Spirit in the hearts of his hearers.

Last Days

This preaching ministry came to an end on 6th February 1564. In increased weakness and sickness, he gave his last lecture in the Academy a few days later, leaving his series on Ezekiel unfinished. On Easter Sunday a few weeks afterwards he went for the last time to the church for communion; and sat patiently through the sermon, and sang at the end with the congregation, the hymn: 'Lord, now lettest thou thy servant depart in peace, according to thy word; for mine eyes have seen thy salvation'. On April 25th he dictated his will; his own testimony in it reads as follows:

I John Calvin, servant of the Word of God in the church of Geneva, weakened by many illnesses . . . thank God that he has not only shown mercy to me, his poor creature . . . and suffered me in all sins and weaknesses, but what is more than that, he has made me a partaker of his grace to serve him through my work . . . I confess to live and die in this faith which he has given me, inasmuch as I have no other hope or refuge than his predestination upon which my entire salvation is grounded. I embrace the grace which he has offered me in our Lord Jesus Christ, and accept the merits of his suffering and dying that through him all my sins are buried; and I humbly beg him to wash me and cleanse me with the blood of our great redeemer, as it was shed for all poor sinners so that I, when I appear before his face, may bear his likeness.

On 27th May 1564, he passed to his eternal reward. He was
buried without ceremony in the cemetery, in an unmarked
grave, so that when foreign students asked to see it some
months later, it could not be distinguished from others like
it. In death, as in life, it was his aim to follow him who made
himself of no reputation, but became a servant of all. Well
did his friend, colleague, and successor, Theodore Beza write:
'*It has pleased God to show us in the life of a single man of our
time how to live and how to die*'. He expressed his personal ambition in a letter to Farel: '*It is enough that I live and die for
Christ, who is to all his followers a gain both in life and in death*'.
The words of the only hymn attributed to him sum up the
devotion of his life:

I greet thee, who my sure Redeemer art,
My only trust and Saviour of my heart,
Who pain didst undergo for my poor sake.
I pray thee from our hearts all cares to take.

Thou art the King of mercy and of grace,
Reigning omnipotent in every place;
So come, O King, and our whole being sway;
Shine on us with the light of thy pure day.

Thou art the life by which alone we live
And all our substance and our strength receive.
Sustain us by thy faith and by thy power
And give us strength in every trying hour.

Our hope is in no other save in thee;
Our faith is built upon thy promise free.
Lord, give us peace, and make us calm and sure
That in thy strength we evermore endure.

I/TO NICOLAS DUCHEMIN.[1]

Calvin at the University of Orleans
His early friendships
He is recalled to Noyon by the illness of his father.

Noyon, 14th May 1531.

As I do not think that you have hitherto been correctly informed of the motives and peculiar circumstances which have brought my punctuality in question, you must at least be willing to admit, that until now you have known me to be a person rather overmuch attentive, not to say troublesome, in the frequency of my correspondence. Nor has my fidelity been so sorely endangered as to leave me altogether inexcusable. For after calm consideration, I came to this conclusion in my own mind, that all the esteem you had conceived for me, during a long acquaintance and daily intercourse, could not vanish in a single moment; and that a certain kindly courtesy, as well as shrewdness, is so much your nature, that nothing is wont unadvisedly to prejudice you. This consideration makes me feel confident that I may be restored to favour, if any has been lost. Receive now, I pray you, in few words, the cause of this delay. The promise made at my departure, that I would return in a short time, while it was my wish to fulfil it, kept me all the longer in a state of suspense. For when I was seriously intending to return to you, my father's illness occasioned the delay. But afterward, when the physicians gave some hope of his restoration to good health, I then thought of nothing

---

1 This letter is the earliest in the series of Calvin's correspondence. Born at Noyon the 10th of July 1509, educated in the *belles lettres* at Paris, in 1527 he went to study law at the University of Orleans, which he left soon afterwards, in order to avail himself of the lectures of the celebrated Alciat at Bourges. In the first mentioned of these towns, he had as fellow-students and friends, several young men who were distinguished no less by their piety than by their abilities and achievements. Nicolas Duchemin was one of them.

else than the anxious desire to rejoin you, to which I had previously been very strongly inclined, but which was much increased after an interval of some days. Meanwhile, my on-waiting in this duty has been prolonged, until at length there remains no hope of recovery, and the approach of death is certain. Whatever happens, I shall see you again.

Remember me to Francis Daniel; to Philip,[1] and your entire household. Have you given in your name yet among the professors of literature? See that your modesty does not enforce indolence upon you. – Adieu, dear Duchemin, my friend dearer to me than my life.

2/TO FRANCIS DANIEL

Calvin's first work
Commentary on Seneca's Treatise, De Clementia

Paris, 22nd April 1532

Well, at length the die is cast. My Commentaries on the Books of Seneca, *De Clementia*,[2] have been printed, but at my own expense, and have drawn from me more money than you can well suppose. At present, I am using every endeavour to collect some of it back. I have stirred up some of the professors of this city to make use of them in lecturing. In the University of Bourges I have induced a friend to do this from the pulpit by a public lecture. You can also help me not a little, if you will not take it amiss; you will do so on the score of our old friendship; especially as, without any damage to your reputation, you may do me this service, which will also tend perhaps to the public good. Should you determine to

1 Philippe Laurent, librarian of the library at Orleans.
2 i.e. *On Mercy.*

oblige me by this benefit, I will send you a hundred copies, or as many as you please. Meanwhile, accept this copy for yourself, while you are not to suppose that by your acceptance of it, I hold you engaged to do what I ask. It is my wish that all may be free and unconstrained between us. Adieu, and let me soon hear from you. I wrote lately to Pigney, but he has not answered. To Brosse I wrote long ago, but to this time have no reply. He who will give Le Roy his copy will dutifully salute him.

3/TO CHRISTOPHER LIBERTET[1]

Calvin in Basle
Revision of the Bible of Robert Olivetan
Treatise on the Immortality of the Soul

Basle, 11th September[2]

When our friend Olivetan[3] had intimated, by the letters which he wrote about the time of his departure, that he had put off his intended publication of the New Testament to another time, it appeared to me that I might make the revision which

1 Christopher Libertet or Fabri, of Vienne in Dauphiny, a minister of the Church of Neuchatel. At an early period he entered into friendly relations with Calvin, was in 1536 pastor of the congregaion at Thonon, took part the same year in the disputation at Lausanne, and was recalled in 1546 by the Church of Neuchatel, which he served until the time of his death, in 1563, with equal wisdom and faithfulness.

2 Undated. This letter, written before the publication of the Bible of Robert Olivetan, refers evidently to the year 1534. Under the necessity of leaving France in order to escape persecution, Calvin had retired to Basle, where, in the year following, he composed his book, *The Institutes of the Christian Religion*.

3 Peter Robert Olivetan, related to Calvin, and translator of the Bible into the French language. Banished from Geneva in 1533, he had retired to Neuchatel, where he published successively (1534-1535) his translation of the New and of the Old Testament. This work, undertaken at the request of the Vaudois of Piedmont, had been revised by Calvin.

had been promised at my leisure, and reserve it to another time. Meanwhile other studies engaged my attention, and I thought no more of the matter, or rather sank down into my wonted languor. As yet, I have scarcely got my hand to work upon it, and besides, the volume which I sent will be necessary in the collation, and yet, though it was brought three months ago, it has not yet been put together. This has not occurred through any indifference on my part, but partly by the slowness of the binder, whom, nevertheless, we have not ceased to call upon daily, partly also because when it was brought to me at first we required a supply of paper to the extent of six sheets, which could not be had immediately. Henceforward, however, I shall set apart an hour every day to be bestowed on this work. And should I throw together any remarks, I will not deposit them with any other person than yourself, unless Olivetan on his return shall anticipate you. Further, word has been brought me by some one, I know not who, at your request, that you did not entirely approve of some things in my treatise on the Immortality of Souls.[1] So far from being offended because of your opinion, I am greatly delighted with this straightforward plainness. Nor does my perversity reach to such a degree as to allow myself in a freedom of opinion, which I would wish to take away from others. That I may not, however, vex or annoy you unnecessarily, by fighting the same battle over and over again, I wish you to understand that the book has been recast by me. Some things have been added, others left out, but altogether in a different form and method. Although some few things have been omitted I have inserted others, and some things I have altered. As for that essay which I had given Olivetan to read, it contained my first thoughts, rather thrown together in the shape of memoranda or commonplaces, than digested after any definite and

---

1 This is the treatise which is entitled, *Psychopannychia, qua refellitur eorum error qui animas post mortem usque ad ultimum iudicium dormire putant.* Paris, 1534. (*Soul-sleep*, in which the error of those who believe that men's souls sleep between death and the Last Judgment is repudiated.)

certain method, although there was some appearance of order. That new book (for so it must be called) I would have sent you, had it been read over again by me. But since it was written out by Gaspar, I have not looked into it. Farewell; may the Lord have you in His keeping, and enrich you always with His own gifts.

Somehow or other it has so happened that in the hurry of writing I omitted what by no means I had intended. It was to exhort you and the other brethren in a few words, but most heartily, to the cultivation of peace, for the preservation of which you ought all of you to strive the more earnestly as Satan watches intently for its overthrow. You can scarce believe how much I was shocked at hearing of that new uproar about the lepers, set a-going by him of whom I would never have suspected such a thing. But at length he vomited out the poison with which he was sweltering from long dissimulation, and having fixed the sting, like a viper fled away. Be not wanting, on your part, I entreat you, so far as lies in you, which, indeed, I was confident would be the case of your own accord, but I was willing at the same time to interpose my prayer for peace.

4/TO FRANCIS DANIEL[1]

Calvin in Geneva
Translation into French of the Institutes of the Christian Religion
Disputation of Lausanne
Establishment of the doctrines of the Reformation in the Pays de Vaud

Lausanne, 13th October [1536]

That you may not, according to old use and wont, lay a long and clamorous accusation against my indolence, seeing that three whole months have passed away during which you have not received a single letter from me, accept now a brief statement as to the state of matters upon the whole. For some days I was detained at Geneva by the brethren, until they extracted from me a promise to return; then after that, I brought back my relative Artois[2] to Basle, and gave offence to several churches in the course of my journey, with whom I was requested to stay for a little while. In the meantime, the August fair was over, which was the most favourable opportunity for the conveyance of letters. Furthermore, as soon as I got back to Geneva, a violent cold attacked me, which afterward settled upon the upper gum, to that there was scarce any relief even after nine days, and after having been twice bled, with a double dose of pills and several fomentations. Nor is it yet completely shaken off. During that lost opportunity, al-

1 This is the first letter of the Reformer after his settlement at Geneva. Having left his retreat of Basle at the beginning of 1536, he had made a rapid tour in the north of Italy, and revisited France, which he had left in the month of July on his return to Switzerland. Not being able, without danger, to traverse Champagne and Lorraine, he went back to Basle by the way of Geneva, (August 1536) when he was detained in that town by the entreaties of Farel. Afterwards he accepted the office of Professor of Theology, and attended the disputation of Lausanne on the 1st of October, which was followed by the establishment of the Reformation in the Pays de Vaud, conquered by the Seigneury of Berne from the Duke of Savoy.

2 Calvin had left Noyon accompanied by his brother Antony and his sister Mary, who went to settle at Basle.

though there was abundant leisure for writing, and the way or channel of correspondence was not entirely closed, yet I was kept continually occupied upon the French version of my little book;[1] and the almost certain expectation began then to arise, that the letters might reach you enriched by that acquisition, rather than that they should come empty-handed. But before my intention could be fulfilled, the day fixed for the disputation at Lausanne had already arrived,[2] at which my presence was required; and at the same time I saw the November fair approaching, which I considered to be a more convenient time for writing, and therefore it seemed to me better to wait for that opportunity. So much to stop your expostulations.

The talk of the disputation above mentioned has, I understand, been spread so far and wide, that I do not doubt some whiff of it has reached your city. The disputation was appointed by a decree of the Council of Berne, accompanied by a solemn Edict,[3] whereby the Senate declared, that it was free to every one, and *that* without the dread of being called in question, to state whatever might concern the matter of disagreement upon the point of religion. They considered that this was the most likely method, by which publicly to expose the unskilfulness of those who try to oppose the Gospel, and that thus they might render of no avail the triumph arising out of this new authority which they have accepted at the hand of the Duke of Savoy. Already in many places, the idols and altars of Popery have begun to disappear, and I hope it will not be long before all remaining superstition shall be effectually cleared away. The Lord grant that idolatry may be entirely uprooted out of the hearts of all. I do not describe to

1 The book here referred to is undoubtedly the *Institutes*, first published in Latin, (Basle, 1536). Calvin thought of giving a translation of that work. The first known edition of the *Institution Chrétienne* in French bears the date 1541.

2 The disputation of Lausanne, in which Farel, Viret, and Calvin took part, began on the 2nd October, and lasted seven days.

3 Edict of July 16, 1536.

you the precise form in which the disputation presents itself, because it is not easy to do so in a brief explanation, and also because I trust it will some time or other be published. To-morrow, if the Lord will, I set out for Berne, about which affair you shall hear from me by other letters; and I am afraid it will be necessary for me to hasten forward as far as Basle: which inconvenience, however, I shall endeavour if it be possible to avoid; more especially taking into account the state of my health, and the very unseasonable time of the year. If those idle bellies with you, who chirp together so sweetly in the shade, were only as well disposed as they are talkative, they would instantly flock hither to take on themselves a share of the labour, to which we must be inadequate, since there are so few of us. You can hardly believe the small number of ministers compared with the very many churches which need pastors. How I wish, seeing the extreme necessity of the Church, that, however few they may be in number, there were at least some right-hearted men among you who may be induced to lend a helping hand. May the Lord preserve you.

Remember me, I entreat you, particularly to your mother and sister, your wife also, if you think proper, your kinsmen, and all the rest.

5/TO LOUIS DU TILLET[1]

Departure of Louis du Tillet from Geneva
Regret of Calvin
Controversy between the two friends about the
character of the Church of Jesus Christ

From Villefranche,[2] 31st January [1538]

Monsieur:

Eight days before I received the letters which you left at your departure to be forwarded to me, John had arrived,[3] so that some weeks before I had any news of you the rumour of your departure had taken wing hither. Although such a state of uncertainty was very great occasion of annoyance to me, nevertheless, I held my judgment in suspense as much as was possible; what troubled and tormented me most was the fear I entertained of having offended you by my imprudence, as

1 Louis du Tillet, curé of Claix in Poitou, canon and archdeacon of Angoulême. He was the brother of John du Tillet, the celebrated registrar of the Parlement de Paris, and of that other Du Tillet who became Bishop of Sainte-Brieuc and of Meaux. Having devoted himself to an ecclesiastical career, his first leanings inclined him towards the Reformed. He became acquainted with Calvin at the University of Paris, formed a friendship with him, shared his perils, and received him in 1534 at Angoulême in his own house. United thenceforth to the young Reformer by a like faith, he resigned his curacy of Claix to follow him, under the name of Hautmont, to Strassburg, to Basle, and into Italy. In August 1536 he was at Geneva, when Calvin was there retained by the earnest entreaties of Farel. But the struggles to which the Reformer was thenceforward condemned were little suited to the mild and contemplative disposition of Louis du Tillet. A prey to indecision, he secretly left Geneva and went to Strassburg, where his anxieties were only brought to an end by his return to the Roman Catholic faith. He wrote to Calvin to inform him of this change, and to submit to him his scruples regarding the lawfulness of the ministry in the Reformed Churches. Calvin replied; and that controversy, free, sincere, but tempered by respect, marked the later relations between these two men, at first united and too soon separated by the religious revolution of the sixteenth century.

2 Ville Affranchie, (Geneva).

3 John du Tillet, brother of Louis, raised at a later period to the honours of the Episcopate. He was charged with various scientific missions by Francis I, and in the course of his travels had visited Geneva.

I know and acknowledge that I have not observed towards you the due consideration which I ought. It is indeed true, that I derived such advantage from your society and conversation, that absence could not be joyous to me; but inasmuch as I saw you were in a somewhat languid state, I bore my loss patiently, considering your comfort as a sufficient recompense. Finally, since the arrival of your letters from two different quarters, by them I have partly understood your intention. While I consider, however, that my company could not be very agreeable in such rudeness and incivility as I used towards you, notwithstanding, I feel confident that that circumstance has neither estranged nor alienated you from us, for which we may certainly rather thank your prudence, which I have had to sustain me in regard to that, than because I conducted myself as became me.

I cannot conceal from you that I have been very much astonished on hearing of your intention, and even the reasons which are put forth along with the declaration of it in your letters. What occasions me the greatest surprise is, that I considered you so settled and resolved in that affair, that it would no way be possible to dislodge you from your purpose, and although you could not have had in the course you have been following very solid reasons, yet this so sudden change has appeared very strange to me, seeing the constancy and firmness which you manifested. May God grant, nevertheless, that your change of opinion may be as benignly construed by others as I endeavour to take it.

As for the reasons which have swayed you in arriving at that determination I cannot perceive them to be very persuasive. I know well that my conscience before God is sufficiently assured of the contrary, and I hope that it will be so until the day when we must appear to give in our account. Besides, I am much misunderstood if I have not manifestly proved the justice of my cause in such a way that every one ought to be content, were it not that the one party pardon themselves too easily, while the others would readily give entrance to Jesus Christ, but only by ways wherein He will in nowise walk. I have never doubted that the eminent persons[1] you mention might in some degree have helped, without intending it, to land you in such a conclusion, while in touching on this point in letters written to me, they concealed it. Certainly their great learning and piety may well lend authority to their consultations. But I am well assured that in this matter, besides substantial grounds, I shall have more colour of reason than they, if I assume a mask to make myself look like them. Both the one and the other constrain me by their conduct to desire in them greater firmness and constancy. However high our reputation may be, it is never well to be so very liberal in bestowing another's property; and if we must beware of being bountiful at the expense of men, what caution ought to be exercised in dispensing the truth of God, which He does not commit to our trust that we may lessen it in anything? I pray the Lord that Himself would give us so much understanding as that we may clearly comprehend that He will not be served by halves, and as our foolishness would divide His portion, but entirely according to His own will.

If you do acknowledge for churches of God those who hold us in execration, I cannot help it. But we should be in a sad plight if it indeed were so. For certainly you cannot give them this title, unless you hold us to be schismatics, in which case you will have to consider how your opinion will agree with the deliverance of our Master, 'whatsoever ye shall bind on earth,' &c. If you consider that there always remains some remnant of the blessing of God, as St. Paul affirms of the Israelites, you may well understand that I agree with you, seeing that I have sometimes declared to you that such was my opinion even as regards the Greek churches. But it does not follow as a consequence from that, that in the assembly we are bound to acknowledge the church; and if we do there

---

1 Bucer and Capito, the Reformers of Strassburg.

acknowledge her, she will be our church, not that of Jesus Christ, who marks His own by other tokens, when He says, my sheep hear my voice; and St Paul, when he calls her the 'pillar of truth.' You will answer me that she will be found nowhere, seeing that everywhere there is ignorance. Yet the ignorance of the children of God is of such a nature, that it does not hinder them from following His will.

Were it a question of comparison of such meetings with the synagogues of the Jews, I should fear to injure the latter in not preferring them to the other, or at least placing them in the background, for their idolatry is not so great, nor their abomination so horrible. What one can see of good, it is common to both, except indeed that it appears to be a great advantage that the name of Jesus Christ is avowed in the one and not in the other. But its influence is not the less abolished. Or if we would find a more suitable comparison, it is such a state as existed among the people of Israel under Jeroboam, or rather under Ahab, at a time when the spirit of the people had been corrupted by long usage. I do not mention these things without good cause, for I perceive how many begin to flatter themselves under the title of The Church, strongly condemning whatever is not like their own, for which they will have to render account. Let them consider by what right they do so, for I know well that our assurance is too certain to yield merely to frivolous objections. As regards yourself I do not think that you can look upon us otherwise than as if you held intercommunion with us, but it is a step towards separation from the Church of God when any one joins that which is opposed to Him.

Moreover, I think that I perceive such a fear of God to be in you that I must see great arguments to move me from the persuasion which I have entertained. Be assured, then, that the first slight reports will not have such power over me as to overturn the experience I have had of you for many long years. But although I may tolerate that infirmity, offering you no more opposition than if you were one of ourselves, I can by no means approve your conduct; and would choose rather that I should be taken out of the world by a bitter death, than approve your deed, which I know to be damnable in itself, and besides that, fraught with ruin, or at least marvellous offence towards many, as well as because I see the readiness with which we justify ourselves, in order to encourage others to follow our example. However, concerning those matters of which at present you are resolved, I will make no long dispute. I would rather entreat the Lord that it may be His pleasure to deliver you from all scruples, so that His way may be quite plain and open in that direction, waiting an opportunity when such shall offer itself.

As for the departure of Louis Dartois, I never had a suspicion that it proceeded from you, inasmuch as I have been lately informed to the contrary. But it has been a poor stratagem on his part to conceal things from me in which he could not deceive God; for it is no light thing to tempt God, which those do who voluntarily bring themselves again under bondage. The miserable excuses with which we are wont to cover even our moral nakedness before men, will never be able to endure the heat of God's judgment.

You have long ago graciously permitted me to consider all things in common between us. Would that it pleased God I could make you a due acknowledgment. My companions charge me to commend them to you, who are of the same mind with me, although I have striven to the utmost, without shewing your letters, to prevent their taking offence. I could give no other counsel to John than that which my conscience warranted, unless I would turn traitor to the truth of God, and to his personal salvation. You will not take it amiss. I entreat you to have special remembrance of us in your prayers, to which although the knowledge you have of our weakness ought sufficiently to stir you up, nevertheless, the difficulties which press upon us ought yet more to arouse you, as they are now greater than ever.[1] After humbly commending my-self to your kind remembrance, I pray the Lord to keep you in His holy protection, and so to direct you that you may not go astray in that slippery path whereon you are, until He shall have manifested to you His complete deliverance.

You will pardon me if this present is very confusedly writ-ten, shortness of time is in part the cause, and partly our troubles, besides that the argument was not very easy to handle.

6/TO HENRY BULLINGER[2]

State of the Church at Geneva
Wish for the union of the Reformed Churches
Mention of Luther

Geneva, 21st February 1538

Grace to you and peace, from God the Father and from Christ the Lord, most respected and learned brother.

Were I to begin to describe to you at length the full narra-tive of our most wretched condition, a long history must be unfolded by me. For I call ours the trouble which for a long

[1] The opposition which the establishment of the ecclesiastical discipline drawn up by Farel and Calvin met with at Geneva became every day more intense and lively. The newly-elected Syndics made common cause with the malcontents, and already gave signs of the forthcoming crisis which was to lead the way to the triumph of the party of the Libertines and the banishment of the ministers.

[2] Henry Bullinger, born July 18, 1504, at Bremgarten, became minister of that parish in 1529. He was a friend of the reformer Zwingli and his successor at Zurich, after the fatal battle of Cappel, 1531. He discharged his ministry in that church with wisdom and prudence for more than forty years, kept up a regular correspondence with the Reformers abroad, was on friendly terms with Melanchthon, Cranmer, Calvin, and Beza. In 1566 he drew up the Swiss Confession of Faith, and through his advice, exercised a decisive influence over the progress of the Reformation in the different countries of Europe. He died at Zurich, September 17, 1575. Bullinger left several valuable works; among others a Chronicle which he wrote in German, Commentaries and Theological Treatises, and a vast Correspondence, preserved largely at Zurich and at Geneva.

time has pressed, and which now severely presses upon that Church over which the Lord has been pleased to set us. But because there is not enough of leisure at present for explaining everything, and these good men can relate somewhat themselves, I will not trouble you with a larger epistle. Although, indeed, they have not perhaps discerned the very source of the evil, nor perceived whither the attempts of the wicked tended, yet they have forecast pretty clearly the state of affairs, how it was likely to turn out. How I wish that we could have a single day for free communication together, for from such a meeting we could not depart without much advantage. I have some things which can neither be treated safely in a letter, nor determined, until they have been weighed and thoroughly discussed on both sides. This, however, I will venture to throw out in passing, that it does appear to me, that we shall have no lasting Church unless that ancient apostolic discipline be completely restored, which in many respects is much needed among us. We have not yet been able to obtain, that the faithful and holy exercise of ecclesiastical excommunication be rescued from the oblivion into which it has fallen; and that the city, which in proportion to its extent is very populous, may be distributed into parishes, as is rendered necessary by the complicated administration of the Church. The generality of men are more ready to acknowledge us as preachers than as pastors. There are many other things besides, which, although we desire intensely to see amended, we can find out no means of doing so, unless that can be accomplished by faith, by diligence, and by perseverance on the part of all. Oh, if a pure and sincere accommodation could be agreed upon at length among us! What, then, would hinder the assembling of some public Synod, where individuals might propose whatever they may conceive to be most for the benefit of the churches? A way might be found out of going to work by common deliberation, and if need be, that the cities and princes also should assist in this undertaking by mutual exhortation and counsel, and also confirm by their authority; but in so great perplexity, the Lord is rather to be inquired of, that Himself may open up a way.

Pellican has informed us that you have received a kind and friendly reply from Luther, from which Grynée affirms that he entertains much hope of seeing peace established.[1] But of what kind we have not been able to divine, seeing that that church, which, from its near neighbourhood, might most easily communicate with us in all things, has not thought us worthy to receive any intelligence whatever. When occasion offers, you must not grudge to let us at least understand the sum of it. Farel greets you. Will you salute for me with no common esteem my highly respected brethren in the Lord, your colleagues, Pellican, Leo, Theodore, Bibliander, and besides, Phyrisius. May the Lord keep you all in safety for the promoting of His kingdom.

1 Bucer and Capito were at this time engaged in very active negotiations to bring about a union between the Reformed Churches of Switzerland and those of Germany. Luther did not oppose this accommodation, and had written (Dec. 1, 1537) to the reformed districts of Switzerland, a letter full of tolerance and conciliation, in which there is the following passage: 'They can easily advise with Bucer also and Capito on all these matters, provided we can lay aside all that is offensive, and in like-minded agreement give room for the leading and guidance of the Holy Spirit, that we may go forward in pious and brotherly concord. Assuredly, in so far as we are concerned, and especially as regards myself, casting aside whatever may be occasion of offence, I shall embrace you in faith, good will, and with love.' In another letter to Capito of the same year (6th Dec. 1537) he says, 'I write these things that you may know that our heart is upright and sincere in the hope of agreement; may the Lord himself complete the work. Amen.'

In a letter to Bullinger, written 4th March 1538, he pays deep-felt homage to the memory of Zwingli and Œcolampadius. 'I can freely declare that, after having seen and heard Zwingli at Marburg, I have considered and esteemed him as a most excellent man, as also Œcolampadius; so that their calamity has well-nigh disheartened me.' These sentiments of true generosity seemed almost to open up an era of reconciliation and of peace between the Churches.

7/TO WILLIAM FAREL[1]

Farel called as minister to the Church of Neuchatel
Sad condition of the Church at Geneva
Uncertainty of Calvin
Bucer's urgency to draw him to Strassburg

Basle, 4th August 1538

The grace of the Lord be with you. The person who had brought back the horse, promised that he would return after three days. When, after the lapse of five days, I had ceased to expect him, I began to look about for a messenger. For I knew that as soon as my silence began to appear to you to be longer than it ought, you would impute it to carelessness as well as indolence. But while these were my thoughts, lo, the messenger presented himself upon the spot, who informed me of your departure two days before he came away. With regard to your letter, that elaborate lament over your own, clownish simplicity with which you furnished me for Grynée, I have

---

1 William Farel, the most illustrious missionary of the Reformation in French Switzerland, was born at Gap, in Dauphiny (1489). He studied at the University of Paris, under the direction of the learned Le Fèvre of Étaples, whose friendship he speedily obtained, and shared with him the same faith. A man of fiery spirit, and gifted with an impetuous eloquence, he preached the doctrines of the Reformation successively at Paris and at Meaux, in Dauphiny. In 1524 he left France, when he retired to Strassburg, and brought over to the new doctrine (as the true doctrine of the Gospel was termed at that time) the Duchy of Montbeliard, Bienne, Morat, Neuchatel, Aigle, Geneva. Driven at first from the latter town in 1532, he reappeared there, and was thereupon banished. On the 27th August 1535, he obtained the famous declaration which restored the Reformation. In less than two years afterwards he was banished from Geneva along with his colleague Calvin, whom he followed to Basle, and became, in the month of July 1538, pastor of the church of Neuchatel, which he served until his death (13th Sept. 1565) with indefatigable activity.

Having been called as minister by the Church of Neuchatel, Farel had left Basle precipitately, without taking leave of Calvin, then on his journey to Strassburg. On returning to Basle, Calvin wrote the following letter to his old colleague, which is one of the earliest in the long correspondence which they kept up with each other.

carefully complied with. When dinner-time arrived, I told Grynée that I observed from your letter the rain somewhat had slackened your wonted speed: whereupon, by your riding so slow a pace, Simon remembered that you were a rustic. Thereafter also I read to him your letter, and added of my own accord, what appeared to me to be required in the way of serious apology. In regard to him, so little need was there of clearing yourself, that he would have complied good-humouredly with your infectious anxiety, if the business in which he is now completely immersed had not stood in the way. How our successors[1] are likely to get on, I can conjecture from the first beginnings. While already they entirely break off every appearance of peace by their want of temper, they suppose that the best course for themselves to pursue was to tear in pieces our estimation, publicly and privately, so as to render us as odious as possible. But if we know that they cannot calumniate us, excepting in so far as God permits, we know also the end God has in view in granting such permission. Let us humble ourselves, therefore, unless we wish to strive with God when He would humble us. Meanwhile, let us wait upon God. For the crown of pride of the drunkards of Ephraim will speedily wither. I could wish that you had not so much anxiety on my account. Since your departure, I have begun to consider more attentively what it may be right to be prepared for in case of emergency. It cannot be told how this apprehension torments me, lest those who measure us by their own standard, because conscience accuses themselves, may think that we have fixed designedly upon our present abode as convenient for the purpose of retaliating injuries, and so may set themselves to contrive some new contests, and take no rest until they have stirred up some fresh disturbances against us. When I am out of the way, suspicion will not be

[1] The new ministers elected at Geneva to replace Calvin, Farel, and Courault, were Antony Marcourt, pastor of the Church of Nyon, and Doctor Morand. Their nomination, approved only by a part of the Church, gave occasion to serious disorder.

so apt to arise. For no one will be so utterly malignant as to suppose that we intend anything farther. But if you do not at once come hither, we must put off until the meeting become hopeless, which the Strassburghers always insist on our requiring; or if we obtain it the result will teach us what we ought to do. This above all, in the name of the Lord, I entreat of you, that you do determine nothing about me without first of all giving me a previous warning. You will perceive, from Bucer's letter, what are his present sentiments. He has communicated certain other matters to Grynée in writing, which I have not yet had an opportunity of reading. I strongly suspect, however, that they tend to the point of my hastening thither, which I shall not comply with, unless a greater necessity convinces me. In so far as I can discover, the person you know has endeavoured most ambitiously, by means of his relations, to pave the way for himself to the office of the ministry. Expressions sometimes are thrown out which afford greater room for conjecture than for any meaning which they contain. But as he hoped that ere long I would take my departure, he advised me to undertake what by and by I might resign to him. He did not know what might be brought to pass with you, and I took care closely to conceal that from him. 'Are you not ashamed,' said he, 'in so great an assemblage to remain silent? Would there be no church here vacant for you?' I replied, that we had an auditory also in our house at home which suited us very well. He, forsooth, would have nought but what was public. Having dined once with us, he wished to be received at table by Grynée through my introduction. Excuse was of no avail, but he must urge the proposal with unseasonable importunity, until Grynée restrained his forwardness by checking him aloud. I have satisfied the owner of the horse; the rest of your commissions are duly attended to. Grynée salutes you in the most friendly manner, and entreats you to pardon him, on account of his business engagements, that he does not write at present. Oporin also,

Stagnaeus, Du Tailly, for the other two have gone from this. May the Lord preserve and protect you, may your soul prosper in the strength of His own Spirit. You will not envy me the reading of Capito's epistle, which I send you unsealed. Will you, if you please, return both the letters of Bucer, or carefully preserve them, as hereafter we shall have occasion for them? Salute not merely with your complaisance, but from my heart, all our brethren, especially such of them as you well know are here meant. If you desire that I should write, arrange that I may have messengers from yourself.

Read after this Bucer's letter, where he advises that we carefully avoid colleaguing together, since it may be suspected that the one urges on the other, to what both are too much inclined to. He even wishes that I may yield to that extent, in order that this irritable disposition may not be disturbed by frequent rumours.

8/TO FAREL

Death of Courault
Calvin's discouragement and trust in God
Answers a question of Saunier regarding the Supper
The faithful at Geneva exhorted not to separate from the new preachers
Affectionate advice given to Farel

Strasburg, 24th October 1538

The death of Courault has so overwhelmed me, that I can set no bounds to my grief.[1] None of my daily occupations can so avail to engage my mind as that they do not seem to turn upon that one thought. Distress and wretchedness during the day seems only to prepare a lodging for the more painful and excruciating thoughts of the night. It is not merely the want of sleep, to which custom has so inured me, by which I am harassed, but I am utterly exhausted by these melancholy thoughts all night long, than which I find there is nothing more destructive of my health. But that atrocious deed chiefly rankles my mind, if indeed the suspicion is well founded, to which, whether I will or nill, I am constrained to allow some weight. To what a degree of wickedness must our posterity at length arrive when in the very commencement such monstrosities rise up before our eyes? I much fear lest this great wickedness may speedily be punished by some great affliction of the Church. Moreover, it is no slight evidence of the anger of God, that amid so great a scarcity of good ministers, the Church should be deprived of one who stood in the foremost

---

1 The aged monk, Augustin Courault, a zealous preacher of the Reformation at Paris and at Geneva. He stood firm with Calvin and Farel, after a short imprisonment was banished from Geneva, found a retreat with Christopher Fabri at Thonon, and was appointed pastor at Orbe, where he died, 4th October 1538. Courault was advanced in years, and had become blind. His death, which was at first attributed to poison, caused the deepest regret both to Farel and Calvin, who were his colleagues in the ministry.

rank of the good. What else, therefore, dear brother, can we do than lament our calamity? although, nevertheless, we are not lacking in solid consolation. This of itself is a great comfort when all do thus testify, by affectionate sorrow as for their own loss, the high esteem in which they held him for courage and uprightness. So neither does the Lord suffer the wickedness of our enemies to remain concealed upon earth. They have not gained the worth of a single hair by his death. For there stands before the judgment-seat of God a witness and avenger of their villainy, whose voice will proclaim their destruction more loudly than if it shook the earth. We, the survivors whom the Lord has left behind for a while, let us persevere in the same path wherein our deceased brother walked until we have finished our course. Whatsoever difficulties may be thrown across our path, they will not prevent our arriving at that rest into which he has been already admitted. Unless this sure hope held us firm and steadfast, what ground of despair encompasses us round about! But since the truth of the Lord remains firm and unshaken, let us stand resolutely upon the watch-tower even to the end, until the kingdom of Christ, which is now hidden and obscured, may shine forth.

Our opponents have already sounded the trumpet on account of the sentence pronounced against the town of Minden.[1] As the interest of religion is concerned in the matter, our friends are necessarily implicated. It will be our surest and invincible defence if the Lord of Hosts shall defend us by His own strength. Otherwise we are scarcely strong enough to repel the assaults of our enemies. Let us therefore take refuge in that one asylum, which, even although the whole earth may be shaken, can never be moved.

---

[1] As one of the cities in league with Schmalkalden for the defence of the Gospel, the town of Minden had just been placed under the ban of the Empire. The Roman Catholic princes of Germany, confederated at Nuremberg, prepared to execute the sentence against which the Protestant princes had solemnly protested.

We do not slacken our endeavour, and continue to cry incessantly for a conference until it shall have been obtained. Saunier[1] wished another question to be discussed by us,—Whether it is lawful for himself, and others similarly situated, to receive the sacrament of the Lord's Supper from the hands of the new ministers, and to partake of it along with such a promiscuous assemblage of unworthy communicants? In this matter I quite agree with Capito. This, in brief, was the sum of our discussion: that among Christians there ought to be so great a dislike of schism, as that they may always avoid it so far as lies in their power. That there ought to prevail among them such a reverence for the ministry of the Word and of the Sacraments, that wherever they perceive these things to be, there they may consider the Church to exist. Whenever therefore it happens, by the Lord's permission, that the Church is administered by pastors, whatever kind of persons they may be, if we see there the marks of the Church, it will be better not to break the unity. Nor need it be any hindrance that some points of doctrine are not quite so pure, seeing that there is scarcely any Church which does not retain some remnants of former ignorance. It is sufficient for us if the doctrine on which the Church of God is founded be recognized and maintain its place. Nor should it prove any obstacle, that he ought not to be reckoned a lawful pastor who shall not only have fraudulently insinuated himself into the office of a true minister, but shall have wickedly usurped it. For there is no reason why every private person should mix himself up with these scruples. The Sacraments are the means of communion with

1 Antony Saunier, countryman and disciple of Farel, was honoured to be his companion in announcing for the first time the Gospel in Geneva, (September 1532). Having been appointed Regent of the college of that town in 1538, he offered a determined opposition to the pastors who were elected in room of Farel and Calvin, and along with his colleague Mathurin Cordier was banished, on account of his refusal, notwithstanding the advice of Calvin himself, to receive the sacrament at the hands of the new ministers. He retired to the Pays de Vaud, and at a later period became pastor of the church at Morges.

the Church; they must needs therefore be administered by the hands of pastors. In regard to those, therefore, who already occupy that position, legitimately or not, and although the right of judging as to that is not denied, it will be well to suspend judgment in the meantime, until the matter shall have been legally adjudicated. Therefore, if men wait upon their ministry, they will run no risk that they should appear either to acknowledge or approve, or in any way to ratify their commission. But by this means they will give a proof of their patience in tolerating those who they know will be condemned by a solemn judgment. The refusal at first of these excellent brethren did not surprise nor even displease me. In truth, at a time of so great excitement, which could not fail to produce an ebullition in the minds of men, a schism in the body of Christ was the infallible result. Besides, they were still uncertain whither at length this tempest would drive them, which for the time put everything in confusion and disorder.

Saunier then proceeded to speak of himself, but with so much contention, that it seemed as if he would never have an end until he had extorted what he sought. There was evident ground of reason why we should deny. For prudence in making a due distinction is required from the minister to whom the dispensation of this sacred mystery belongs. Moreover, he who has not from the first repudiated their fellowship plainly approves their ministry. Lastly, the question having been reduced to these conditions,—whether it were better to yield or to refuse, I forced him into this dilemma: If the minister does his duty, all will at once go well; if not, it will beget a scandal which must not be endured, whatever supposed advantages might arise therefrom. But when he perceived that I was firmly determined to accomplish what I sought to effect, he readily acquiesced therein, whatever it was. We know by our experience how difficult it is to keep within due bounds those who are puffed up with a silly opinion of their own wisdom.

When we all thought this particular time very unreasonable for discussing the points in dispute among the brethren, the Lord has surpassed our utmost expectation. Whatever we sought has been obtained. Saunier at first seemed to dislike that any formula of confession should be required. He supposed that our friends would be satisfied for this alone, because they had been taught by himself. Afterwards, however, he relaxed his opposition and approved without further controversy, such as I have drawn it in their name. I fear that the person will give you most trouble whose business it ought to be to help you; however, by patient sufferance you will struggle through. I entreat of you, my dear brother, in so great iniquity of the time in which we live, that you will use your utmost endeavour to keep together all who are any way bearable. As to the trifling ceremonies, strive to induce the brethren not to dispute the point with those of their neighbourhood with so much of stiffnecked obstinacy. It will then come to pass that we may carry our point, ourselves free from all, that we may only serve the interests of peace and Christian agreement. If I omit any important points, it is because your letter, which I had given to Capito to read, has not yet been returned to me. May the Lord perserve and strengthen you by His Spirit, confirm you in the enduring of all things, my most beloved brother in the Lord. Your anxiety on my account admonishes me in my turn to recommend your taking care of your health, for all accounts report that you appear very much worn out. I beg and entreat of you, my dear brother, have such regard to others as at the same time to keep in mind that the Church of Christ cannot yet spare you. Greet a thousand times for me all the brethren who are with you; Viret, Francis also and James, when you write to them. Capito, Sturm, and Firmin, desire to salute you in the most friendly way.

9/TO FAREL

Second edition of The Institutes
Death of Robert Olivetan
State of religion in Germany
First lectures of Calvin at Strassburg

Month of January 1539

The grace of the Lord be with you, most sound-hearted brother.

You would have received a longer letter from me had not grief of mind so distracted me that I had neither heart nor hand capable of discharging duty. When I thought that the edition of my work was quietly going forward,[1] lo and behold! a copy is forwarded to me by my brother in the same state in which I had sent it; therefore it must be put off to the next fair-time. This kindness has been repaid to me by Robert. Although there is privately no reason why I should vex myself on this account; yet since I supposed that it would be of public advantage that it should go forth as soon as possible, I could not be otherwise than greatly annoyed that the expectation and desire of many good men should be frustrated by the cross humour of a single individual; for I do not wish to say anything more severe. The death of our friend Olivetan followed upon that other vexation, of which the wife of Sinapi informed me by letter.[2] You will therefore bear with me in my reasonable sorrow, if my letters are not only confused, but also somewhat concise. What you mention about the reply of Konzen cheered me as much as was possible in such sadness. I entreat you, my dear brother, that we may

1 He refers here to the second edition of the *Institution Chrétienne*, which appeared in 1539 at Strassburg.

2 Robert Olivetan died, in 1538, at Ferrara. The news was given to Calvin by Francesca Bucyronia, wife of the physician, John Sinapi, a German, settled at the Court of the Duchess of Ferrara as the preceptress of her children.

follow up such favourable and auspicious beginnings. Now, for the first time, our spirit can be raised to entertain good hope of the result; but, as you observe, we must have a conferential meeting, without which the fallen and miserably scattered churches cannot be built up. Scarcely could I have dared to hope for any good until I understood that this opening had occurred. Now am I led to entertain the sure hope of an excellent result, if we have once an opportunity of meeting together. We must wait, however, for the return of Bucer, who, when he was arrived at no great distance from home, was drawn back again upon a new piece of business, a secret indeed, but which I will whisper in your ear. Duke George of Saxony,[1] beyond all expectation, intimated that he wished to have some consultation with him and Melanchthon about religion and the reformation of the Church, and appointed a day for them to come to Leipsig, on which he promised that he would be present; therefore both secretly set out thither. If he comes to any determination he will draw many others after his example. Some of the princes are impelled by a fierce desire of stirring up war against us, and already they are prepared with all requisite munition. They are, however, kept in some restraint by the more prudent, who foresee that the Turk will not remain quiet if he sees Germany engaged in civil war. Already he has possession of Upper and Lower Wallachia, and has declared war upon the King of Poland unless he allow him free passage through his territories. As soon as Bucer returns I will tire you with a long story, for I am very confident that he will bring along with him a great store of news. He has loaded Saunier and the brethren with superfluous expense, and has hence fatigued them with labour to no purpose. I am too much intent on the success of this project to have any need to be goaded on regarding it; but what

1 George Duke of Saxony, cousin of the Elector of Saxony, John Frederick. Although the princes of his family had adopted the (so called) new doctrines, this prince had constantly opposed the Reformation, which he persecuted in his states. He died in 1539.

could I do, since the proposed Diet of the princes and free cities on whom the charge was laid has not yet been held? There met lately a council of the cities at Erlangen, but that concerned other matters; nor was it composed only of those of our persuasion, although the cities sent deputies, but of all promiscuously. The Diet of those of our side, both of the princes and of the cities, is called for the eighth of February, before which day ambassadors from the Duke of Saxony and the Landgrave are to come hither. We are so cordial in the undertaking that we shall omit no opportunity of promoting it so far as lies in us.

Having lately been induced by Capito, against my inclination, to lecture publicly, I either lecture or preach daily. Michael writes you. Others more fitted for the work will fall in afterwards, if they have only a little time given them. All send you their most friendly greetings, and specially Capito, who does not write only because he thinks my letter sufficient. Sturm, also, and Firmin, and Gaspar, and Henry, and the others. Adieu, most excellent brother; may the Lord preserve you for Himself and His people. Salute all the brethren from me.

You may hence be able to conjecture my state of composure, from the circumstance that I have altogether forgotten in writing to you what I ought to have told you at the first: I mean, that I had written to you and Zebedeus by Dr Ulrich. He avers that he entrusted the letters to a faithful hand. Do let me hear by the first opportunity whether they have reached you, and how you were pleased with the contents; for I would willingly hear that you were satisfied with reference to the offence which my letters had given among the brethren at Geneva.

10/TO FAREL

Impressions of Calvin on his recall to Geneva
Rigorous application of discipline in his church
News of Germany, of France, and of England

Strassburg, 29th March 1540

I have already waited so long for your letter that I may well doubt whether I ought to wait any longer. My anxious wish to hear from you kept alive my expectation, and shall even yet sustain my hope for some few days; but if at length my hope shall give way, you will see how indignantly I have borne this disappointment; and your neglect is all the less to be tolerated, because Geneva at this present time affords you such abundant material for correspondence. Du Tailly, however, has written to me, and yet I do not clearly understand from his expressions what has been the catastrophe of this drama. Michael, also, the printer, has communicated to me at Blecheret, that my return thitherward might be brought about; but rather would I submit to death a hundred times than to that cross, on which one had to perish daily a thousand times over. This piece of information I have wished incidentally to communicate to you, that to the utmost of your power you may set yourself to oppose the measures of those who shall endeavour to draw me back thither. And that I may not appear to be looking in one direction and rowing in another, I will lay open my mind to you whenever at any time you ask me to do so. We are as yet in a state of suspense as to the marriage,[1] and this annoys me exceedingly, forasmuch as the relations of that young lady of rank are so urgent that I may

1 Calvin's own marriage with Idelette de Bure, which was delayed until August.

take her unto myself, which, indeed, I would never think of doing, unless the Lord had altogether demented me. But because it is unpleasant to refuse, especially in the case of such persons, who overwhelm me altogether with their kindness, most earnestly do I desire to be delivered out of this difficulty. We hope, however, that this will very shortly be the case; and during the next four or five days another engagement will turn away my mind from the subject, and itself will engross all my attention.

In this place hitherto many individuals were in the habit of making a rash approach to the sacrament of the Supper. On Easter-day, when I gave out the intimation that we were to celebrate the Supper on next Lord's-day, I announced, at the same time, that no one would be admitted to the table of the Lord by me, who had not beforehand presented himself for examination. The greatest difficulty will arise in correcting that silly eagerness to press forward which has taken possession of some Frenchmen, so that it can scarcely be driven out of them. You are aware of those regulations that have been made for the Academy, that the young men confining themselves to the distinction of the student's gown must lay aside the wearing of a sword, that they must give up their names to the rector, and such like. Now, in order to evade these rules they renounce entirely the profession of the belles-lettres; but as this bears upon it the face of manifest contumacy, I have resolved on no account to allow it, for I would rather that the whole of them should go away than that they should remain at the expense of discipline. Leo Juda[1] lately requested of me to allow him to publish, in German, with the addition of my name, the first of those two Epistles which I wrote four years ago; that one, indeed, (I mean the one in which I am made to coax and flatter the Popish bishops,) he has published at this fair-time without the name. The answer I gave was very

[1] Minister of the Church of Zurich.

friendly, but, at the same time, contained some rather cutting admonition. A little before that I had written almost to the same purpose to Bullinger. If it shall succeed I will let you know the course I may take. Our friends are hitherto at a standstill as to what they intend to do. The reason of their dilemma is because they have not as yet received any certain return by way of answer from the Emperor, who, however, begins to be much more tractable. The meeting of the King of England with our sovereign has somewhat tamed his arrogance, which may have considerable influence in changing the whole of his measures.[1] He made use of this sophism, that he would not bind himself to the King by promise on any account, but that he would inflate him with empty hopes for the future. Already the King seemed to himself to have possession of Milan. Lately, however, when the Emperor's inclination was put to proof by the ambassador, he found that it was not easy to bring him that length. It is said, indeed, that in everything he has given the King his choice, provided only that he does not ask Milan. On that account, therefore, it is that the Constable is gone to him, and if he does not get what he seeks, we suspect that they will be more ready to go to war than ever. Neither, indeed, will the King of England, in such a crisis of affairs, yield in any point, much less the admiral,[2] who is now restored to his former post of honour and favour. Before few months are over we shall see, if I am not mistaken, a wonderful change of scene, but, in the meanwhile, the Lord must be entreated that in this turn of affairs he would both hasten forward the decision and also confirm the resolution of our friends. May the Lord keep you all in safety,

1 This interview, which had been proposed to be held at Calais, in reference to fresh matrimonial projects of Henry VIII, did not take place, and after apparent hesitation on the part of the English monarch between an alliance with Francis I and one with the Emperor, he turned to Charles V, sacrificing at once the friendship of the King of France and that of the German Princes.

2 Sir William Fitz-William, high admiral, recently created Earl of Southampton.

continually under His protection. And foremost of them all, adieu, my very excellent and right trusty brother. Capito, Sturm, Bedrot, Claude, and my brother, salute you. Nicolas and the others do not know that I am writing.

11/TO PETER VIRET

Excuses for his silence
Sad news from France
Repugnance of Calvin to return to Geneva
His comparative estimate of Capito, Zwingli, Luther, and Œcolampadius

Strassburg, 19th May 1540

At length somewhat has been gained by my expostulation, for I have in some measure broken that unkind silence of so many months; but I do not take it so well, that when you ought plainly to have sought pardon, you chose rather to make a return in kind; for you make out that we are equally to blame except in this one point, that when both had come short in duty, I seized the opportunity and was the first to write. You thought, forsooth, to get out of the scrape in this way, as if in the meanwhile I had not written a hundred times to Farel, on condition that he would communicate with you, during which period I neither received a single letter from you, nor did you send even a salutation, except that which you once wrote at the end of a letter to Bucer. Therefore, true it is and of verity, that I cannot acquit you until you shall have approved your diligence for the future, on condition that if, as you are wont, you begin to grow slack in your correspondence, I shall be entitled to lay a double fine upon you. But that I may not appear to press too severely, I do hereby freely remit whatever there is of failure on your part, provided, for the future, you both perform your own share of duty, and pardon me if, perhaps, I shall have become too negligent.

Your letter was a very sad one to me, and all the more so because I can well imagine that cruel butchery to boil over without measure, as always happens whenever it has once burst forth, and there is no way of putting a stop to it. I wrote, however, to Farel, under the apprehension that what so long kept us in suspense would at length come to pass. Wherefore, unless the Lord open up some new outlet, there is no other way of helping our unhappy brethren than by our prayers and exhortations, which are, besides, so dangerous to their lives, that it is more discreet to abstain. The only remedy which almost alone remains, therefore, seems to be, that we commit their safety to the Lord.[1]

I read that passage of your letter, certainly not without a smile, where you show so much concern about my health, and recommend Geneva on that ground! Why could you not have said at the cross? for it would have been far preferable to perish once for all than to be tormented again in that place of torture. Therefore, my dear Viret, if you wish well to me, make no mention of such a proposal. It was, however, most agreeable to me to understand that the brothers La Fontaine were so anxious concerning my safety, and that you also had turned your mind to it: for, indeed, I can scarcely persuade myself that I am worth so much trouble. It is impossible for

1 While he sought the alliance of the Protestant princes of Germany, Francis I. persecuted the Protestants in his own dominions with an extreme rigour. The year 1540 witnessed numerous burnings at the stake, in the provinces of Dauphiny, Vivarais, at Paris, and in the valleys of Provence. There dwelt for many centuries a pastoral population, which was only known to the world by simplicity of manners and the purity of its faith. The Vaudois of Cabrières and Merindol, hated by the Roman Catholic clergy on account of their being estranged from the superstitions of the time, were devoted to death by the fanatical fury of the parliament of Aix. The arrest which condemned in the mass an innocent and inoffensive people to extermination, was dated 18th November 1540. The intercession of the Senate of Strasburg, of the Swiss Cantons, and of the German princes, suspended the execution of it until the year 1545.

me, however, not to be rejoiced by that kindness of good men towards me.

Capito, in his lectures, has some things which may be of much use to you in the illustration of Isaiah. But as he does not dictate any part to his hearers, and has not yet reached beyond the fourteenth chapter, his assistance cannot at present much help you. Zwingli, although he is not wanting in a fit and ready exposition, yet, because he takes too much liberty, often wanders far from the meaning of the Prophet. Luther is not so particular as to propriety of expression or the historical accuracy; he is satisfied when he can draw from it some fruitful doctrine. No one, as I think, has hitherto more diligently applied himself to this pursuit than Œcolampadius, who has not always, however, reached the full scope or meaning. It is true that you may now and then find the need of having appliances at hand, nevertheless I feel confident that the Lord has not deserted you.

About our affairs I do not write, in order that there may be more material for writing to Farel. All here greet you in the most friendly manner, Capito, Bucer, Matthias, Sturm, Bedrot. Hedio I have not seen since your letter was delivered to me. In return, on my part, salute Conrad, Corneille, James, Isnard, and the others; your aunt also, and your wife, whom, one and all, I wish to see.

The mention of Conrad, which had occurred to me, brings to mind that Gaspar, who lived with him for some time, was lately here, and has complained much to Sturm that I had defamed him in an offensive manner among good people, at the instigation of Grynée. He said nought about it to me, and merely saluted when he left my lecture. I wished you to know this, that in future you may be more on your guard. Adieu, most excellent and kind brother.

12/TO FAREL[1]

> *Prepares to depart for Geneva*
> *Self-denial of Calvin*
> *Absolute submission to the will of God*

Strassburg

When your letter was brought to me mine was already written; and although you will find that it does not agree in all points to what you require of me, I have thought it best to forward it to you, that you may be aware what my feelings were at the time when it arrived. Now, however, after that I have seen you press the matter further, and that our former guests associate openly in the same cause, I have again had recourse to our magistracy. Having read over your letter and those of the Genevese, I asked what in their opinion was now to be done. They answered, that there could be no doubt that, without calling any previous meeting, I ought immediately to set out thither; for that the question was not now open or doubtful, although it had not been formally settled. Therefore we prepare to start on the journey. In order, however, that the present supply of that Church may be provided for, which we are not willing should continue destitute, they are of opinion that Viret should by all means be sent for thither, in the meantime, while I am for the present distracted between two charges. When we come back our friends here will not refuse their consent to my return to Geneva. Moreover, Bucer has pledged himself that he will accompany me. I have written to them to that effect; and in order to make the promise all the more certain, Bucer has accompanied my letter by one from himself. As to my intended course of proceeding, this

---

1 Undated, but written most probably in the month of August 1541. It informs us about the last inward struggles of the Reformer on the eve of quitting Strassburg to return to Geneva.

is my present feeling; had I the choice at my own disposal, nothing would be less agreeable to me than to follow your advice. But when I remember that I am not my own, I offer up my heart, presented as a sacrifice to the Lord. Therefore there is no ground for your apprehension that you will only get fine words. Our friends are in earnest, and promise sincerely. And for myself, I protest that I have no other desire than that, setting aside all consideration of me, they may look only to what is most for the glory of God and the advantage of the Church. Although I am not very ingenious, I would not lack pretexts by which I might adroitly slip away, so that I should easily excuse myself in the sight of men, and show that it was no fault of mine. I am well aware, however, that it is God with whom I have to do, from whose sight such crafty imaginations cannot be withheld. Therefore I submit my will and my affections, subdued and held fast, to the obedience of God; and whenever I am at a loss for counsel of my own, I submit myself to those by whom I hope that the Lord himself will speak to me. When Capito wrote, he supposed, as I perceive, that I would, in a lengthy and tiresome narrative, relate to you the whole course of our deliberation; but it is enough that you have the sum of it; although I would have done that also had there been time. But the whole day was taken up in various avocations. At this present, after supper, I am not much inclined to trifle, by longer sitting up, with my health, which is at best in a doubtful state. This messenger has promised to return here at Christmas with the carriage, in which he can bring along with him to Wendelin, of the books which belong to him, ten copies of *The Institutes*, six of the *Commentaries on Jeremiah*: these you will give to be brought away with him.

13/TO FAREL[1]

Details of the death of the first Syndic, Amy Porral

Geneva, 16th June 1542

Would that I might attain to that discipline in contempt of this present life, and in the meditation of a holy death, as the experience of the past year, in the deaths of many pious persons, may well have brought me. Porral, the chief magistrate of the city, has departed to the Lord; his death, which could not be other than occasion of sadness to us, has been bitterly lamented. The manner of his decease, as it was in some respects consolatory to me, so, on the other hand, it increased my sorrow when I considered how great has been our loss in the bereavement of that one man. The day after he became unwell, when we were calling upon him, that is, Viret and myself, he told us that he considered himself in danger, for that the disease with which he was afflicted had been fatal in his family. Thereupon he had a long conversation on a variety of matters: he talked about them just as though he had been in sound and perfect health. During the two following days his sufferings were more acute, but, notwithstanding, his intellect was stronger, and he exhibited more fluency of speech than he had ever manifested in his life hitherto. Whoever called to see him, heard some suitable exhortation; and that you may not suppose it to have been mere talkative vanity, as far as was possible he applied to each individual what was best adapted to his circumstances, and most likely to be of use to him. Afterward he began to feel somewhat better, so that very much hope was entertained that he would be forthwith

[1] The Republic of Geneva incurred the loss of an excellent magistrate and friend in Porral, who had been named first Syndic of this year. He had concurred with Calvin in drawing up the Ecclesiastical Ordinances adopted the preceding year.

restored to health. In this state he continued for three days; at length, however, the disease began to grow more severe, so that it was evident that he was in the greatest danger. The more he was afflicted in body, the more animated and vivid was the spirit. I say nothing about the intermediate period; but upon the day of his death, about nine in the morning, we went thither, I and Viret. When I had spoken a few words, to set before him the cross, the grace of Christ, and the hope of eternal life – for we were unwilling to weary him with tedious addresses – he replied, that he received God's message as became him; that he knew the efficacy of the power of Christ for confirming the consciences of true believers. Thereupon he spoke in such a luminous manner on the work of the ministry, and all the benefits which accompany or flow from it as the means of grace, that we were both of us in a sort of stupor of astonishment; and whenever it recurs to my memory, even yet I grow bewildered. For he spoke in such a way that it seemed to reflect some discourse by one of ourselves after long and careful meditation. He concluded this part of his address by declaring, that the remission of sins which we promised on the authority of Christ, he received just the same as if an angel had appeared to him from heaven. After that he spoke of the unity of the Church, which he commended with marvellous praise; he bore testimony that, in his own experience, he had found no better or more certain source of consolation, in the struggle of death, than from having already been confirmed in the assurance of this unity. He had summoned, a little before, our two colleagues, and had been reconciled with them,[1] lest, having persisted in that dispute, others might make a bad use of it in following his example.

1 Two years before, he had a keen religious dispute with the minister Henri de la Mare, and James Bernard had supported his colleague. De la Mare upheld that the magistrate should not punish sins; that no one can have assurance of his election; that no one could go more gladly to his wedding than Jesus went to death. Amy Porral pronounced these opinions to be false and dangerous. This dispute, degenerating into a quarrel, had embroiled the two ministers with the magistrate.

And he had, moreover, said to ourselves, since the public edification of the Church compels you to bear with them as brethren, why might not I acknowledge them as pastors? He had previously, however, seriously admonished them, and reminded them of their sins. But I return to that last address. Turning himself to those who stood around, he exhorted every one to prize very highly the communion of the Church; such of them as are superstitious in the observance of days and ceremonies, he advised to lay aside their perverse opposition, and to agree with us, for that we better understood, and saw more clearly what was the prudent course than they did; that he had himself, also, been rather obstinate in these things, but that his eyes were at length opened to perceive how injurious contention might become. After that he made a short, serious, as well as sincere and lucid confession. Thence he proceeded to exhort us both, as well regarding the other departments of our charge as ministers, as also to constancy and firmness; and when he discoursed at some length on the future difficulties of the ministers of the Gospel, he seemed inspired with the foresight of a prophet. It was wonderful how wisely he spoke to purpose on what concerned the public good. He recommended as a most important step that we ought to lose no time in devoting our utmost attention to bring about a reconciliation among the cities in alliance with us.[1] 'However loudly some noisy people may clamour,' he said, 'don't trouble yourselves about it, and do not be discouraged.' My time will not admit of my relating everything. After we had submitted a few observations we engaged in prayer, and then took our leave and departed.

On the second afternoon, when my wife arrived, he told her to be of good courage whatever might happen, that she ought to consider that she had not been rashly led hither, but brought by the wonderful counsel of God, that she also might

[1] The disputes which had fallen out between Geneva and Berne had not yet been finally settled.

serve in the Gospel. A little while after he signified that his voice was gone; but even when his speech entirely failed he intimated that he retained a perfect consciousness of the confession which he had previously made, and in that same he would die. At the same time, having repeated the song of Simeon, with application of it to himself, 'I have seen,' he said, 'and have touched with my hand, that saving merciful Redeemer.' He then composed himself to rest. From that time he was speechless, but indicated at times, by a nod, that he had lost nothing of his strength of mind. About four o'clock I went thither with the Syndics; when, as often as he attempted to speak, and was hindered by obstruction in the throat, I requested that he would not further disturb himself, for that his confession was abundantly satisfactory. At length I began to speak as well as I could; he hearkened with a very composed and tranquil countenance. Scarcely had we left when he gave up his pious soul to Christ. This narrative, when you weigh the character of the man, will hardly appear credible to you; but I would have you understand that he had been thoroughly renewed in the spirit of his mind.

We are at present very much occupied in the choice of new colleagues, and the more so because, when we thought that we had fallen upon a very suitable one we afterwards discovered that he did not answer our expectation. When we fix anything definitely you shall receive information. There is no reason, although you may be absent, why you may not aid us with your counsel.—Adieu.

14/TO LUTHER[1]

Calvin submits to Luther several of his writings, of which he desires to obtain his approval

January 21, 1545

To the very excellent pastor of the Christian Church, Dr M. Luther, my much respected father.

When I saw that my French fellow-countrymen, as many of them as had been brought out from the darkness of the Papacy to soundness of the faith, had altered nothing as to their public profession, and that they continued to defile themselves with the sacrilegious worship of the Papists, as if they had never tasted the savour of true doctrine, I was altogether unable to restrain myself from reproving so great sloth and negligence, in the way that I thought it deserved. How, indeed, can this faith, which lies buried in the heart within, do otherwise than break forth in the confession of the faith? What kind of religion can that be, which lies submerged under seeming idolatry? I do not undertake, however, to handle the argument here, because I have done so at large already in two little tractates, wherein, if it shall not be troublesome to you to glance over them, you will more clearly perceive both

---

1 Special interest attaches to this letter, the only one which the French Reformer had written to the German Reformer. Inspired by the deep conviction of the unity of the reformed churches, written with as much moderation as respect, the message of conciliation was not even listened to. Soured by the quarrel about the sacraments, in which he took too great a share during the latter years of his life, Luther evinced daily more and more irritation against the theologians of Switzerland, and Melanchthon did not even venture to present the letter of Calvin, to whom he wrote in sadness: 'I have not shown your letter to Dr Martin, for he takes up many things suspiciously, and does not like his replies to questions of the kind you have proposed to him, to be carried round and handed from one to another . . . At present I am looking forward to exile and other sorrows. Farewell. On the day upon which, 3846 years ago, Noah entered into the ark, by which God gave testimony of his purpose never to forsake his Church even when she quivers under the shock of the great sea billows.'

what I think, and the reasons which have compelled me to form that opinion. By the reading of them, indeed, some of our people, while hitherto they were fast asleep in a false security, having been awakened, have begun to consider what they ought to do. But because it is difficult either casting aside all consideration of self to expose their lives to danger, or having roused the displeasure of mankind to encounter the hatred of the world, or having abandoned their prospects at home in their native land, to enter upon a life of voluntary exile, they are withheld or kept back by these difficulties from coming to a settled determination. They put forth other reasons, however, and those somewhat specious, whereby one may perceive that they only seek to find some sort of pretext or other. In these circumstances, because they hang somehow in suspense, they are desirous to hear your opinion, which as they do deservedly hold in reverence, so it shall serve greatly to confirm them. They have therefore requested me, that I would undertake to send a trusty messenger to you, who might report your answer to us upon this question. And because I thought it was of very great consequence for them to have the benefit of your authority, that they might not fluctuate thus continually, and I myself stood besides in need of it, I was unwilling to refuse what they required. Now, therefore, much respected father in the Lord, I beseech you by Christ, that you will not grudge to take the trouble for their sake and mine, first, that you would peruse the epistle written in their name, and my little books, cursorily and at leisure hours, or that you would request some one to take the trouble of reading, and report the substance of them to you. Lastly, that you would write back your opinion in a few words. Indeed, I am unwilling to give you this trouble in the midst of so many weighty and various employments; but such is your sense of justice, that you cannot suppose me to have done this unless compelled by the necessity of the case; I therefore trust that you will pardon me. Would that I could fly to you, that

I might even for a few hours enjoy the happiness of your society; for I would prefer, and it would be far better, not only upon this question, but also about others, to converse personally with yourself; but seeing that it is not granted to us on earth, I hope that shortly it will come to pass in the kingdom of God. Adieu, most renowned sir, most distinguished minister of Christ, and my ever-honoured father. The Lord himself rule and direct you by his own Spirit, that you may persevere even unto the end, for the common benefit and good of his own Church.

15/TO MELANCHTHON[1]

He complains of Luther's tyranny, and affectionately exhorts Melanchthon to manifest greater decision and firmness

June 28, 1545

Would that the fellow-feeling which enables me to condole with you, and to sympathize in your heaviness, might also impart the power in some degrees, at least, to lighten your sorrow. If the matter stands as the Zurichers say it does, then they have just occasion for their writing. Your Pericles[2] allows himself to be carried beyond all due bounds with his love of thunder, especially seeing that his own case is by no means the better of the two. We all of us do acknowledge that we are much indebted to him. Neither shall I submit myself unwillingly, but be quite content, that he may bear the chief

1 Hurt at the new attacks which Luther began to direct against their doctrine in his Short Confession upon the Supper, the ministers of Zurich published an Apology in 1545. Provoked by Luther's violence, this reply irritated the zealous Lutherans, afflicted Melanchthon, and delighted the adversaries of the Reform by the unseemly divisions which had got the upper hand among them.

2 Pericles (*c.* 495–429 B.C.) Athenian statesman and military leader under whom Athens reached the height of her power.

sway, provided that he can manage to conduct himself with moderation. Howbeit, in the Church we must always be upon our guard, lest we pay too great a deference to men. For it is all over with her, when a single individual, be he whosoever you please, has more authority than all the rest, especially where this very person does not scruple to try how far he may go. Where there exists so much division and separation as we now see, it is indeed no easy matter to still the troubled waters and bring about composure. But were we all of that mind we ought to be, some remedy might, perhaps, be discovered; most certainly we convey a mean example to posterity, while we rather prefer, of our own accord, entirely to throw away our liberty, than to irritate a single individual by the slightest offence. But, you will say, his disposition is vehement, and his impetuosity is ungovernable; – as if that very vehemence did not break forth with all the greater violence when all shew themselves alike indulgent to him, and allow him to have his way, unquestioned. If this specimen of overbearing tyranny has sprung forth already as the early blossom in the springtide of a reviving Church, what must we expect in a short time, when affairs have fallen into a far worse condition? Let us therefore bewail the calamity of the Church, and not devour our grief in silence, but venture boldly to groan for freedom. Consider, besides, whether the Lord may not have permitted you to be reduced to these straits, in order that you may be brought to a yet fuller confession upon this very article. It is indeed most true, as I acknowledge it to be, that which you teach, and also that hitherto by a kindly method of instruction, you have studiously endeavoured to recall the minds of men from strife and contention. I applaud your prudence and moderation. While, however, you dread, as you would some hidden rock, to meddle with this question from the fear of giving offence, you are leaving in perplexity and suspense very many persons who require from you somewhat of a more certain sound, on which they can repose; and besides, as I remember I have sometimes said to you, it is not over-creditable to us, that we refuse to sign, even with ink, that very doctrine which many saints have not hesitated to leave witnessed with their blood. Perhaps, therefore, it is now the will of God thus to open up the way for a full and satisfactory declaration of your own mind, that those who look up to your authority may not be brought to a stand, and kept in a state of perpetual doubt and hesitation. These, as you are aware, amount to a very great number of persons. Nor do I mention this so much for the purpose of arousing you to freedom of action, as for the sake of comforting you; for indeed, unless I could entertain the hope, that out of this vexatious collision some benefit shall have arisen, I would be utterly worn out by far deeper distress. Howbeit, let us wait patiently for a peaceable conclusion, such as it shall please the Lord to vouchsafe. In the meanwhile, let us run the race set before us with deliberate courage. I return you very many thanks for your reply, and at the same time, for the extraordinary kindness which Claude assures me had been shewn to him by you.[1] I can form a conjecture what you would have been to myself, from your having given so kind and courteous a reception to my friend. I do not cease however, to offer my chief thanks to God, who hath vouchsafed us that agreement in opinion upon the whole of that question about which we had both been examined; for although there is a slight difference in certain particulars, we are, notwithstanding, very well agreed upon the general question itself.

[1] Claude de Senarclens returned to Geneva loaded with testimonials of affection from the German Reformers.

16/TO MONSIEUR DE FALAIS[1]

Exhortation to glorify God amid poverty and persecution.

Monsieur:

Although I do not know the state of mind or body in which you are at present, nevertheless, I have good confidence in God that, whether in health or sickness, He gives you strength to overcome all the annoyance you may have to encounter. For you are no novice in the fight, seeing that for a long time past this good Lord has begun to prepare you for it; and nothing has happened to you which you had not looked for beforehand. But it is time to show in reality that when you have set yourself frankly to follow Jesus Christ, you have not done so without being resolved to hold fellowship with Him at the cross, since He has done us that honour to be crucified in us, to glorify us with Himself. And there is no doubt, even at the time when you were in your own mansion, and in the peaceable enjoyment of your property, you would have had the courage to quit everything had it so pleased Him, and that you were of the number of those who *use the things of this world as not abusing them*, [1 Cor 7. 31]. But, forasmuch as it is very reasonable that one should be taught by experience discernment of what our affection is most set upon, you are to consider that it has been our Lord's will to give you to

1 Letter without date, written at the same time as the following (September 1545). Summoned in the name of the Emperor to leave Strassburg and return to Brabant, M. de Falais had not obeyed that command. This refusal, in stirring up the imperial displeasure against him, had exposed him, without defence, to the interested denunciations of his enemies. The butt of slanderous accusations, he saw his character misunderstood, his name outraged, his property put under sequestration, while he pined away himself, a prey to sickness and discouragement.

many others for an example, and, by this means, to glorify
His name in you.

On the other hand, we know not what it is to part with
everything for the love of Him, until He has brought us to
the test. True it is, that he who has taken off his affection from
the goods of this world has already sold all, and has made
himself poor, so far as depends upon himself; but the fruit
and the proof of this spiritual poverty are, patiently to endure
the loss of worldly goods, and without any regret, when it
pleases our heavenly Father that we should be despoiled of
them. I do not set these things before you as to one who is
ignorant, or who has need of lengthy remonstrances, but for
the love that I bear you, of which God is my witness. I take
comfort along with you, as I also suffer in your person.

The time then is arrived when you must manifest that you
reckon all things no more than dung, that you may reach
forward to Him who not only has bestowed on you all His
benefits, but also Himself. And since God has permitted that
you should be disburdened of a part of your worldly goods,
you are to consider that He has clearly perceived that, for the
present, they would prove a useless burden for you. I say a part,
albeit that, as it were, the whole has been snatched away from
you, yet, so that there remains, as I hope, an abundance for
your use. These whirlpools, however, which engulf the whole
world, have daily greater want than those whose substance
they have swallowed down.

In short, you have not been lessened one whit, seeing that
our Lord, while teaching you that your inheritance is in
heaven, has made provision for what might be useful for the
life of the body, by bestowing contentment upon you, and,
as regards property, more than was needful to make you contented. If the whole should be taken away from you, there
would yet remain the consolation to which we must chiefly
betake ourselves, namely, to yield ourselves up entirely. It is

certain, that having the Son of God, we suffer no injury in being deprived of all else: for thus highly ought we indeed to prize Him. But further, since this kind Saviour has so benignly upheld you, that while calling you to the fellowship of His cross, He has provided for your worldly comfort, it is quite fitting that you submit yourself to His good pleasure, and, besides, rejoice that in being minished, so far as the world is concerned, you are thereby so much the more exalted before Him and His angels. For howsoever the world strives, by all means, to bury Jesus Christ in ignominy, His burial cannot be otherwise than glorious, not only in Himself, but also in His members. Let us therefore endure personal humiliation, as shall seem good to Him. But my letters would never come to an end were I to follow out the drift of this discourse. Therefore, Monseigneur, after having humbly commended me to your kind favour, I pray our good Lord that He would so work in you now more powerfully than ever, to make you despise all that is in the world, and to make you breathe upwards direct to Him with your whole heart, without being turned aside by anything whatsoever, making you taste what is the worth of the hope which He reserves for us in heaven; and that it may please Him to lighten your burden as regards the body, in order that you may be all the better disposed, well to meditate upon the favours He has bestowed upon you, and to take delight in them, acknowledging the love which He has shewn you. My wife, who is sick in bed, begs also to be humbly commended to your kind remembrance. This bearer, who is of the better sort, and of the stamp such as you require, will inform you more at large concerning our state.

17/TO JOHN FRELLON

Rupture of the Relations between Calvin and Servetus.

This 13th of February 1546.

Seigneur Jehan:

By cause that your last letter was brought to me at my going away, I had not leisure to reply to what was inclosed therein. Since my return, at the first leisure that I have had, I have been quite willing to satisfy your desire; not that I have had great hope of late of being profitable to a certain person,[1] judging from the disposition in which I see him to be; but in order to try once more if there shall be any means of bringing him back, which will be, when God shall have wrought in him so effectually, that he has become entirely another man. Since he has written to me in so proud a spirit, I would fain have beaten down his pride a little, speaking more harshly to him than is my wont; but I could scarcely do otherwise. For I do assure you that there is no lesson which is more necessary for him than to learn humility, which must come to him from the Spirit of God, not otherwise. But we must observe a measure here also. If God grants that favour to him and to us, that the present answer turns to his profit, I shall have whereof to rejoice. If he persists in the same style as he has now done, you will lose time in asking me to bestow labour

---

[1] The mysterious person who is pointed at in this letter, is no other than Michel Servetus — seven years before the trial which was to attach so fatal a celebrity to his name. Settled as a physician at Vienne, in Dauphiny, he kept up a correspondence with Calvin, under the pseudonym of John Frellon, and he had just sent the Reformer an extract of the work which was in preparation under the title of *Christianismi Restitutio (The Reconstruction of Christianity)*, expressing at the same time the desire of coming to Geneva. See the following letter.

upon him, for I have other affairs which press upon me more closely; and I would make a matter of conscience of it, not to busy myself further, having no doubt that it was a temptation of Satan to distract and withdraw me from other more useful reading. And therefore I beg you to content yourself with what I have done in the matter, unless you see some better order to be taken therein.

Wherefore, after my commendation to you, I beseech our good Lord to have you in his keeping.

18/TO FAREL

> *Reply to various questions*
> *Threat against Servetus*
> *Imprisonment of one of the leaders of the Libertines*

Geneva, 13th February 1546

You will be at ease regarding your brothers since you received the letter of Claude. The messenger who brought it asked whether mine would be ready when I returned from sermon, after three o'clock. I replied in the negative; but I bid him dine at my house with my wife, as I myself had been invited to dine with Macrin. I promised to be with him immediately after dinner, to make a brief reply. He did not come [to my house,] but hurried away without waiting a moment, so that I was confounded by so sudden a departure. And yet the youth had not appeared to me to behave badly in general. I trust the reflection may occur to your brothers, that they have been thus extricated from all their difficulties by the hand of God, in order that they make the greater haste [in the work.] It did not become the Israelites, when a way was opened up to them, to show remissness in immediately girding themselves for flight.[1] Such would have been the burden of my epistle had not the messenger deceived me; but I am confident that they are burning with ardour of their own accord. I now come to your own contests.[2] If the ungodly still occasion you some trouble, when that letter shall arrive, I have briefly expressed in it what I think should be your mode of proceeding. I should wish, however, the matter to be discussed *viva voce*; and that, thereupon, the result, or something like it, be committed to writing. You will perhaps smile because I suggest nothing out of the common, as you looked for something recondite and elevated at my hands: but I do not wish, nor, besides, is it right to be fettered by your estimate of me. I had rather, however, be foolish by so writing, than by my silence lead you to suppose that your entreaties were neglected by me. If nothing can be effected by reasoning, and in this lawful way, the Bernese must be privately prevailed upon not to allow that wild beast to go out of its den. I do not sufficiently comprehend your meaning regarding a treaty, unless it be, as I conjecture, that you are turning your thoughts to some sort of alliance, with a view to your receiving the assistance of the Bernese; and that just as they guard the liberty of the people by the law of the state, so they may protect ministers in their office by some title which commands respect. If that be provided for, I do not disapprove of [the alliance.] Bear in mind, that recourse should be had to those extraordinary remedies only when there is the exculpatory plea of an ultimate necessity. In the next place, be very cautious lest anything you do be such as may injure your interests in time to come. You may have greater cause of regret in that you once received aid, and were parties to a compact, than if you were to remain in your original servitude. Marcourt has, without doubt,

1 Decimated by cruel persecution, the faithful of Dauphiné, the native country of Farel, had inquired of the ministers of French Switzerland, whether it was lawful for them to have recourse to flight, in order to escape the fury of their adversaries. Numerous refugees had already settled at Geneva.

2 Ecclesiastical embroilments with the Seigneury of Berne.

already promised a place for himself; for he publicly proclaims that he does not regard the consent of the brethren,
since he is desired, both by magistrates and people, and he
has no doubt but that they are indignant against you. Finally,
since he prematurely discloses the wickedness of his character,
he must be repulsed by all artifices, lest he rise to a position
in which he is able to perform what he threatens. With regard
to those who gave out that we were establishing here a per-
manent seat of despotism, under colour of defence, let us
suffer this rumour to spread on both sides. Their impudence
has been met with civility and mildness, so that they ought
to be ashamed of themselves. I trust that they will keep quiet.
I seek, as far as I am able, to persuade our friends to remain
unconcerned. Servetus lately wrote to me, and coupled with
his letter a long volume of his delirious fancies, with the
Thrasonic boast, that I should see something astonishing and
unheard of. He takes it upon him to come hither, if it be
agreeable to me. But I am unwilling to pledge my word for
his safety, for if he shall come, I shall never permit him to
depart alive, provided my authority be of any avail.[1]

More than fifteen days have now elapsed since Cartelier[2]
was imprisoned, for having, at supper in his own house, raged
against me with such insolence as to make it clear that he was
not then in his right senses. I concealed what I felt, but I
testified to the judge that it would be agreeable to me were
he proceeded against with the utmost rigour of the law. I
wished to go to see him. Access was prohibited by decree of
the Senate; and yet some good men accuse me of cruelty, for-

1 See the preceding letter. It appears that relations between Calvin and Servetus continued in a state of interruption, as is proved by the following
passage of a letter of Calvin to Viret, dated 1st September 1548: 'I think I once
read to you my answer to Servetus. I was at length disinclined from striving
longer with the incurable obstinacy of a heretic; and, indeed, I ought to have
followed the advice of Paul. He now attacks you. You will see how long you
ought to persist in rebutting his follies. He will twist nothing out of me henceforward.'

2 One of the most violent members of the party that combated the influence
and institutions of the reformer at Geneva.

sooth, because I so pertinaciously revenge my injuries.[1] I have been requested by his friends to undertake the part of intercessor. I refused to do so, except on these two conditions, viz., that no suspicion should attach to me, and that the honour of Christ should remain intact. I have now done. I abide the judgment of the Council. Adieu, brother, and most sincere friend. We all salute you and your sisters. You will convey to the brethren the best salutations in my name, and that of my brethren in the ministry. May God ever bless you and prosper your labours.

19/TO VIRET[2]

Calvin invites his friend to Geneva after the death of his wife

Geneva, 8th March 1546

Come, on this condition, that you disengage your mind not only from grief, but also from every annoyance. Do not fear that I will impose any burden upon you, for through my means you will be allowed to take whatever rest is agreeable to you. If any one prove troublesome to you, I will interpose. The brethren, also, make the same promise to you as I do. I

1 Calvin showed himself, on more than one occasion, disposed to forgive personal injuries, as the Registers of Council testify: 'A woman having abused M. Calvin, it is directed that she be consigned to prison. Liberated at the request of the said M. Calvin, and discharged with a reproof.' 12th December 1545.

2 Viret was at that time plunged into the deepest affliction. He had just lost, after a long illness, his wife, Elizabeth Turtaz, of Orbe. The grief which he felt on that occasion is expressed in a very touching manner in a letter written many years afterwards to Calvin: 'I was so completely dispirited and prostrated by that arrow of affliction, that the whole world appeared to me nothing but a burden. There was nothing pleasant, nothing that could mitigate my grief of mind.' The friends of Viret, and especially Farel and Calvin, lavished upon him, during that trial, marks of the most brotherly affection. The correspondence of Calvin furnishes us with illustrations of this affection.

will also be surety that the citizens do not interfere with your wishes.

I know not what I ought to imprecate on the wretches who had spread a report of your death. Never did a letter from you arrive more opportunely. Although your death was announced, yet as mention was made of poison, Textor was already in the midst of preparations for the journey, that he might speed to Orbe on fleet horses. A great part of the brethren were present, all overwhelmed with deep affliction. Shortly afterward your letter made its appearance, and such exultation instantly broke forth, that we were hardly masters of our senses. It was fortunate that we did not pass a night of sorrow, else I should not have borne it without danger. But why do I detain you, and not rather incite you to hasten hither as quickly as possible? Adieu, brother and most agreeable friend. Salute respectfully the brethren James, Ribitti, Hubert, Cordier, Celio, Francis, Merlin. The Lord protect you and the remainder of your family.

20/TO FAREL

False report of Calvin's death
Proposition (query) by the wife of Amy Perrin
Calumnious accusation against Idelette de Bure
Journey of Farel to Geneva

Geneva, 21st August 1547

I am more grateful to you than words can readily express, for having spontaneously transferred to us your credit and service, when you thought that we were pressed by great difficulties. In this, however, you did nothing that was novel or unexpected. The reason why I did not avail myself of your offer, was that various rumours were everywhere flying about which I thought had been extinguished, but which would have been the more increased had I summoned hither you and Viret. You know with what sort of men we have to deal, and how eager they are for an opportunity of speaking against us. Letters were daily arriving, especially from Lyons, from which I learned that I had been more than ten times killed.[1] It was therefore proper that the ungodly should be deprived of the occasion of talking. The senate is now quieted, and is favourably disposed to the good cause. Amy, our friend, is still in France.[2] His wife is with her father, where she carries on her revels in her usual fashion, and yet we requested the Senate that all past offences might be forgiven her, if she shewed anything to warrant a hope of repentence. That petition has not been granted, for she has gone so far as to have cut off all hope of pardon for herself. As the day of the [Lord's] Supper draws near, I may meet with Penthesilaea. Froment lately made a movement about a reconciliation, but he wished the matter to be settled according to his own arbitration. I replied that our church was not so destitute but that there were brethren competent to undertake that duty. We shall make every effort. And yet she has cruelly wounded me. For when at the baptism of our child James, I had admitted the truth about the fault of my wife and her former husband,[3] she

1 'M. Calvin has represented that letters have been written to him, as well from Bourgoyne as from Lyons, to the effect that the children of Geneva were willing to give five hundred crowns to have him put to death; he does not know who these are.' *Registers of the Consistory*, 1st September 1547.

2 Charged with an important mission to the court of King Henry II, Perrin, on his return, was subjected to the accusation of treason in the carrying out of his commission. The King of France had said that he would give two millions to be master of Geneva. Perrin was accused of having replied, that two hundred horse would be sufficient to conquer the city. It could not however be proved that he had contracted secret engagements with France. He was nevertheless imprisoned, but afterwards released at the request of the Seigneury of Berne, and stripped of his offices.

3 Idelette de Bure's late husband, Jean Storder, had originally been an Anabaptist. According to the doctrines of that sect, the marriage to be legitimate had no need of the sanction of the magistrate.

calumniously asserted among her own friends, that my wife was therefore a harlot; such is her bold impudence. I shall treat her not according to what she deserves, but according to what my office demands. Add that N. had invented a most calumnious fable, to the effect, that I had received a severe reprimand from you and Viret, on the ground that, having been placed here by you in your room, and by way of deputy, I abused my precarious authority. You will now, however, come at a much more opportune time than you would have done before. You would hear everything that cannot be committed to writing. You might apply your hand to wounds that are not yet well healed. We might consult together about the remedying of occult diseases. You will therefore see whether you will have any leisure. I have commenced work upon the Fathers of Trent;[1] but the beginnings proceed slowly. The reason is, I have not an hour that is free from incessant interruptions. Adieu, most sound-hearted brother, and matchless friend; salute respectfully fellow-ministers and your family in my name. May the Lord be always present with you, direct you, and bless your labours. Amen.

---

[1] Allusion to the work which Calvin was at that time preparing against the Council of Trent, and which appeared at the end of the year.

21/TO THE PROTECTOR SOMERSET[1]

Duties imposed on the Protector by the high office which he holds
Plan of a complete reformation in England
Preaching of the pure Word of God
Rooting out of abuses
Correction of vices and scandalous offences.

Geneva, 22nd October 1548

Monseigneur:

Although God has endowed you with singular prudence, largeness of mind, and other virtues required in that station wherein He has set you, and for the affairs which He has put into your hand; nevertheless, inasmuch as you deem me to be a servant of His Son, whom you desire above all else to obey, I feel assured, that for the love of Him you will receive with courtesy that which I write in His name, as indeed I have no other end in view, save only, that in following out yet more and more what you have begun, you may advance His honour, until you have established His kingdom in as great perfection as is to be looked for in the world. And you will perceive likewise as you read, that without advancing any-

1 Edward Seymour, Earl of Hertford, Duke of Somerset was Regent of England, under the minority of Edward VI. It was under his administration that the reformation was victoriously established in England. Supported by Parliament, he suppressed the troubles which arose in some parts of the kingdom after the death of Henry VIII, confirmed the king's supremacy, abolished private masses and the worship of images, and restored the communion in both kinds. He held a correspondence with Calvin, who dedicated to him (June 24, 1548) his *Commentary on the First Epistle of Paul to Timothy*; and by advice of the reformer, he offered asylum to the exiles, Bucer, Fagi, Ochino, and Peter Martyr, banished for the sake of their religion from the Continent. Loved by the people, hated by the nobles, he made himself unpopular by his lack of success in the war which he kept up against the Scots, and in France; was overthrown by a conspiracy of the nobility, imprisoned in the Tower of London, (October 1549) and only recovered his liberty the year following, to perish in 1552 on the scaffold, victim of the ambition of Warwick, Duke of Northumberland.

thing of my own, the whole is drawn from His own pure doctrine. Were I to look merely at the dignity and grandeur of your position, there would seem no access whatsoever for a man of my quality. But since you do not refuse to be taught of the Master whom I serve, but rather prize above all else the grace which He has bestowed in numbering you among His disciples, methinks I have no need to make you any long excuse or preface, because I deem you well disposed to receive whatsoever proceeds from Him.

We have all reason to be thankful to our God and Father, that He has been pleased to employ you in so excellent a work as that of setting up the purity and right order of His worship in England by your means, and establishing the doctrine of salvation, that it may there be faithfully proclaimed to all those who shall consent to hear it; that He has vouchsafed you such firmness and constancy to persevere hitherto, in spite of so many trials and difficulties; that He has helped you with His mighty arm, in blessing all your counsels and your labours, to make them prosper. These are grounds of thankfulness which stir up all true believers to magnify His name. Seeing however, that Satan never ceases to upheave new conflicts, and that it is a thing in itself so difficult, that nothing can be more so, to cause the truth of God to have peaceable dominion among men, who by nature are most prone to falsehood; while on the other hand, there are so many circumstances which prevent its having free course; and most of all, that the superstitions of Antichrist, having taken root for so long time, cannot be easily uprooted from men's hearts, – you have much need, methinks, to be confirmed by holy exhortations. I cannot doubt, indeed, that you have felt this from experience; and shall therefore deal all the more frankly with you, because, as I hope, my deliberate opinion will correspond with your own desire. Were my exhortations even uncalled for, you would bear with the zeal and earnestness which has led me to offer them. I believe, therefore, that the need of them which you feel, will make them all the more welcome. However this may be, Monseigneur, may it please you to grant me audience in some particular reformations which I propose to lay here briefly before you, in the hope that, when you shall have listened to them, you will at least find some savour of consolation therein, and feel the more encouraged to prosecute the holy and noble enterprise in which God has hitherto been pleased to employ you.

I have no doubt that the great troubles which have fallen out for some time past, must have been very severe and annoying to you, and especially as many may have found in them occasion of offence, forasmuch as they were partly excited under cover of the change of religion. Wherefore you must necessarily have felt them very keenly, as well on account of the apprehensions they may have raised in your mind, as of the murmurs of the ignorant or disaffected, and also of the alarm of the well-disposed. Indeed, the mere rumour which I heard from afar, caused me heartfelt anxiety, until I was informed that God had begun to apply a remedy thereto. However, since perhaps they are not yet entirely allayed, or seeing that the devil may have kindled them anew, it will be well that you call to mind what the sacred history relates of good King Hezekiah, (2 *Chron* 32.,) namely, that after he had abolished the superstitions throughout Judea, reformed the state of the church according to the law of God, he was even then so pressed by his enemies, that it almost seemed as if he was a lost and ruined man. It is not without reason that the Holy Spirit pointedly declares, that such an affliction happened to him immediately after having re-established the true religion in his realm; for it may well have seemed reasonable to himself, that having striven with all his might to set up the reign of God, he should have peace within his own kingdom. Thus, all faithful princes and governors of countries are forewarned by that example, that however earnest they may be in banishing idolatry and in promoting the true worship of

God, their faith may yet be tried by diverse temptations. So God permits and wills it to be thus, to manifest the constancy of his people, and to lead them to look above the world. Meanwhile, the devil also does his work, endeavouring to ruin sound doctrine by indirect means, working as it were underground, forasmuch as he could not openly attain his end. But according to the admonition of St James, [James 5. 11,] who tells us, that in considering the patience of Job, we must look to the end of it, so ought we, Monseigneur, to look to the end which was vouchsafed to this good king. We see there that God was a present help in all his perplexities, and that at length he came off victorious. Wherefore, seeing that His arm is not shortened, and that in the present day He has the defence of the truth and the salvation of His own as much at heart as ever, never doubt that He will come to your aid, and that not once only, but in all the trials He may send you.

If the majority of the world oppose the Gospel and even strive with rage and violence to hinder its progress, we ought not to think it strange. It proceeds from the ingratitude of men, which has always shown itself, and ever will, in drawing back when God comes near, and even in kicking against Him when He would put His yoke upon them. More than that, because by nature they are wholly given to hypocrisy, they cannot bear to be brought to the clear light of the Word of God, which lays bare their baseness and shame, nor to be drawn forth out of their superstitions, which serve them as a hiding-hole and shady covert. It is nothing new, then, if we meet with contradiction when we attempt to lead men back to the pure worship of God. And we have, besides, the clear announcement of our Lord Jesus, who tells us that He has brought a sword along with His Gospel. But let not this daunt us, nor make us shrink and be fearful, for at last, when men shall have rebelled most stoutly, and vomited forth all their rage, they shall be put to confusion in a moment, and shall destroy themselves by the fury of their own onset. That is a true saying, in the second Psalm, that God shall only laugh at their commotion; that is to say, that seeming to connive, He will let them bluster, as if the affair did not at all concern Him. But it always happens, that at length they are driven back by His power, wherewith if we be armed, we have a sure and invincible munition, whatsoever plots the devil may frame against us, and shall know by experience in the end, that even as the Gospel is the message of peace and of reconciliation between God and us, it will also avail us to pacify men; and in this way we shall understand, that it is not in vain that Isaiah has said, [Is 2. 4,] that when Jesus Christ shall rule in the midst of us by His doctrine, the swords shall be turned into ploughshares, and the spears into pruning-hooks.

Albeit, however, the wickedness and opposition of men may be the cause of the sedition and rebellion which rises up against the Gospel, let us look to ourselves, and acknowledge that God chastises our faults by those who would otherwise serve Satan only. It is an old complaint, that the Gospel is the cause of all the ills and calamities that befall mankind. We see, in fact, from history, that shortly after Christianity had been everywhere spread abroad, there was not, so to speak, a corner of the earth which was not horribly afflicted. The uproar of war, like a universal fire, was kindled in all lands. Land-floods on the one hand, and famine and pestilence on the other, a chaotic confusion of order and civil polity to such a degree, that it seemed as if the world was presently about to be overturned. In like manner we have seen in our times, since the Gospel has begun to be set up, much misery; to such an extent, indeed, that every one complains we are come upon an unhappy period, and there are very few who do not *groan* under this burden. While, then, we feel the blow, we ought to look upward to the hand of Him who strikes, and ought also to consider why the blow is sent. The reason why He makes us thus to feel His rod is neither very obscure nor difficult to be understood. We know that the Word, by which He would guide us to salvation, is an invaluable treasure; with what reverence do we receive it when He presents it to us? Seeing, then, that we make no great account of that which is so precious, God has good reason to avenge Himself of our ingratitude. We hear also what Jesus Christ announces [*Luke* 12. 47], that the servant knowing the will of his Master, and not doing it, deserves double chastisement. Since, therefore, we are so remiss in obeying the will of our God, who has declared it to us more than a hundred times already, let us not think it strange if His anger rage more severely against us, seeing that we are all the more inexcusable. When we do not cultivate the good seed, there is much reason that the thorns and thistles of Satan should spring up to trouble and annoy us. Since we do not render to our Creator the submission which is due to Him, it is no wonder that men rise up against us.

From what I am given to understand, Monseigneur, there are two kinds of rebels who have risen up against the King and the Estates of the Kingdom. The one, a fantastical sort of persons, who, under colour of the Gospel, would put all into confusion. The others are persons who persist in the superstitions of the Roman Antichrist. Both alike deserve to be repressed by the sword which is committed to you, since they not only attack the King, but strive with God, who has placed him upon a royal throne, and has committed to you the protection as well of his person as of his majesty. But the chief point is, to endeavour as much as possible, that those who have some savour of a liking for the doctrine of the Gospel, so as to hold fast, should receive it with such humility and godly fear, as to renounce self in order to serve God; for they ought seriously to consider that God would awaken them all, so that in good earnest they may profit far more from His Word than they have ever yet done. These madmen, who would have the whole world turned back into a chaos of licentiousness, are hired by Satan to defame the Gospel, as if

it bred nothing but revolt against princes, and all sorts of disorder in the world. Wherefore, all the faithful ought to be
deeply grieved. The Papists, in endeavouring to maintain the
corruptions and abominations of their Romish idol, show
themselves to be the open enemies of the grace of Jesus Christ,
and of all His ordinances. That ought likewise to occasion
great sickness at heart among all those who have a single drop
of godly zeal. And therefore they ought every one of them
earnestly to consider, that these are the rods of God for their
correction. And wherefore? Just because they do not set a
proper value on the doctrine of salvation. Herein lies the chief
remedy for the silencing of such calumnies, that those who
make profession of the Gospel be indeed renewed after the
image of God, so as to make manifest that our Christianity
does not occasion any interruption of the humanities of social
life, and to give good evidence, by their temperance and
moderation, that being governed by the Word of God, we
are not unruly people subject to no restraint, and so by an
upright holy life shut the mouth of all the evil speakers. For
by this means God, being pacified, shall withdraw His hand,
and instead of, as at this day, punishing the contempt with
which they have treated His Word, He will reward their
obedience with all prosperity. It would be well were all the
nobility and those who administer justice, to submit themselves, in uprightness and all humility, to this great King,
Jesus Christ, paying Him sincere homage, and with faith un-
feigned, in body, soul, and spirit, so that He may correct and
beat down the arrogance and rashness of those who would
rise up against them. Thus ought earthly princes to rule and
govern, serving Jesus Christ, and taking order that He may
have His own sovereign authority over all, both small and
great. Wherefore, Monseigneur, as you hold dear and in regard the estate of your royal nephew, as indeed you show
plainly that you do, I beseech you, in the name of God, to
apply your chief care and watchfulness to this end, that the

doctrine of God may be proclaimed with efficacy and power, so as to produce its fruit, and never to grow weary, whatsoever may happen, in following out fully an open and complete reformation of the Church. The better to explain to you what I mean, I shall arrange the whole under three heads.

The first shall treat of the sound instruction of the people; the second shall regard the rooting out of abuses which have prevailed hitherto; the third, the careful repression and correction of vice, and to take strict heed that scandals and loose conversation may not grow into a fashion, so as to cause the name of God to be blasphemed.

As concerning the first article, I do not mean to pronounce what doctrine ought to have place. Rather do I offer thanks to God for his goodness, that after having enlightened you in the pure knowledge of Himself, He has given you wisdom and direction to take measures that His pure truth may be preached. Praise be to God, you have not to learn what is the true faith of Christians, and the doctrine which they ought to hold, seeing that by your means the true purity of the faith has been restored. That is, that we hold God alone to be the sole Governor of our souls, that we hold His law to be the only rule and spiritual directory for our consciences, not serving Him according to the foolish inventions of men. Also, that according to His nature He would be worshipped in spirit and in purity of heart. On the other hand, acknowledging that there is nothing but all wretchedness in ourselves, and that we are corrupt in all our feelings and affections, so that our souls are a very abyss of iniquity, utterly despairing of ourselves; and that, having exhausted every presumption of our own wisdom, worth, or power of well-doing, we must have recourse to the fountain of every blessing, which is in Christ Jesus, accepting that which He confers on us, that is to say, the merit of His death and passion, that by this means we may be reconciled to God; that being washed in His blood, we may have no fear lest our spots prevent us from finding grace at the heavenly throne; that being assured that our sins are pardoned freely in virtue of his sacrifice, we may lean, yea rest upon, that for assurance of our salvation; that we may be sanctified by His Spirit, and so consecrate ourselves to the obedience of the righteousness of God; that being strengthened by His grace, we may overcome Satan, the world, and the flesh; finally, that being members of His body, we may never doubt that God reckons us among the number of His children, and that we may confidently call upon Him as *our* Father; that we may be careful to recognize and bear in mind this purpose in whatsoever is said or done in the Church, namely, that being separated from the world, we should rise to heaven with our Head and Saviour. Seeing then that God has given you grace to re-establish the knowledge of this doctrine, which has been so long buried out of sight by Antichrist, I forbear from entering further on the subject.

What I have thus suggested as to the manner of instruction, is only that the people be so taught as to be touched to the quick, and that they may feel that what the Apostle says is true [*Heb* 4.12], that 'the Word of God is a two-edged sword, piercing even through the thoughts and affections to the very marrow of the bones.' I speak thus, Monseigneur, because it appears to me that there is very little preaching of a lively kind in the kingdom, but that the greater part deliver it by way of reading from a written discourse. I see very well the necessity which constrains you to that; for in the first place you have not, as I believe, such well-approved and competent pastors as you desire. Wherefore, you need forthwith to supply this want. Secondly, there may very likely be among them many flighty persons who would go beyond all bounds, sowing their own silly fancies, as often happens on occasion of a change. But all these considerations ought not to hinder the ordinance of Jesus Christ from having free course in the preaching of the Gospel. Now, this preaching ought not to be lifeless but lively, to teach, to exhort, to reprove, as Saint

Paul says in speaking thereof to Timothy [2 *Tim* 4]. So indeed, that if an unbeliever enter, he may be so effectually arrested and convinced, as to give glory to God, as Paul says in another passage [1 *Cor* 14]. You are also aware, Monseigneur, how he speaks of the lively power and energy with which they ought to speak, who would approve themselves as good and faithful ministers of God, who must not make a parade of rhetoric only to gain esteem for themselves; but that the Spirit of God ought to sound forth by their voice, so as to work with mighty energy. Whatever may be the amount of danger to be feared, that ought not to hinder the Spirit of God from having liberty and free course in those to whom He has given grace for the edifying of the Church.

True it is, nevertheless, that it is both right and fitting to oppose the levity of some fantastic minds, who allow themselves in too great license, and also to shut the door against all eccentricities and new doctrines; but the method to be taken, which God has pointed out to us, for dealing with such occurrences, is well fitted to dispose of them. In the first place, there ought to be an explicit summary of the doctrine which all ought to preach, which all prelates and curates swear to follow, and no one should be received to any ecclesiastic charge who does not promise to preserve such agreement. Next, that they have a common *formula* of instruction for little children and for ignorant persons, serving to make them familiar with sound doctrine, so that they may be able to discern the difference between it and the falsehood and corruptions which may be brought forward in opposition to it. Believe me, Monseigneur, the Church of God will never preserve itself without a Catechism, for it is like the seed to keep the good grain from dying out, and causing it to multiply from age to age. And therefore, if you desire to build an edifice which shall be of long duration, and which shall not soon fall into decay, make provision for the children being instructed in a good Catechism, which may show them briefly, and in language suited to their tender age, wherein true Christianity consists. This Catechism will serve two purposes, to wit, as an introduction to the whole people, so that every one may profit from what shall be preached, and also to enable them to discern when any presumptuous person puts forward strange doctrine. Indeed, I do not say that it may not be well, and even necessary, to bind down the pastors and curates to a certain written form, as well for the sake of supplementing the ignorance and deficiencies of some, as the better to manifest the conformity and agreement between all the churches; thirdly, to take away all ground of pretence for bringing in any eccentricity or new-fangled doctrine on the part of those who only seek to indulge an idle fancy; as I have already said, the Catechism ought to serve as a check upon such people. There is, besides, the form and manner of administration of the sacraments; also the public prayers. But whatever, in the meantime, be the arrangement in regard to these matters, care must be taken not to quench the efficacy which ought to attend the preaching of the Gospel. And the utmost care should be taken, that so far as possible you have good trumpets, which shall sound into the very depths of the heart. For there is some danger that you may see no great profit from all the reformation which you shall have brought about, however sound and godly it may have been, unless this powerful instrument of preaching be developed more and more. It is not said without a meaning, that *Jesus Christ shall smite the earth with the rod of his mouth, and with the breath of his lips shall he slay the wicked* [*Is* 11. 4]. The way by which He is pleased to subdue us is, by destroying whatsoever is contrary to Himself. And herein you may also perceive why the Gospel is called the Kingdom of God. Even so, albeit the edicts and statutes of princes are good helps for advancing and upholding the state of Christianity, yet God is pleased to declare His sovereign power by this spiritual sword of His Word, when it is made known by the pastors.

Not to tire you, Monseigneur, I shall now come to the second point which I propose to touch upon; that is, the abolition and entire uprooting of the abuses and corruptions which Satan had aforetime mixed up with the ordinances of God. We know well that under the Pope there is a bastard sort of Christianity, and that God will disavow it at the last day, seeing that He now condemns it by His Word. If we desire to rescue the world from such an abyss, there is no better method than to follow the example of St Paul, who, wishing to correct what the Corinthians had improperly added to the Supper of our Lord, tells them [1 *Cor* 11], *I have received of the Lord that which I have delivered to you*. Thence we are bound to take a general instruction, to return to the strict and natural meaning of the commandment of God, if we would have a sound reformation and by Him approven. For whatsoever mixtures men have brought in of their own devising, have been just so many pollutions which turn us aside from the sanctified use of what God has bestowed for our salvation. Therefore, to lop off such abuses by halves will by no means restore things to a state of purity, for then we shall always have a dressed-up Christianity. I say this, because there are some who, under pretence of moderation, are in favour of sparing many abuses, without meddling with them at all, and to whom it appears enough to have rooted out the principal one. But on the contrary, we see how fertile is the seed of falsehood, and that only a single grain is needed to fill the world with them in three days' time, to such an extent are men inclined and addicted thereto. Our Lord teaches quite another method of procedure, for when David speaks of the idols he says [*Psalm* 16], *Their names will I not take up into my lips*, to intimate in what degree of detestation we ought to hold them. Above all, if we consider how we have offended God in the days of our ignorance, we ought to feel doubly bound to flee from the inventions of Satan, which have led us into the commission of evil, as from baits which serve only to seduce souls. On the other hand, we see, even when we remonstrate with men about their faults and errors, though we warn them as earnestly as possible, they are nevertheless so hardened that we can produce no effect. If, therefore, we were to leave them any remnant of abuse, that would only serve to nourish their obstinacy the more, and become a veil to darken all the doctrine which we might set before them. I willingly acknowledge that we must observe moderation, and that overdoing is neither discreet nor useful; indeed, that forms of worship need to be accommodated to the condition and tastes of the people. But the corruptions of Satan and of Antichrist must not be admitted under that pretext. Therefore it is that Holy Scripture, when praising those kings who had cast down the idols and their worshippers, not having swept them entirely away, notes it as a blemish, that nevertheless they had not cast down the chapelries and places of silly devotion.

Wherefore, Monseigneur, seeing that God has brought you so far, take order, I beseech you, that so without any exception He may approve you as a repairer of His temple, so that the times of the king your nephew may be compared to those of Josiah, and that you put things in such condition, that he may only need to maintain the goodly order which God shall have prepared for him by your means. I will mention to you an instance of such corruptions, as, if they were allowed to remain, would become a little leaven, to sour in the end the whole lump. In your country, some prayer is made for the departed on occasion of communicating in the Lord's Supper. I am well aware that it is not done in admission of the purgatory of the Pope. I am also aware that ancient custom can be pleaded for making some mention of the departed, for the sake of uniting together all the members of the one body. But there is a peremptory ground of objection against it, that the Supper of Jesus Christ is an action so sacred, that it ought not to be soiled by any human inventions whatsoever. And besides, in prayer to God, we must not take an unbounded licence in our devotions, but observe the rule which St Paul give us [*Rom* 10], which is, that we must be founded upon the Word of God; therefore, such commemoration of the dead as imports a commending of them to His grace, is contrary to the due form and manner of prayer; it is a hurtful addition to the Supper of our Lord. There are other things which possibly may be less open to reproof, which however are not to be excused: such as the ceremony of chrism and unction. The chrism has been invented out of a frivolous humour by those who, not content with the institution of Jesus Christ, desired to counterfeit the Holy Spirit by a new sign, as if water were not sufficient for the purpose. What they call extreme unction, has been retained by the inconsiderate zeal of those, who have wished to follow the apostles without being gifted as they were. When the apostles used oil in the case of the sick, it was for the healing of them miraculously. Now, when the gift of miracles has ceased, the figure ought no longer to be employed. Wherefore, it would be much better that these things should be pruned away, so that you might have nothing which is not conformed to the Word of God, and serviceable for the edification of the Church. It is quite true we ought to bear with the weak; but in order to strengthen them, and to lead them to greater perfection. That does not mean, however, that we are to humour blockheads who wish for this or that, without knowing why. I know the consideration which keeps back many is, that they are afraid too great a change could not be carried through. It is admitted, that when we have to do with neighbours with whom we desire to cherish friendly feeling, one is disposed to gratify them by giving way in many things. In worldly matters, that may be quite bearable, wherein it is allowable to yield one to another, and to forego one's right for the sake of peace; but it is not altogether the same thing in regard to the spiritual governance of the Church, which ought to be according to the ordinance of the Word of God. Herein, we are not at liberty to yield up anything to men, nor to turn aside on either hand in their favour. Indeed there is nought that is more displeasing to God, than when we would, in accordance with our own human wisdom, modify or curtail, advance or retreat, otherwise than He would have us. Wherefore, if we do not wish to displease Him, we must shut our eyes to the opinion of men. As for the dangers which may arise, we ought to avoid them so far as we can, but never by going aside from the straight road. While we walk uprightly, we have His promise that He will help us. Therefore, what remains for us is to do our duty, humbly committing the event unto Himself. And here we may perceive wherefore the wise men of this world are oft-times disappointed in their expectation, because God is not with them, when, in distrust of Him and His aid, they seek out crooked paths and such as He condemns. Do we then wish to feel that we have the power of God upon our side? Let us simply follow what he tells us. Above all, we must cling to this maxim, that the reformation of His Church is the work of His hand. Wherefore, in such matters, men must leave themselves to be guided by Him. What is more, whether in restoring or in preserving the Church, He thinks fit for the most part, to proceed after a method marvellous, and beyond human conception. And, therefore, it were unseemly to confine that restoration, which must be Divine, to the measure of our understanding, and to bring that which is heavenly into subjection to what is earthly and of this world's fashion. I do not thus exclude the prudence which is so much needed, to take all appropriate and right means, not falling into extremes either on the one side or upon the other, to gain over the whole world to God, if that were possible. But the wisdom of the Spirit, not that of the flesh, must overrule all; and having inquired at the mouth of the Lord, we must ask Him to guide and lead us, rather than follow the bent of our own understanding. When we take this method, it will be easy to cut off much occasion of temptation, which might otherwise stop our progress midway.

Wherefore, Monseigneur, as you have begun to bring back Christianity to the place which belongs to it, throughout the realm of England, not at all in self-confidence, but upheld by the hand of God, as hitherto you have had sensible experience of that powerful arm, you must not doubt that it shall continue with you to the end. If God upholds the kingdoms and the principalities of the infidels who are His enemies, far more certainly will He have in safeguard those who range themselves on His side and seek Him for their superior.

I come now to the last point, which concerns the chastisement of vice and the repression of scandals. I have no doubt that there are laws and statutes of the kingdom both good and laudable, to keep the people within the bounds of decency. But the great and boundless licentiousness which I see everywhere throughout the world, constrains me to beseech you, that you would earnestly turn your attention to keeping men within the restraint of sound and wholesome discipline. That, above all, you would hold yourself charged, for the honour of God, to punish those crimes of which men have been in the habit of making no very great account. I speak of this, because sometimes larcenies, assault, and extortions are more severely punished, because thereby men are wronged, whereas they will tolerate whoredom and adultery, drunkenness, and blaspheming of the name of God, as if these were things quite allowable, or at least of very small importance. Let us hear, however, what God thinks of them. He proclaims aloud, how precious His name is unto Him. Meanwhile, it is as if torn in pieces and trampled under foot. It can never be that He will allow such shameful reproach to remain unpunished. More than this, Scripture clearly points out to us, that by reason of blasphemies a whole country is defiled. As concerning adulteries, we, who call ourselves Christians, ought to take great shame to ourselves that even the heathen have exercised greater rigour in their punishment of such than we do, seeing even that some among us only laugh at them. When holy matrimony, which ought to be a lively image of the sacred union which we have with the Son of God, is polluted, and the covenant, which ought to stand more firm and indissoluble than any in this world, is disloyally rent asunder, if we do not lay to heart that sin against God, it is a token that our zeal for God is very low indeed. As for whoredom, it ought to be quite enough for us that St Paul compares it to sacrilege, inasmuch as by its means the temples of God, which our bodies are, are profaned. Be it remembered also, that whoremongers and drunkards are banished from the kingdom of God, on such terms that we are forbidden to converse with them, whence it clearly follows, that they ought not to be endured in the Church. We see herein the cause why so many rods of judgment are at this very day lifted up over the earth. For the more easily men pardon themselves in such enormities, the more certainly will God take vengeance on them. Wherefore, to prevent His wrath, I entreat of you, Monseigneur, to hold a tight rein, and to take order, that those who hear the doctrine of the Gospel, approve their Christianity by a life of holiness. For as doctrine is the soul of the Church for quickening, so discipline and the correction of vices are like the nerves to sustain the body in a state of health and vigour. The duty of bishops and curates is to keep watch over that, to the end that the Supper of our Lord may not be polluted by people of scandalous lives. But in the authority where God has set you, the chief responsibility returns upon you, who have a special charge given you to set the others in motion, on purpose that every one discharge himself of duty, and diligently to look to it, that the order which shall have been established may be duly observed.

Now, Monseigneur, agreeably to the protestation which I made above, I shall make no further excuse, neither of the tiresomeness of my letter, nor on account of my having thus freely laid open to you what I had so much at heart. For I feel assured that my affection is well known to you, while in your wisdom, and as you are well versed in the Holy Scriptures, you perceive from what fountain I have drawn all that is herein contained. Wherefore, I do not fear to have been troublesome or importunate to you, in making manifest, according as I could, the hearty desire I have that the name of God may always be more and more glorified by you, which is my daily supplication, beseeching Him that He would please to increase His grace in you, to confirm you by His Spirit in a true unconquerable constancy, upholding you against all enemies, having yourself with your whole household under His holy protection, enabling you successfully to administer the charge which is committed to you, that so the King may have whereof to praise this gracious God for having had such a governor in his childhood, both for his person and for his kingdom.

Whereupon I shall make an end, Monseigneur, very humbly commending me to your kind favour.

22/TO VIRET[1]

Death of Idelette de Bure, the wife of Calvin

April 7, 1549

Although the death of my wife has been exceedingly painful to me, yet I subdue my grief as well as I can. Friends, also, are earnest in their duty to me. It might be wished, indeed,

1 A special interest attaches to this and the following letter, written under great personal affliction. Early in April 1549, Calvin lost Idelette de Bure, whose frail and delicate health gave way under the pressure of a protracted illness, and whose last hours are known to us by the touching picture given of them

that they could profit me and themselves more; yet one can scarcely say how much I am supported by their attentions. But you know well enough how tender, or rather soft, my mind is. Had not a powerful self-control, therefore, been vouchsafed to me, I could not have borne up so long. And truly mine is no common source of grief. I have been bereaved of the best companion of my life, of one who, had it been so ordered, would not only have been the willing sharer of my indigence, but even of my death. During her life she was the faithful helper of my ministry. From her I never experienced the slightest hindrance. She was never troublesome to me throughout the entire course of her illness; she was more anxious about her children than about herself.[1] As I feared these private cares might annoy her to no purpose, I took occasion, on the third day before her death, to mention that I would not fail in discharging my duty to her children. Taking up the matter immediately, she said, 'I have already committed them to God.' When I said that that was not to prevent me from caring for them, she replied, 'I know you will not neglect what you know has been committed to God.' Lately, also, when a certain woman insisted that she should talk with me regarding these matters, I, for the first time, heard her give the following brief answer: 'Assuredly the principal thing is that they live a pious and holy life. My husband is not to be urged to instruct them in religious know-

by the Reformer. The consolations of friendship, and the consideration of the important duties he had to discharge, supported Calvin in this affliction, and the self-control which he manifested during the first days of his bereavement, excited the admiration of his friends. Viret wrote him on this occasion as follows: 'Wonderfully and incredibly have I been refreshed, not by empty rumours alone, but especially by numerous messengers who have informed me how you, with a heart so broken and lacerated, have attended to all your duties even better than hitherto . . . and that, above all, at a time when grief so fresh, and on that account all the more severe, might have prostrated your mind. Go on then as you have begun . . . and I pray God most earnestly that you may be enabled to do so, and that you may receive daily greater comfort and be strengthened more and more.' Letter of 10th April 1549.

1 By her first marriage with Jean Storder, Idelette de Bure already had children known to us only by her concern for them during her last illness.

ledge and in the fear of God. If they be pious, I am sure he
will gladly be a father to them; but if not, they do not deserve
that I should ask for aught in their behalf.' This nobleness of
mind will weigh more with me than a hundred recommendations. Many thanks for your friendly consolation. Adieu,
most excellent and honest brother. May the Lord Jesus watch
over and direct yourself and your wife.[1] Present my best
wishes to her and to the brethren.

23/TO FAREL

Further details regarding the death of Idelette de Bure

Geneva, 11th April 1549

Intelligence of my wife's death has perhaps reached you before now. I do what I can to keep myself from being overwhelmed with grief. My friends also leave nothing undone
that may administer relief to my mental suffering. When your
brother left, her life was all but despaired of. When the
brethren were assembled on Tuesday, they thought it best that
we should join together in prayer. This was done. When
Abel, in the name of the rest, exhorted her to faith and patience,
she briefly (for she was now greatly worn) stated her frame of
mind. I afterwards added an exhortation, which seemed to
me appropriate to the occasion. And then, as she had made no
allusion to her children, I, fearing that, restrained by modesty,
she might be feeling an anxiety concerning them, which would
cause her greater suffering than the disease itself, declared in

1 We read in Viret's letter to Calvin already referred to, – 'My wife salutes
you most courteously; she has been grieved in no ordinary way by the death
of her very dear sister, and she and I feel it to be a loss to us all.' Idelette de
Bure kept up with Viret's wife a correspondence which has unfortunately
not been preserved.

the presence of the brethren, that I should henceforth care for them as if they were my own. She replied, 'I have already committed them to the Lord.' When I replied, that that was not to hinder me from doing my duty, she immediately answered, 'If the Lord shall care for them, I know they will be commended to you.' Her magnanimity was so great, that she seemed to have already left the world. About the sixth hour of the day, on which she yielded up her soul to the Lord, our brother Bourgouin[1] addressed some pious words to her, and while he was doing so, she spoke aloud, so that all saw that her heart was raised far above the world. For these were her words: 'O glorious resurrection! O God of Abraham and of all our fathers, in thee have the faithful trusted during so many past ages, and none of them have trusted in vain. I also will hope.' These short sentences were rather ejaculated than distinctly spoken. This did not come from the suggestion of others, but from her own reflections, so that she made it obvious in few words what were her own meditations. I had to go out at six o'clock. Having been removed to another apartment after seven, she immediately began to decline. When she felt her voice suddenly failing her she said: 'Let us pray: let us pray. All pray for me.' I had now returned. She was unable to speak, and her mind seemed to be troubled. I having spoken a few words about the love of Christ, the hope of eternal life, concerning our married life, and her departure, engaged in prayer. In full possession of her mind, she both heard the prayer, and attended to it. Before eight she expired, so calmly, that those present could scarcely distinguish between her life and her death. I at present control my sorrow so that my duties may not be interfered with. But in the meanwhile the Lord has sent other trials upon me. Adieu, brother, and very excellent friend. May the Lord Jesus strengthen you by His Spirit; and may He support me also under this heavy affliction, which would certainly have overcome me, had not

1 The minister Francis Bourgouin.

He, who raises up the prostrate, strengthens the weak, and re-freshes the weary, stretched forth His hand from heaven to me. Salute all the brethren and your whole family.

24/TO MADAME DE CANY[1]

Account of the instructive death of Madame Laurent de Normandie

This 29th of April 1549

Madame:

Although the news which I communicate is sad, and must also sadden the person to whom I beg you to impart it, never-theless I hope that my letter will not be unwelcome to you. It has pleased my God to withdraw from this world the wife of my kind brother, M. de Normandie.[2] Our consolation is, that He has gathered her unto Himself; for He has guided her even to the last sigh, as if visibly He had held out the hand to

1 Peronne de Pisseleu, wife of Michel de Barbançon, Seigneur de Cany, one of the personages of most importance in Picardy. This lady, instructed in the reformed faith by Laurent de Normandie, lieutenant of the king at Noyon, and the friend of Calvin, had for a long time to endure the severity of her husband, who afterwards came at a later period to be a partaker of like faith. – Beza, *Hist. Eccl.*, tom. ii. p. 244; De Thou, lib. xxv. Madame de Cany, sister of the Duchess d'Etampes, favourite of the late king, had possessed an un-bounded influence at court, which she always used for generous purposes. Her ordinary residence was the Château de Varannes, situated on the Oise, near to Noyon.

2 Laurent de Normandie, sprung from a noble family of Picardy, fellow countryman and friend of Calvin, discharged the functions of master of re-quests and of lieutenant of the king at Noyon, before retiring to Geneva. Received inhabitant of the town, 2nd May 1547, burgess, the 25th April 1555, he lived there in intimacy with Calvin, who dedicated to him in 1550 his *Treatise on Scandals*. He had married for his first wife Anne de la Vacquerie, of a noble family, which had merged in that of the Dukes of Saint Simon, and illustrious during the reign of Louis XI, by the first president Jacques de la Vacquerie. A short time after his arrival at Geneva he lost his wife, whose edifying death is the subject of Calvin's letter to Madame de Cany, and he married a second time (14th September 1550).

her. Now, forasmuch as her father must needs be informed,[1] we have thought there was no way more suitable than to request that you would please take the trouble to request him to call on you, that the painful intelligence may be broken to him by your communication of it. What the gentleman has written to us who lately presented our letter to you, has emboldened us to take this step, viz., that you had introduced the good man in question to the right way of salvation, and that you had given him understanding of the pure and sound doctrine which we must maintain. We do not doubt, therefore, that you are willing to continue your good offices, and that even in this present need. For we cannot employ ourselves better, than in carrying this message in the name of God, to comfort him to whom you have already done so much good, that he may not be beyond measure disconsolate. Therefore, Madame, I leave you to set before him the arguments and reasons which you know to be suitable for exhorting to submission. Only I shall shortly relate to you the history which will furnish you with ample matter for showing him that he has reason to be thankful. And, according to the grace and wisdom that God has given you, you will draw thence for his comfort as opportunity shall require.

Having heard of the illness of the good woman, we were amazed how she could have been able to bear so well the fatigue of the journey, for she arrived quite fresh, and without showing any sign of weariness. Indeed she acknowledged that God had singularly supported her during that time. Weak as she was, she kept well enough until a little before Christmas. The eager desire which she had to hear the Word of God upheld her until the month of January. She then began to take to bed, not because the complaint was as yet thought to be mortal, but to prevent the danger which might arise. Although expecting a favourable termination, and hoping to recover her health, she nevertheless prepared for death, saying

[1] Eloi de la Vacquerie.

often, that if this was not the finishing blow, it could not be long delayed. As for remedies, all was done that could be. And if her bodily comfort was provided for, that which she prized most highly was nowise wanting, to wit, pious admonitions to confirm her in the fear of God, in the faith of Jesus Christ, in patience, in the hope of salvation. On her part she always gave clear evidence that the labour was not in vain, for in her discourse you could see that she had the whole deeply imprinted upon her heart. In short, throughout the course of her sickness, she proved herself to be a true sheep of our Lord Jesus, letting herself be quietly led by the Great Shepherd. Two or three days before death, as her heart was more raised to God, she also spoke with more earnest affection than ever. Even the day before, while she was exhorting her people, she said to her attendant, that he must take good heed never to return thither where he had polluted himself with idolatry; and that since God had led him to a Christian Church, he should be careful to live therein a holy life. The night following, she was oppressed with great and continual pain. Yet never did one hear any other cry from her, than the prayer to God that He would have pity upon her, and that He would deliver her out of the world, vouchsafing grace to persevere always in the faith which He had bestowed. Toward five o'clock in the morning I went to her. After she had listened very patiently to the doctrine which I set before her, such as the occasion called for, she said: 'The hour draws near, I must needs depart from the world; this flesh asks only to go away into corruption; but I feel certain that my God is withdrawing my soul into His kingdom. I know what a poor sinful woman I am, but my confidence is in His goodness, and in the death and passion of His Son. Therefore, I do not doubt of my salvation, since He has assured me of it. I go to Him as to a Father.' While she was thus discoursing, a considerable number of persons came in. I threw in from time to time some words, such as seemed suitable; and we also made supplication to God as the exigency of her need required. After once more declaring the sense she had of her sins, to ask the pardon of them from God, and the certainty which she entertained of her salvation, putting her sole confidence in Jesus, and having her whole trust in Him, without being invited by any one to do so, she began to pronounce the *Miserere* as we sing it in church and continued with a loud and strong voice, not without great difficulty, but she entreated that we would allow her to continue. Whereupon, I made her a short recapitulation of the whole argument of the psalm, seeing the pleasure she took in it. Afterwards, taking me by the hand, she said to me, 'How happy I am, and how am I beholden to God, for having brought me here to die. Had I been in that wretched prison, I could not have ventured to open my mouth to make confession of my Christianity. Here I have not only liberty to glorify God, but I have so many sound arguments to confirm me in my salvation.' Sometimes, indeed, she said, 'I am not able for more.' When I answered her, 'God is able to help you; He has, indeed, shown you how He is a present aid to His own;' she said immediately, 'I do believe so, and He makes me feel His help.' Her husband was there, striving to keep up in such sort that we were all sorry for him, while he made us wonder in amazement at his fortitude. For while possessed with such grief as I know it to have been, and weighed down by extremity of sorrow, he had so far gained the mastery over self, as to exhort his better part as freely as if they were going to make a most joyful journey together. The conversation I have related took place in the midst of the great torment she endured from pains in her stomach. Towards nine or ten o'clock they abated. Availing herself of this relaxation, she never ceased to glorify God, humbly seeking her salvation and all her well-being in Jesus Christ. When speech failed her, her countenance told how intently she was interested as well in the prayers as in the exhortations which were made. Otherwise she was so motionless, that sight alone gave indication of life. Towards the end, considering that she was gone, I said, 'Now let us pray God that He would give us grace to follow her.' As I rose, she turned her eyes upon us, as if charging us to persevere in prayer and consolation; after that, we perceived no motion, and she passed away so gracefully, that it was as if she had fallen asleep.

I pray you, Madame, to excuse me if I have been too tedious. But I thought that the father would be well pleased to be fully informed of the whole, as if he himself had been upon the spot. And I hope that in so good a work you will find nothing troublesome. St Paul, in treating of charity, does not forget that we ought to weep with those who weep; that is to say, that if we are Christians, we ought to have such compassion and sorrow for our neighbours, that we should willingly take part in their tears, and thus comfort them. It cannot otherwise be but the good man must, at the first, be wrung with grief. Howbeit he must already have been long prepared to receive the news, considering that his daughter's sickness had increased so much, that her recovery was despaired of. But the great consolation is, the example which she has afforded to him and to all of us, of bowing to the will of God. And thus, seeing that she has presented herself so peaceably to death, let us herein follow her, willingly complying with the disposal of God; and if her father loved her, let him show his love in conforming himself to the desire which she exhibited of submitting herself to God. And seeing that her dismissal has been so happy, let him rejoice in the grace of God vouchsafed to her, which far surpasses all the comforts we can possess in this world.

In conclusion, Madame, having humbly commended me to your kind favour, I beseech our good Lord to be always your protector, to increase you with all spiritual blessing, and to cause you to glorify His name even to the end.

25/TO THE PROTECTOR SOMERSET[1]

Congratulations on the royal favour shown to the Duke of Somerset
Use to be made of his influence for spreading the Gospel in England

February/March 1550

Monseigneur:

That I have so long delayed to write to you, has been from
no want of good-will, but to my great regret I have refrained,
fearing lest, during the troubles which have been of late, my
letters should be the occasion of annoyance. I thank my God
that He has now afforded me the opportunity which hitherto
I have been waiting for. It is not I alone who rejoice at the
good issue which God has given to your affliction, but all true
believers, who desire the advancement of the kingdom of our
Lord Jesus Christ, forasmuch as they know the solicitude
with which you have laboured for the re-establishing of the
Gospel in all its purity in England, and that every kind of
superstition might be abolished. And I do not doubt that you
are prepared to persevere in the same course, in so far as you
shall have the means. On your own part, Monseigneur, not
only have you to acknowledge the favour God has shown
you in stretching out His hand for your deliverance, but also
to bear His dealing with you in remembrance, that you may
profit by it.[2] I know the regret which you may well entertain, and how you may be tempted to render the like to those

1 This letter was addressed to the Duke of Somerset after his first disgrace.
Set at liberty, the 6th February 1550, by the favour of the king his nephew.
he resumed his place in the Privy Council, but losing the title and dignity of
Protector. The letter of Calvin is without any doubt of February or March
1550.
2 During his disgrace, which was regarded as a public calamity by the
friends of the Reformation in England and throughout Europe, the Duke of
Somerset had sought consolation in reading and meditation. He translated
into English a work on patience, to which he added a preface containing the

whom you reckon to have meditated greater mischief against you than what has come to pass. But you know the admonition which Saint Paul has given us on that head, that is, that we have not to fight against flesh and blood, but against the hidden wiles of our spiritual enemy. Wherefore let us not waste our energies upon men, but rather let us set ourselves against Satan to resist all his machinations against us, as there is no doubt whatever that he was the author of the evil which impended over you, in order that the course of the Gospel might thereby be hindered, and even that all should be brought to confusion. Therefore, Monseigneur, forgetting and pardoning the faults of those whom you may conceive to have been your enemies, apply your whole mind to repel his malice who thus engaged them to their own destruction in setting themselves to seek your ruin. This magnanimity will not only be pleasing to God, but it will make you the more loved among men; and I do not doubt that you have such regard to that as you ought. But if your humane disposition itself impels you to this course, so much the more may I be confident that you will receive kindly what I say, knowing that nothing induces me to tender such advice to you, but the love I bear you, and the care which I have for your honour and welfare. And besides, it is so difficult a virtue so to overcome our passions as to render good for evil, that we can never be too much exhorted to do so. Moreover, seeing that the Lord has directed the issue so much better than many expected, keep in mind, Monseigneur, the example of Joseph. It would be difficult to find in our day such a mirror of integrity. For he, seeing that God had turned to good the evil which they had plotted against him, is unwearied in showing himself the minister of the goodness of God towards his brethren who had persecuted him. This victory will be more

---

expression of the most elevated sentiments. He received also exhortations from Peter Martyr, and showed himself no less constant in his attachment to the Gospel, than resigned to the loss of fortune and credit.

glorious than that which God has already given you, when He saved and secured your person, and your property, and your honours. However, Monseigneur, you have also to consider that if God has been pleased to humble you for a little while, it has not been without a motive. For although you might be innocent in regard to men, you know that before this great Heavenly Judge there is no one living who is not chargeable. Thus, then, it is that the saints have honoured the rod of God, by yielding their neck, and bowing low their head under His discipline. David had walked very uprightly, but yet he confessed that it had been good for him to be humbled by the hand of God. For which reason, as soon as we feel any chastisement, of whatsoever kind it may be, the first step should be to retire into ourselves, and well to examine our own lives, that we may apprehend those blessings which had been hidden from us: for sometimes too much prosperity so dazzles our eyes, that we cannot perceive wherefore God chastises us. It is but reasonable that we should do Him at least as much honour as we would to a physician, for it is His to heal our inward maladies, which are unknown to ourselves, and to pursue a course of healing, not according to our liking, but as He knows and judges to be fitting. What is more, it must needs happen sometimes that He makes use of preservative remedies, not waiting till we have already fallen into evil, but preventing it before it comes. God, besides your native rank, having assigned you a high dignity, has performed great things by your hand, and which shall possibly be more applauded after your death than they are duly appreciated during your lifetime. Moreover, He has caused His name to be magnified by you. Now, the most virtuous and excellent persons are in greater danger than any others of being tempted to forget themselves. You are aware, Monseigneur, of what is written concerning the good King Hezekiah, that after having performed such memorable actions, as well for religion and the worship of God as for the common weal of the country, his heart was lifted up. If God has been pleased to prevent that in you, it is a special favour He has shown you. Were there no other reason for it, save that He would be glorified in your deliverance, and that He would be recognized by you, as well as by all in your person, as the true protector of His own, that alone ought to be all-sufficient to you.

It remains, Monseigneur, that since He has thus given you the upper hand, you do render homage to Him for this benefit, as is due. If we are recovered out of a dangerous sickness, we ought to be doubly careful, and to honour this merciful God, just as if He had bestowed a new life upon us. You may not do less in your present circumstances. Your zeal to exalt the name of God, and to restore the purity of His Gospel, has been great. But you know, Monseigneur, that in so great and worthy a cause, even when we have put forth all our strength, we come very far short of what is required. However, if God, in thus binding you to Himself anew, has meant, in this way, to induce you to do better than ever, your duty is to strive to the uttermost and with all your energy, so that so holy a work as that which He has begun by you may be carried forward. I doubt not that you do so: but I am also confident, that knowing the affection which induces me to exhort you thereunto, you will receive all my solicitation with your wonted benignity. If the honour of God be thus esteemed by you above all else, He will assuredly watch over you and your whole household, to pour out His grace there more abundantly, and will make you know the value of His blessing. For that promise can never fail: *Those who honour me, I will render honourable.* True it is, that those who best do their duty are oftentimes troubled the most by many violent onsets. But this is quite enough for them, that God is at hand to succour and relieve them. Now, although it is enough for you to look to God and to feel the assurance that your service is pleasing to Him, nevertheless, Monseigneur, it is a great comfort to you to see the King so well disposed that he prefers the restoration of the Church, and of pure doctrine, to everything else, seeing it is a virtue greatly to be admired in him, and a peculiar blessing for the kingdom,[1] that in a youth of such tender age the vanities of this world do not hinder the fear of God and true religion from ruling in his heart. This also ought to be a great help and confirmation, that you discharge the principal service which he desires and asks, in serving our heavenly King, the Son of God.

Monseigneur, having very humbly commended me to your kind favour, I beseech our good Lord, that, upholding you in His holy keeping, He would increase in you yet more and more the gifts of His Holy Spirit, for the furtherance of His own glory, so that we may all have whereof to rejoice.

26/TO WILLIAM RABOT[2]

Exhortation to the study of the Scriptures.

24th July 1550

Although we have been unknown to each other by sight, yet since you recognize the Master Christ in my ministry, and submit yourself cheerfully and calmly to His teaching, this is

---

1 The young King Edward VI. Instructed by the most able masters, he gave early proof of a strong mind and of a lively piety.

2 It appears from a letter of Rabot's to Calvin, preserved in the Library of Gotha, that, exiled from his native country from conscientious motives, this young man was then engaged in the study of law at the University of Padua, in company with a number of gentlemen, among others Charles de Jonvillers, and François and Louis de Budé. Their studies were intermingled with religious discourses, which contributed to the spread of the Gospel in certain distinguished families. The increasing rigours of persecution soon scattered this focus of Evangelism, and led some of those youthful missionaries to Geneva, where Charles de Jonvillers, one of their number, gained the friendship of Calvin, and became his secretary.

a sufficient reason why I should, on the other hand, esteem you as a brother and fellow-disciple, But, as I understand from your letter, that it is not very long since the Lord shed the light of His gospel on you, I could not give a fitter expression of my love towards you, than by exhorting and encouraging you to daily exercises. For we see sparks of piety immediately disappear which had shone forth on many occasions; because, instead of increasing the flame, they rather extinguish what little light the Spirit of God had enkindled in them, by the empty allurements of the world, or the irregular desires of the flesh. That nothing of this kind may happen to you, you must first of all give devoted submission to the will of the Lord, and in the next place, you must fortify yourself by His sacred doctrines. But as this is too extensive a theme to be embraced in a letter, it is better for you to draw from the fountain-head itself. For if you make a constant study of the word of the Lord, you will be quite able to guide your life to the highest excellence. You have faithful commentaries, which will furnish the best assistance. I wish very much you could find it convenient at some time to pay us a visit; for, I flatter myself, you would never regret the journey. Whatever you do, see that you follow the Lord, and at no time turn aside from the chief end.

27/TO THE KING OF ENGLAND[1]

He exhorts him to persevere in the work of the Reformation in his kingdom
Enumeration of abuses, ceremonies, ecclesiastical elections
Universities.

From Geneva, (January 1551)

Sire:

If I must excuse myself towards your Majesty for having used the boldness to dedicate these books which I now present to you, I would need to find an advocate to speak a word for me. For so far would my letter be from having credit enough to do that, that it would even stand in need of a fresh excuse. And, indeed, as I never should have taken upon me to address the Commentaries to you which I have published with your name, neither should I have ventured now to write to you, but for the confidence I had already conceived, that both would be well received. For inasmuch as, holding me to be among the number of those who are zealous for the advancement of the kingdom of the Son of God. you have not disdained to read what I did not specially present to your Majesty, I have thought, that if, while serving Jesus Christ my Master,

---

1 Edward VI, son of Henry VIII and Jane Seymour, King of England, born in 1537, died, in his sixteenth year, the 6th of July 1553. Gifted with a precocious strength of reason, and a lively sensibility, instructed in the ancient languages and foreign literature, this young prince did not live long enough to realize the hopes to which his accession to the throne had given birth. 'His virtues,' says the historian Hume, 'had made him an object of tender affection to the public. He possessed mildness of disposition, application to study and business, a capacity to learn and judge, and an attachment to equity and justice.' Devotional reading had a particular attraction for this prince, who was heartily devoted to the cause of the Reformation. Calvin dedicated two of his commentaries to him, *Isaiah*, and *The Canonical Epistles*. The dedication of the first of these commentaries (25th December 1550) furnishes us the date of the letter of Calvin, written in the month of January 1551, and brought to the King by the minister Nicolas des Gallars.

I could likewise testify to the reverence and singular affection which I bear you, I could not fail to find a kind and courteous acceptance.

Moreover, Sire, holding myself assured that my letter will have such a reception from you as I desire, I shall not hesitate to pray and beseech you in the name of Him to whom you ascribe all authority and power, to take courage in following out what you have so well and happily begun, as well in your own person as in the state of your kingdom; namely, the consecration of all to God and to our blessed Saviour, who has so dearly purchased us. For as regards general reformation, it is not yet so well established, as that it would be wise to look on it as achieved. And, in fact, it would be very difficult to purge in a day such an abyss of superstition as there is in the papacy. Its root is too deep, and has expanded itself too widely, to get so soon to the bottom of it. But whatsoever difficulties or delays there may be, the excellency of the work is well worthy of unwearying pursuit.

I have no doubt, Sire, but Satan will put many hindrances in the way before you to slacken your pace, and to make your zeal grow cold. Your subjects, for the most part, do not know the blessing which you procure for them. The great, who are raised to honour, are sometimes too wise in their own conceits to make much account of the world, far less to look to God at all. And new and unexpected conflicts arise daily. Now I hope, indeed, Sire, that God has stored you with such greatness and constancy of mind, that you will neither be weakened nor wearied by all that. But the thing itself is of so great importance, that it well deserves that one should apply to it far more than human strength and energy. And then, after all, when we shall have striven to the very uttermost, there will always remain more waiting to be done.

We see how, in the time of the good king Josiah, who has the special testimony of the Holy Spirit, that he approved himself a prince excellent in faith, in zeal, and in all godliness;

nevertheless, the Prophet Zephaniah shows, that there was still some remainder of bygone superstitions, yea, even in the city of Jerusalem. Even so, however you may labour with your Council, Sire, you will find it very difficult completely to uproot all the mischief which would well deserve to be corrected. But this ought to be a great confirmation to animate and spur you on; and even if you should not accomplish all that could be desired, it is a very sufficient consolation to you when you hear that the pains which this good king took is a service pleasing to God, insomuch that the Holy Spirit magnifies the reformation effected by him, as if nothing more had been desired. Let me entreat you then, Sire, to reach forward to the mark which is set before you in the example of this godly king, that you may have the honour, not only of having overthrown impieties which are clearly repugnant to the honour and service of God, but also of having abolished and razed to the ground, whatsoever served merely to nourish superstition. For when God would praise as with an open mouth the faithful princes who have restored and again set up the purity of His service, He expressly adds this word, that they have also *taken away the high places*, that the memory of foolish devotions might be utterly obliterated.

True it is, Sire, that there are things indifferent which one may allowably tolerate. But then we must always carefully insist that simplicity and order be observed in the use of ceremonies, so that the clear light of the Gospel be not obscured by them, as if we were still under the shadows of the law; and then that there may be nothing allowed that is not in agreement and conformity to the order established by the Son of God, and that the whole may serve and be suited to the edification of the Church. For God does not allow His name to be trifled with,—mixing up silly frivolities with His holy and sacred ordinances. Then there are manifest abuses which cannot be endured, such as prayer for the souls of the departed, of putting forward to God the intercession of saints in our prayers, as also of joining them to God in invocation. I do not doubt, Sire, that you are aware that these are so many corruptions of true Christianity. I beseech you, in the name of God, that you may please look to that matter, so that the whole may be restored to a sound and wholesome state.

There is another point, Sire, of which you ought to take a special charge, namely, that the poor flocks may not be destitute of pastors. Ignorance and barbarism have lain so heavy on this accursed popery, that it is not easy to obtain all at once men fit and duly qualified to discharge that office. Notwithstanding, the object is well worth pains, and that your officers, Sire, should have an eye upon it, as they ought. Without that, all the good and holy ordinances which you can make, will scarce avail for the reformation of the heart in good earnest.

Further, inasmuch as the schools contain the seeds of the ministry, there is much need to keep them pure and thoroughly free from all ill weeds. I speak thus, Sire, because in your universities, it is commonly said, there are many young people supported on the college bursaries, who, instead of giving good hope of service in the Church, rather show an inclination to do mischief, and to ruin it, not even concealing that they are opposed to the true religion. Wherefore, Sire, I beseech you anew, in the name of God, that you may please to take order therein, to the effect, that property which ought to be held sacred, be not converted to profane uses, and far less to nourish venomous reptiles, who would desire nought better than to infect everything for the future. For, in this way, the Gospel would always be kept back by these schools, which ought to be the very pillars thereof.

Meanwhile, Sire, all honest hearts praise God, and feel themselves greatly obliged to you, that it hath pleased you of your favour to grant churches to your subjects who use the French and German languages.[1] In so far as regards the use of

1 The privilege granted by King Edward VI to the Church of the foreign Protestants formed at London 1550. The royal patent was thus expressed: —

the Sacraments, and spiritual order, I hope that the permission which you have been pleased to confer upon them will bear fruit. Howbeit, Sire, I cannot help beseeching you once more, feeling so deeply how needful it is, not only that you would secure the rest and contentment of the godly who desire to serve God and to live peaceably in obedience to you, but also that you would restrain vagabond and dissolute people, should such withdraw into your kingdom.

I know well, Sire, that you have people of distinguished learning at hand, who can make known to you these things by word of mouth, far better than myself by writing; also, that in your council you have men of prudence and zeal to suggest all that is expedient. Among the others, I have no doubt that Monsieur the Duke of Somerset spares no trouble to follow out that wherein he has employed himself so faithfully hitherto. But I believe, Sire, that all that shall be no hindrance to prevent your kind reception of what you will recognize as proceeding from a like source.

To conclude, Sire, forasmuch as I fear to have already wearied you with my tediousness, I pray you, in respect of that as in everything else, that you would please excuse and pardon me of your kind favour, to which very humbly I beg to be commended, having besought our gracious God and Father to maintain and uphold you in His holy protection, to guide you by His Spirit, and to cause His name to be more and more glorified by you.

'Considering that it is the duty of a Christian prince well to administer the affairs of his kingdom, to provide for religion, and for the unhappy exiles, afflicted and banished by reason thereof, we would have you to know, that having compassion on the condition of those who have for some considerable time past been domiciled in our kingdom, and come there daily, of our special grace ... will and ordain that henceforward they may have in our city of London a church, to be called the Church of the Lord Jesus, where the assembly of the Germans and other strangers can meet and worship, for the purpose of having the Gospel purely interpreted by the ministers of their church, and the Sacraments administered according to the Word of God and the apostolic ordinance.'

28/TO A FRENCH GENTLEMAN[1]

Sickness of Theodore Beza
Calvin's grief.

30th June 1551

When the messenger presented himself with your letter to Beza, I was seized with fresh alarm, and, at the same time, weighed down with a load of grief. For I was informed, the day before, that he had been seized with the plague. I was therefore not only troubled about the danger he was in, but from my very great affection for him I felt almost over-powered, as if I was already lamenting his death; although, indeed, this grief did not rise so much from private regard, as from my public anxiety for the prosperity of the Church. Indeed, I were destitute of human feeling, did I not return the affection of one who loves me with more than a brother's love, and reveres me like a very father. But the Church's loss afflicted me more deeply, when I pictured a man, of whom I had so very high expectations, suddenly snatched away from us by death, at the very outset of his career – a man whose gentle disposition, polished manners, and native candour, had endeared him to all good men. Should you ever happen to make a secret and hasty journey hither – which I am very anxious you should – you will find him far superior in those respects to anything I have stated. I trust that melancholy foreboding is far distant, of an event which you say would be an irreparable loss to you. Your coming would be the more desirable, as he was very anxious to see you when he left. What should we delight in but Christ? Yet I confidently

1 This letter, without an address, was written to a friend, perhaps to one of the members of the family of Beza in France, during an illness which endangered his life, in 1551, and which called forth from the Reformer the most touching testimonies of his affection.

trust that the life of man will not be denied to our prayers. For although he has not yet escaped danger, yet yesterday's messenger brought us more hopeful accounts of him. To-morrow I hope to hear what will remove all doubt. Adieu, distinguished Sir, and take in good part this voluntary service of mine, seeing I write with so much familiarity to one with whom I am not acquainted. May the Lord guide you by His Spirit, and shield you by His protection!

29/TO THE DUKE OF SOMERSET[1]

Protestations of attachment
Reforms required in the Church of England
Squandering of the revenues of benefices and of the universities.

From Geneva, this 25th July 1551

Monseigneur:

I know not how to thank you enough for the kind reception which my messenger has met with from you, not merely in that you have been pleased to take the trouble of offering my books to the King, but for all other proofs of the singular friendly affection which you have hitherto graciously shown me. As for the youth whom you have taken into your service, I should not have had the boldness to write to you about him, had I not thought, as was generally expected, that he was likely to turn out remarkably well. But so much the more am I obliged to you, since I find that my recommendation has been of use in this quarter. As however all that I could write would be but very feeble compared with what is in my heart,

1 See the letter to the King, January, 1551. The minister, Nicolas des Gallars, charged to present to the King the letter and the Commentaries of Calvin, had met with the most flattering reception at Court.

and what your benefits deserve, I prefer to desist from further comment on them. Only I pray you, Monseigneur, to consider me so wholly yours, that had I any way of doing you service, it would not be my fault if you lacked proof of more goodwill than I know how to express. I would have made these excuses to you sooner, or rather these thanks, if it may please you to hold them such, had it not been for the desire which this gentleman had, himself to present my letter to you. And in this also, I can perceive the friendship you are pleased to show towards me, since those who well deserve to have access to you, hope to be the more welcome by means of my letters.

Nevertheless, Monseigneur, I shall not cease to commend to your attention that which is of itself dear and precious enough to you. It is, that you provide and take heed that God may be faithfully honoured and served; above all, that better order be established in the Church than heretofore. Albeit it may not be easy to obtain people specially qualified to discharge this office; yet, from what I hear, there are two great hindrances against which it would be essential to provide. The first is, that the revenues of the universities which have been founded for the maintenance of scholars, are ill distributed; many being thus supported who openly profess to resist the Gospel, so far are they from affording any hopes of upholding that which has been there built up with great pains and labour.

The second evil is, that the revenue of the cures is diverted and wasted, so that there is not wherewithal to support worthy men who might be fit to discharge the office of true pastors. And thus ignorant priests are installed, who bring in great confusion. For the character of individuals begets a great contempt of the Word of God; and thus whatever their authority, they cannot exercise it. I pray you, therefore, Monseigneur, to advance and improve the Reformation, and so give it permanence; be pleased to exert all your might in correcting this abuse. I quite believe that it has not been your fault that matters have not been better regulated in the first instance. But since it is very difficult all at once to organize an establishment as well as might be desirable, it only remains that we persevere, so as to perfect in time what has been well begun.

It ought not to be ill taken by those who at the present time derive profit from Church property, that the pastors be adequately supported; seeing that every one ought to strive to support them out of his own private means, were there no public ones. It would even be to their own advantage to discharge themselves of this debt, for they cannot expect to prosper while defrauding the people of God of their spiritual pasturage, by depriving the churches of good pastors. And on your part, Monseigneur, I have no doubt, when you have faithfully laboured to reduce these matters to order, that God will the more multiply His blessings upon you. But since I feel assured that you are so well inclined of yourself that I need not longer to exhort, I shall conclude, after having besought our good Lord, that it may please Him to guide you always by His Spirit, to increase you in all well-doing, and to cause His name to be more and more glorified by you. Even so, Monseigneur, I commend myself very humbly to your gracious favour.

30/TO LAELIUS SOCINUS[1]

Refusal to reply to the curious questions proposed to him by Socinus.

[1551.]

You are deceived in so far as you entertain the impression that Melanchthon does not agree with us on the doctrine of predestination. I only said briefly that I had a letter written by his own hand, in which he confessed that his opinion agreed with mine. But I can believe all you say, as it is nothing new for him to deceive in this matter, the better to rid himself of troublesome inquiries. Certainly no one can be more averse to paradox than I am, and in subtleties I find no delight at all. Yet nothing shall ever hinder me from openly avowing what I have learned from the word of God; for nothing but what is useful is taught in the school of this master. It is my only guide, and to acquiesce in its plain doctrines shall be my constant rule of wisdom. Would that you also, my

1 Laelius Socinus, founder of the celebrated sect which bears his name, was born at Sienna of a distinguished family: his father, Marianus Socinus, a professor in the University of Bologna, was one of the most learned jurisconsults of his age. Of a bold and active mind, which found pleasure in the most subtle speculations, and which would not stop short of the interpretation of mysteries, Laelius left his native country in 1548, and joined the Reformers of Switzerland and Germany, whose friendship he won by the politeness of his manners, the purity of his life, and his zeal for learning. He resided by turns at Zurich and Wittenberg, and was not slow, by correspondence or conversation, to express his doubts on the common doctrines, which he skilfully advanced rather in the form of questions than as opinions which he was prepared to maintain and to teach. He was beloved by Bullinger, who did not suspect the heterodoxy of his beliefs, and who wrote to Calvin regarding him, 'I restrain as far as I can this man's curiosity;' and Calvin himself, after having repeatedly broken off correspondence with Socinus, could not forbear renewing it, and giving a friendly reply to the doubts which he had expressed on the resurrection, baptism, the trinity, etc. The letter throws valuable light on the relation of the Reformer to the founder of a sect to which even Socinus himself was yet a stranger, and whose doubts were afterwards to be set up as dogmas by his disciples. Laelius Socinus died in 1562, before he had completed his thirty-seventh year.

dear Laelius, would learn to regulate your powers with the same moderation! You have no reason to expect a reply from me so long as you bring forward those monstrous questions. If you are gratified by floating among those airy speculations, permit me, I beseech you, an humble disciple of Christ, to meditate on those things which tend towards the building up of my faith. And indeed I shall hereafter follow out my wishes in silence, that you may not be troubled by me. And in truth, I am very greatly grieved that the fine talents with which God has endowed you, should be occupied not only with what is vain and fruitless, but that they should also be injured by pernicious figments. What I warned you of long ago, I must again seriously repeat, that unless you correct in time this itching after investigation, it is to be feared you will bring upon yourself severe suffering. I should be cruel towards you did I treat with a show of indulgence what I believe to be a very dangerous error. I should prefer, accordingly, offending you a little at present by my severity, rather than allow you to indulge unchecked in the fascinating allurements of curiosity. The time will come, I hope, when you will rejoice in having been so violently admonished. Adieu, brother very highly esteemed by me; and if this rebuke is harsher than it ought to be, ascribe it to my love to you.[1]

1 This letter, without a date, appears to belong to the last months of the year 1551. Laelius Socinus was living at that time at Wittenberg.

31/TO CRANMER[1]

*Agreement to the proposal for assembling a General Synod for the more
close union of the Reformed Churches.*

Geneva, [April 1552]

Your opinion, most distinguished Sir, is indeed just and wise,
that in the present disordered condition of the Church, no
remedy can be devised more suitable than if a general meeting
were held of the devout and the prudent, of those properly

1 Thomas Cranmer, Archbishop of Canterbury and Primate of England,
took an important part in the Reformation of his country during the reigns of
Henry VIII and Edward VI. He laboured assiduously with the Reformers of
the Continent, who esteemed his learning and honoured his character, to
establish a bond of union between the foreign churches and his own; and if he
did not live to see his efforts crowned with success, he at least left behind him
an example worthy of imitation. What is most notable in these endeavours is
to be found in Cranmer's Letters to the leading theologians of Switzerland
and Germany, reproduced in the Collections of his Works published by the
Parker Society. They are likewise to be found in the Collection of *Zurich Letters*,
1st series, vol. i. p. 21–26, from which we borrow the following letter to Calvin,
which furnishes us with the date of the Reformer's reply to the Prelate:

As nothing tends more injuriously to the separation of the Churches than
heresies and disputes respecting the doctrines of religion, so nothing tends
more effectually to unite the Churches of God, and more powerfully to defend
the fold of Christ, than the pure teaching of the Gospel and harmony of doctrine. Wherefore I have often wished, and still continue to do so, that learned
and godly men, who are eminent for erudition and judgment, might meet
together, and, comparing their respective opinions, might handle all the heads
of ecclesiastical doctrine, and hand down to posterity, under the weight of
their authority, some work not only upon the subjects themselves, but upon
the forms of expressing them. Our adversaries are now holding their councils
at Trent, for the establishment of their errors; and shall we neglect to call together a godly synod, for the refutation of error, and for restoring and propa-
gating the truth? They are, as I am informed, making decrees respecting the
worship of the host; wherefore we ought to leave no stone unturned, not
only that we may guard others against this idolatry, but also that we may ourselves come to an agreement upon the doctrine of this sacrament. It cannot
escape your prudence how exceedingly the Church of God has been injured
by dissensions and varieties of opinion respecting the sacrament of unity; and
though they are now in some measure removed, yet I could wish for an agreement in this doctrine, not only as regards the subject itself, but also with respect to the words and forms of expression. You have now my wish, about
which I have also written to Masters Philip [Melanchthon] and Bullinger;

exercised in the school of God, and of those who are confessedly at one on the doctrine of holiness. For we see how Satan is attempting, by various devices, to extinguish the light of the Gospel, which, by the wonderful goodness of God, having risen upon us, is shining in many a quarter. The hireling dogs of the Pope cease not to bark, in order to prevent the pure Gospel of Christ from being heard: so great is the licentiousness that is here and there breaking forth, and the ungodliness that is spreading abroad, that religion is become a mere mockery; and those who are not professed enemies of the truth, nevertheless conduct themselves with an impropriety which will create in a short time, unless it be obviated, terrible disorder among us. And not only among the common herd of men here does the distemper of a stupid inquisitiveness alternate with that of fearless extravagance, but, what is more lamentable, in the ranks of the pastors also the malady is now gaining ground. It is too well known with what mad actions Osiander is deceiving himself and deluding certain others. Yet the Lord, as he has done even from the beginning of the world, will preserve in a miraculous manner, and in a way unknown to us, the unity of a pure faith from being destroyed by the dissensions of men. And those whom He has placed on His watchtower He wishes least of all to be inactive, seeing that He has appointed them to be His ministers, through whose labours He may preserve from all corruptions sound doctrine in the Church, and transmit it safe to posterity. Especially, most illustrious Archbishop, is it necessary for you, in proportion to the distinguished position you occupy, to turn your attention as you are doing towards this object. I do not say this as if to spur you on to greater exertions, who are not only, of your own accord, in advance of others,

---

and I pray you to deliberate among yourselves as to the means by which this synod can be assembled with the greatest convenience. Farewell.—Your very dear brother in Christ,

THOMAS CANTUAR.

LAMBETH, *20th March* 1552.

but are also, as a voluntary encourager, urging them on; I say it in order that, by my congratulations, you may be strengthened in a pursuit so auspicious and noble. I hear that the success of the Gospel in England is indeed cheering; but you will experience there also, I doubt not, what Paul experienced in his time, that by means of the door that has been opened for the reception of pure doctrine, many enemies will suddenly rise up against it. Although I am really ignorant of how many suitable defenders you may have at hand to repel the lies of Satan, still the ungodliness of whose who are wholly taken up in creating disturbances, causes the assiduity of the well-disposed to be at no time either too much or superfluous. And then I am aware that English matters are not so all-important in your eyes, but that you, at the same time, regard the interests of the whole world. Moreover, the rare piety of the English King, as well as his noble disposition, is worthy of the highest commendation, in that, of his own inclination, he entertains the pious design of holding a convention of the nature referred to, and offers a place for it also in his own kingdom. And would that it were attainable to bring together into some place, from various Churches, men eminent for their learning, and that after having carefully discussed the main points of belief one by one, they should, from their united judgments, hand down to posterity the true doctrine of Scripture. This other thing also is to be ranked among the chief evils of our time, viz., that the Churches are so divided, that human fellowship is scarcely now in any repute amongst us, far less that Christian intercourse which all make a profession of, but few sincerely practise. If men of learning conduct themselves with more reserve than is seemly, the very heaviest blame attaches to the leaders themselves, who, either engrossed in their own sinful pursuits, are indifferent to the safety and entire piety of the Church, or who, individually satisfied with their own private peace, have no regard for others. Thus it is that the members of the Church being severed, the body lies bleeding. So much does this concern me, that, could I be of any service, I would not grudge to cross even ten seas, if need were, on account of it. If it were but a question regarding the rendering of assistance to the kingdom of England, such a motive would at present be to me a sufficiently just one. Now, seeing that a serious and properly adjusted agreement between men of learning upon the rule of Scripture is still a desideratum, by means of which Churches, though divided on other questions, might be made to unite, I think it right for me, at whatever cost of toil and trouble, to seek to attain this object. But I hope my own insignificance will cause me to be passed by. If I earnestly pray that it may be undertaken by others, I hope I shall have discharged my duty. Mr Philip [Melanchthon] is at too great a distance to admit of a speedy interchange of letters. Mr Bullinger has likely written you before this time. Would that I were as able as I am willing to exert myself! Moreover, the very difficulty of the thing which you feel, compels me to do what, at the outset, I affirmed I would not do, viz., not only to encourage, but also to implore you to increase your exertions, until something at least shall have been accomplished, if not all that we could desire. – Adieu, very distinguished Archbishop, deserving of my hearty reverence. May the Lord continue to guide you by His Spirit, and to bless your holy labours!

32/TO THE FIVE PRISONERS OF LYONS,—
MARTIAL ALBA, PETER ESCRIVAIN,
CHARLES FAVRE, PETER NAVIHÈRES,
BERNARD SEGUIN[1]

Information on various doctrinal points,
and assurances of Christian sympathy.

From Geneva, this 10th of June, 1552

My very dear Brethren:

Hitherto I have put off writing to you, fearing that if the letter fell into bad hands, it might give fresh occasion to the enemy to afflict you. And besides, I had been informed how that God wrought so powerfully in you by His grace, that you stood in no great need of my letters. However, we have not forgotten you, neither I nor all the brethren hereabouts, as to whatever we have been able to do for you. As soon as you were taken, we heard of it, and knew how it had come to pass. We took care that help might be sent you with all speed, and are now waiting the result. Those who have in-

1 In the month of April 1552, five young Frenchmen, instructed at the school of theology of Lausanne, and devoted to the functions of the ministry, made arrangements for returning to their own country. These were Martial Alba of Montauban, Peter Ecrivain of Gascony, Charles Favre of Blanzac in Angoumois, Peter Navihères of Limousin, and Bernard Seguin of La Reole. After having spent some days at Geneva, they set out for Lyons, and met on the way at the Bourg de Colonges, near L'Écluse, a stranger, who offered himself as their fellow-traveller. They consented without harbouring any suspicion. Arriving at Lyons, they parted with their travelling companion, who pressed them to visit him at his dwelling of Ainay. They went there without any distrust, were arrested and led away to the prisons of that jurisdiction. Such was the origin of a long and doleful process, which held the Churches of France and Switzerland for a long time in suspense, and during which, the bloodthirsty cruelty of the judges was only equalled by the constancy of the victims. On the first rumour of the arrest of the five students, the Church of Geneva took the matter up, and lavished upon the captives, by the voice of Calvin, the most lively testimonies of their sympathy.

fluence with the prince in whose power God has put your lives, are faithfully exerting themselves on your behalf, but we do not yet know how far they have succeeded in their suit. Meanwhile, all the children of God pray for you as they are bound to do, not only on account of the mutual compassion which ought to exist between members of the same body, but because they know well that you labour for them, in maintaining the cause of their salvation. We hope, come what may, that God of His goodness will give a happy issue to your captivity, so that we shall have reason to rejoice. You see to what He has called you; doubt not, therefore, that according as He employs you, He will give you strength to fulfil His work, for He has promised this, and we know by experience that He has never failed those who allow themselves to be governed by Him. Even now you have proof of this in yourselves, for He has shown His power, by giving you so much constancy in withstanding the first assaults. Be confident, therefore, that He will not leave the work of His hand imperfect. You know what Scripture sets before us, to encourage us to fight for the cause of the Son of God; meditate upon what you have both heard and seen formerly on this head, so as to put it in practice. For all that I could say would be of little service to you, were it not drawn from this fountain. And truly we have need of a much more firm support than that of men, to make us victorious over such strong enemies as the devil, death, and the world; but the firmness which is in Christ Jesus is sufficient for this, and all else that might shake us were we not established in Him. Knowing, then, in whom ye have believed, manifest what authority He deserves to have over you.

As I hope to write to you again, I shall not at present lengthen my letter. I shall only reply briefly to the point which brother Bernard has asked me to solve. Concerning vows, we must hold to this rule, that it is not lawful to vow to God anything but what He approves. Now the fact is, that monastic vows tend only to corrupt His service. As for the second question, we must hold that it is devilish presumption for a man to vow beyond the measure of his vocation. Now, the Scripture declares, both in the nineteenth of St Matthew and in the seventh of the First to the Corinthians, that the gift of continence is a special grace. It follows, then, that those who put themselves in the position and under the necessity of renouncing marriage for the whole of their life, cannot be acquitted of rashness, and that by so doing they tempt God. The question might very easily be spun out to a greater length, by stating that we ought to consider, first, who He is to whom we vow; secondly, the nature of that vow; and thirdly, the party making the vow. For God is too great a Master for us to trifle with, and man is bound to consider his own capabilities; for to present a sacrifice without obedience, is nothing but thorough pollution. However, this one point may suffice you to prove to them that the gift of continence is a special gift, and in such-wise special, that for the most part it is only for a season. So that he who possessed it for thirty years, like Isaac, may not do so for the remainder of his life. Hence you may conclude, that the monks, in binding themselves never to marry, attempt without faith to promise what is not given to them. As for their poverty, it is quite the reverse of that which our Lord enjoined upon his followers.

Concerning the nature of a glorified body, true it is, that the qualities thereof are changed, but not entirely. For we must distinguish between the qualities which proceed from the corruption of sin, and those which belong to and are inseparable from the nature of the body. St Paul, in the third chapter of the Epistle to the Philippians, says that our vile or weak body shall be made like to the glorious body of Christ. By this humble expression or *Tapinosis*, he points out which of the qualities that we at present bear about with us in our bodies are to be changed; those, namely, which are of the corruptible and fading nature of this world. And on this subject St Augustine says, in the *Epistle of Dardanus*, which in number is the 57th, '*He shall come again in the same form and substance of the flesh, to which certainly he gave immortality; he hath not taken away the nature. In this form he must not be supposed to be everywhere diffused.*' This argument he follows out at greater length, showing that the body of Christ is contained within its own dimensions. And in fact our glorified bodies will not be ubiquitous, although they will have that likeness of which St Paul speaks. As for the passage of the Apocalypse, the words are these in the fifth chapter: '*And every creature which is in heaven, and on the earth, and under the earth, and such as are in the sea, and all that are in them, heard I saying, Blessing, and honour, and glory, and power, be unto Him that sitteth upon the throne, and unto the Lamb, for ever and ever.*' Now you see that it is a childish cavil to apply this to souls in purgatory; for St John, by the figure which is called *Prosopopœia*, rather conveys that even the fishes blessed God. And in regard to the passages of the Doctors, refer your people to the 27th Epistle of St Augustine, *To Boniface*, where he states, towards the end, *that the sacraments have a certain similitude of those things which they represent. From whence it comes to pass, that after some fashion the sacrament of the body of Christ may be the body of Christ.* Also that which he treats of in the third book, *Of Christian Doctrine*, where he says, among other things in the fifth chapter: '*Such is the completely miserable bondage of the soul in conceiving of the signs in place of the things signified, and never lifting up the eye of the understanding above the corporeal creature to breathe eternal light.*' Similarly, in the ninth chapter: '*The believer knows by experience, and understands* [agnoscit] *to what the mystery of baptism, and the celebration of the body and blood of the Lord, may be referred, so that the soul can offer religious worship, not in the bondage of the flesh, but rather in the liberty of the spirit. So to follow the literal sense, and in suchwise to conceive of the signs instead of the things sealed or signified by them, is a slavish weakness; that mere symbols should be so un-*

profitably interpreted, is the result of vague error.' I do not heap up quotations, because these will be quite enough for your purpose. In conclusion, I beseech our good Lord that He would be pleased to make you feel in every way the worth of His protection of His own, to fill you with His Holy Spirit, who gives you prudence and virtue, and brings you peace, joy, and contentment; and may the name of our Lord Jesus be glorified by you to the edification of His Church!

33/TO EDWARD VI[1]

Dedication of a new work, and Christian exhortations.

From Geneva, this 4th July 1552

Sire:

Although I ought to fear lest my importunity may prove troublesome to your Majesty, and have indeed on that account abstained from writing to you more frequently, nevertheless, I have had the boldness to send you, together with my letters, a short exposition which I have composed of the 78th (87th)[2] Psalm, hoping that you would take pleasure in it, and also that the reading thereof might be profitable to you. As I was one day expounding it in a sermon to the people, the argument appeared to me so appropriate for you, that I was forth-

1 Calvin wrote this letter to King Edward VI, when dedicating to him the following little work: Four Sermons of Master John Calvin, treating of matters very profitable for our time, with a Brief Exposition of Psalm lxxvii. These four sermons have been translated at different times into English. In the first, Calvin exhorts the faithful to flee from idolatry; in the second, he encourages them to suffer everything for Jesus Christ; in the third, he shows how highly believers ought to prize the privilege of being in the Church of God, where they are at liberty to worship Him purely; in the last, he shows that this liberty cannot be purchased at too high a price.

2 An error in the original; it is 87 which we must read.

with moved to draw up a summary of it, such as you will see, when it shall please your Majesty to devote to it one hour only. It is very true, that I treat the subject generally, without addressing you personally. But as I have mainly had regard to you in the writing of it, so in the prudent application and appropriation of it, you will find that it contains a very profitable lesson for your Majesty.

You know, Sire, how much danger kings and princes are in, lest the height to which they are raised should dazzle their eyes, and amuse them here below, while making them forgetful of the heavenly kingdom; and I doubt not that God hath so warned you against this evil, to preserve you therefrom, that you are a hundred times more impressed with it, than those who have no personal experience of it. Now, in the present Psalm mention is made of the nobleness and dignity of the Church, which ought so to enrapture both great and small, that no earthly honours and possessions should hold them back, or hinder them from aiming to be enrolled among the people of God. It is indeed a great thing to be a king, and yet more, over such a country; nevertheless, I have no doubt that you reckon it beyond comparison better to be a Christian. It is therefore an invaluable privilege that God has vouchsafed you, Sire, to be a Christian king, to serve as his lieutenant in ordering and maintaining the kingdom of Jesus Christ in England. You see then, that in acknowledgment of such great benefits received from His infinite goodness, you ought to be stirred up to employ all your energies to His honour and service, setting to your subjects an example of homage to this great King, to whom your Majesty is not ashamed to submit yourself with all humility and reverence beneath the spiritual sceptre of His gospel; and if hitherto you have done this, so that we have cause to glorify God for his goodness, the present Psalm will always serve you as a support and a buckler. Meanwhile, I humbly entreat you, Sire, that this short letter may serve as a protest and testimony to your Majesty of the hearty desire I have to do better, if the means were given me.

Sire, after having very humbly commended me to your kind favour, I pray our Lord to fill you with the gifts of his Holy Spirit, to guide you in all prudence and virtue, to make you prosper and flourish to the glory of His name.

34/TO CRANMER[1]

Calvin exhorts him to prosecute with fresh zeal the reformation of the Church in England, by purging it of the relics of Popery.

[July 1552]

Seeing that, at the present time, that which is most of all to be desired is least likely to be attained, viz., that an assembly of the most eminent men of learning, from all the various Churches which have embraced the pure doctrine of the Gospel, after having discussed separately the controverted topics of the day, might transmit to posterity, out of the pure Word of God, a true and distinct confession; I nevertheless highly commend the plan which you, reverend Sir, have adopted, to make the English frame for themselves, without delay, a religious constitution, lest, by matters remaining longer in an unsettled state, or not being sufficiently adjusted, the minds of the common people should be confirmed in their suspense. And it is the duty of all in your country, who have any influence, to direct their energies with united zeal towards this object, so that your duties may still be special. You see what such a position as yours demands, or rather what God may legitimately require of you in consideration of the nature of the office which He has imposed on you.

1 This letter bears no date, but it refers to the subject set forth in the previous letter of Calvin to Cranmer.

Supreme authority is vested in you – an authority which your high rank entitles you to, not more than the previously entertained opinion regarding your wisdom and integrity. The eyes of many are fixed upon you, either to second your exertions, or to imitate your lukewarmness. And sincerely do I desire that, under your leadership, they may be advanced to such an extent during the next three years, that the difficulties and contests of the present time, caused by the removing of the grossest superstition, shall have ceased to exist. I, for my part, acknowledge that our cause has made no little progress during the short period the Gospel has flourished in England. But if you reflect on what yet remains to be done, and how very remiss you have been in many matters, you will discover that you have no reason to advance towards the goal with less rapidity, even although the most of the course has, as it were, been gone over; for I need not inform you that I, as it were, take note of your assiduity, lest, after having escaped danger, you should become self-indulgent. But to speak freely, I greatly fear, and this fear is abiding, that so many autumns will be spent in procrastinating, that by and by the cold of a perpetual winter will set in. You are now somewhat advanced in years, and this ought to stimulate you to increased exertions, so as to save yourself the regret of having been consciously dilatory, and that you may not leave the world while matters remain in so disordered a condition. I say matters are still in a disorganized state, for external religious abuses have been corrected in such a way as to leave remaining innumerable young shoots, which are constantly sprouting forth. In fact, I am informed that such a mass of Papal corruptions remain, as not only to hide, but almost to extinguish the pure worship of God. Meanwhile the life of the whole ecclesiastical order is all but extinct, or at least is not sufficiently vigorous: take, for example, the preaching of doctrine. Assuredly pure and undefiled religion will never flourish, until the Churches shall have been at greater pains to secure suitable pastors, and such as shall conscientiously discharge the duties of teaching. Satan, indeed, opposes his secret wiles to the accomplishment of this. I understand that there is still one shameful obstacle, viz., that the revenues of the Church have been plundered; truly an insufferable evil. But iniquitous as this is, there appears to me to be another vice of equal magnitude, viz., that out of the public revenues of the Church, idle gluttons are supported who chant vespers in an unknown tongue. I shall say nothing farther on this point, except that it is inconsistent for you to approve of such mockery, and it is openly incompatible with the proper arrangements of the Church; besides, it is in itself exceedingly ridiculous. I do not doubt, however, but that these considerations will immediately occur to your own mind, and will be suggested to you by that most upright man Peter Martyr, whose counsel I am exceedingly glad to know you enjoy. Difficulties so numerous and so trying as those against which you are contending, appear to me a sufficient excuse for the exhortations I have offered. – Adieu, most distinguished and esteemed Primate. May the Lord long preserve you in safety; may He fill you more and more with the Spirit of wisdom and fortitude, and bless your labours! Amen.

35/TO THE FIVE PRISONERS OF LYONS[1]

Exhortations to constancy
Mention of Oritz, the Inquisitor.

7th March 1553

My Brethren:

We have been for some days past in deeper anxiety and sadness than ever, having heard of the resolve taken by the enemies of the truth. When the gentleman you know of passed this way,[2] while he was dining very hurriedly, to avoid all delay, I drew up such a form of letters as seemed to me expedient to write. God has given, both to you and all His people, some farther respite; we await the event as it shall please Him to dispose it, always praying Him to uphold you, and not permit you to fall away; in short, to have you in His keeping. I feel well assured that nothing shakes the firmness which he has put within you. Doubtless, for a long time past, you have meditated upon the last conflict which you will have to sustain, if it be His good pleasure to lead you thereto, and have even so fought hitherto that long practice has inured you to fill up what remains. It cannot be but that you feel some twinges of frailty; yet, be confident that He whose service

1 Declared guilty of the crime of heresy, and delivered over to the secular arm by the Judge Ordinary of Lyons, the five students made their appeal to the Parlement de Paris, while the authorities of Berne strove in vain to save them. Transferred from dungeon to dungeon, during a trial which lasted for more than a year, brought back at last from Paris to Lyons, to await the sentence of their judges, the constancy of these young men never faltered for a single day. At length, the 1st March 1553, they received the communication of the decree of the Parlement de Paris, which gave them over to the stake. This information soon spread around, and brought mourning to Lausanne and to Geneva.

2 This was the pious merchant, John Liner, of Saint Gall. He was present with the prisoners at the bar of Roanne when they received their sentence of death. He set out immediately for Berne, in order to try a last application on the part of the seigneury of that town to the King of France.

you are upon will so rule in your hearts by His Holy Spirit, that His grace shall overcome all temptations. If He has promised to strengthen with patience those who suffer chastisement for their sins, how much less will He be found wanting to those who maintain his quarrel,—those whom He employs on so worthy a mission as being witnesses for His truth. You must therefore keep this sentence in mind, that *He who dwells in you is stronger than the world*. We who are here shall do our duty in praying that He would glorify Himself more and more by your constancy, and that He may, by the consolation of His Spirit, sweeten and endear all that is bitter to the flesh, and so absorb your spirits in Himself, that in contemplating that heavenly crown, you may be ready without regret to leave all that belongs to this world.

I have received a certain paper containing some very subtle arguments of that unhappy animal Oritz,[1] to prove that it is allowable to make idols. I do not know whether it is you who have sent it me, and whether you would have me to reply to it. I have not thought it worth while to do so, because I was in some doubt about it, and really I do believe that you have no great need of it. But if you like you shall have an answer to it by the first. There is one thing which I have to request of you; you saw some time ago the letters of a paltry mocker of God in this place, who does nothing but trouble the Church, and has never ceased to deal in that trade for five years past. I wish much that by the first, you would write a word of warning to make known his malice, as there is really no end to him. And this I beseech you, as you love the repose of this Church, which is more teased than you can well believe by internal foes.

And now, my brethren, after having besought our good Lord to have charge over you, to assist you in everything and

1 The inquisitor, Nicolas Oritz, who presided at the trial of the five students. The paper here mentioned still exists in the library of Geneva, 113, with this title: 'Copy of a paper of the Inquisitor Houriz, given to the prisoners for the Word at Lyons, to be conveyed to M. Calvin to retain.'

through everything, to make you taste by experience how kind a Father He is, and how careful of the salvation of his own, I pray to be remembered in your prayers.

36/TO EDWARD VI

Recommendation of a French gentleman,
a prisoner for the sake of the Gospel.

From Geneva, this 12th March 1553

Sire:

Although I had a petition to make to you for myself, I should not have the boldness to urge it, yet I think that you will not take it amiss that I should make a request for another, when you are informed of the necessity which constrains me, and the merits of the case, which commends itself to you not less than to myself. It is, Sire, that there is a French gentleman detained prisoner in Paris[1] on account of some intercepted letters written by him to one of our friends, who was the king's lieutenant in the town of Noyon (of which I am a native), and retired to these parts;[2] added to which the said gentleman was already held suspect in the matter of religion. And being a man of some rank they kept an eye upon him, which has been the occasion of his seizure. Now, if my testimony has any weight with your Majesty, I can assure you, Sire, that he is as right-minded a man as you could anywhere meet with,

1 This gentleman, whose name is not known, corresponded by letter with Calvin, his countryman and friend. Shortly before his arrest he wrote to Calvin on the subject of a fire, which had almost entirely destroyed the town of Noyon, sparing, however, the house of the reformer: 'I have no doubt that God has left this testimony against those of your town, who eight or ten days before had burnt in effigy Monsieur de Normandie and the rest.'
2 Laurent de Normandie.

excelling in all honour and virtue, endowed with graces which deserve to be loved and valued, and above all, confirmed in the fear of God. I know very well that this is great praise; but did you know him, Sire, I have no doubt that you would form a like judgment, and discover that I do not exceed due measure. Now, as he is beloved of all, both high and low, even of Monseiur de Vendosme and other princes, there is nothing save the cause of Jesus Christ on account of which he can be hated or rejected, which cause is so dear to you, Sire, that I hope you will not refuse to help him, if there be any means of doing so. I am aware that your Majesty cannot aid as might be wished, all those who labour and are persecuted on account of the Gospel. But should it be your good pleasure to exert yourself for him of whom I treat, be assured, Sire, that in the person of one man you will console many who are at present greatly dismayed, while the foes of truth are fully intending to triumph if they succeed. But not to be too troublesome to your Majesty, I shall enter no further upon facts, which, if it seem good to you, you can better learn from the statements of the gentleman who delivers this. Only I beseech you, in the name of God, with all possible affection, yea, as eagerly as I would on behalf of my own life, that it may please you to grant this request, namely, to ask the King of France to let him depart out of his country, together with his wife, also detained, and with as much of his property as can be withdrawn. In doing which you will not only lay me under obligation more and more to pray God to prosper you, but an infinite number of believers besides.

Sire, after having commended myself as humbly as I can to your kind favour, I pray our good Lord to keep you under His holy protection, and to govern you by his Spirit in all prudence, uprightness, and strength of purpose, and to make your crown to flourish more and more.

37/TO CRANMER

He entreats his influence in favour of the person already recommended to the King.

March 1553

When I lately wrote to you my last letter[1] – which may not perhaps be put into your hands until after you have received the present one—nothing was farther from my mind than that I should again trouble you so soon. An unexpected necessity has arisen, however, which compels me, even before I have penned a single friendly letter to you, to solicit you regarding a matter of great importance. A certain man, of a noble family, has been lately thrown into prison, whose kind heart and generous nature render him still more worthy of commendation for his virtues, than for the nobility of his descent. Thinking there was no danger, he had written to a common friend, who came among us as a voluntary exile when the royal prefect was at Noyon, the town in which I was born. Owing to the perfidy of the messenger, the letter was seized. He was arrested by a royal order. The Chancellor, and some others, were appointed judges extraordinary. Seeing that this occurrence has caused many good men to be seized with no ordinary alarm, and that the enemies of the whole Church are ferociously insulting Christ in the person of a man of sincere piety, it is our duty to do all we can to restrain their fury, and bring relief to such a distinguished servant of God. I was not at all afraid, therefore, of any one accusing me of indiscretion in engaging in the pious duty of commending the life of this person to your most serene king. And the same necessity which drove me to this, leads me to exhort you to use your

---

1 The letter to which allusion is here made is lost; it might well have shed a fuller light on the relations of Calvin with the Reformer of England.

interest, as far as may be lawful, for furthering the end of my petition. And while I am confident that you will be glad to do it of your own accord, I nevertheless ask and beseech of you, most earnestly to do it for my sake all the more speedily. Adieu, most distinguished Sir, deserving in many ways of my hearty reverence.

38/TO THE FIVE PRISONERS OF LYONS[1]

He exhorts them to steadfastness unto the end, in the assurance of eternal joy reserved in heaven.

From Geneva, 15 May 1553

My very dear Brothers:

We have at length heard why the herald of Berne did not return that way. It was because he had not such an answer as we much desired. For the King has peremptorily refused all the requests made by Messieurs of Berne, as you will see by

1 This letter must have preceded by some days the last conflict of the five prisoners. Foreseeing their end near, they wrote, on the 5th May to the Seigneury of Berne, to thank them for the testimonials of affection which they had received from them. 'If it has not pleased God to preserve life by your means, it has at least been prolonged thereby ... in spite of the fury of all those who would have desired long ago to put us to death. Since, then, that He is pleased that our blood should soon be shed for the confession of His holy name, we reckon ourselves far happier than if we were set at liberty, for as he is true and all-powerful He will strengthen us, and will not permit us to be tormented beyond our strength; and after that we have suffered awhile, He will receive us into His heavenly kingdom, and will bestow upon us eternal rest with Himself. ...' It was the 16th May when the five scholars were told to prepare for death; they received that intelligence with a pious serenity. The stake was set up upon the *Place des Terreaux;* they proceeded thither, singing psalms, and repeating passages of holy writ. Having arrived at the place of death, they cheerfully mounted on the heap of wood, the two youngest first ... The last who went up was Martial Alba, the eldest of the five, who had been a long time on both his knees in prayer to the Lord. He earnestly requested Lieutenant Tignac to grant him a favour. The lieutenant

the copies of the letters, so that nothing further is to be looked for from that quarter. Nay, wherever we look here below, God has stopped the way. This is well, however, that we cannot be frustrated of the hope which we have in Him, and in His holy promises. You have always been settled on that sure foundation, even when it seemed as though you might be helped by men, and that we too thought so; but whatever prospect of escape you may have had by human means, yet your eyes have never been dazzled so as to divert your heart and trust, either on this side or that. Now, at this present hour, necessity itself exhorts you more then ever to turn your whole mind heavenward. As yet, we know not what will be the event. But since it appears as though God would use your blood to sign His truth, there is nothing better than for you to prepare yourselves to that end, beseeching Him so to subdue you to His good pleasure, that nothing may hinder you from following whithersoever he shall call. For you know, my brothers, that it behoves us to be thus mortified, in order to be offered to Him in sacrifice. It cannot be but that you sustain hard conflicts, in order that what was declared to Peter may be accomplished in you, namely, that they shall carry you whither ye would not. You know, however, in what strength you have to fight – a strength on which all those who trust, shall never be daunted, much less confounded. Even so, my brothers, be confident that you shall be strengthened, according to your need, by the Spirit of our Lord Jesus, so that you shall not faint under the load of temptations, however heavy it be, any more than He did who won so glorious a victory, that in the midst of our miseries it is an

---

said to him: What would you? He said to him: That I might kiss my brethren before I die. The lieutenant granted his wish. Then the said Martial kissed the other four who were already bound, saying to each of them, *Adieu, adieu, my brother*. The fire was kindled; the voice of the five confessors was heard, still exhorting one another in the midst of the flames: *Courage, my brothers; courage*. . . . These were the last audible words of these five valiant champions and martyrs of the Lord.

unfailing pledge of our triumph. Since it pleases Him to employ you to the death in maintaining His quarrel, He will strengthen your hands in the fight, and will not suffer a single drop of your blood to be spent in vain. And though the fruit may not all at once appear, yet in time it shall spring up more abundantly than we can express. But as He hath vouchsafed you this privilege, that your bonds have been renowned, and that the noise of them has been everywhere spread abroad, it must needs be, in despite of Satan, that your death should resound far more powerfully, so that the name of our Lord be magnified thereby. For my part, I have no doubt, if it please this kind Father to take you unto Himself, that He has preserved you hitherto, in order that your long-continued imprisonment might serve as a preparation for the better awakening of those whom He has determined to edify by your end. For let enemies do their utmost, they never shall be able to bury out of sight that light which God has made to shine in you, in order to be contemplated from afar.

I shall not console, nor exhort you more at length, knowing that our heavenly Father gives you to experience how precious His consolations are, and that you are sufficiently careful to meditate upon what He sets before you in His Word. He has already so shown how His Spirit dwells in you, that we are well assured that He will perfect you to the end. That in leaving this world we do not go away at a venture, you know not only from the certainty you have, that there is a heavenly life, but also because from being assured of the gratuitous adoption of our God, you go thither as to your inheritance. That God should have appointed you His Son's martyrs, is a token to you of superabounding grace. There now remains the conflict, to which the Spirit of God not only exhorts us to go, but even to run. It is indeed a hard and grievous trial, to see the pride of the enemies of truth so enormous, without its getting any check from on high; their rage so unbridled, without God's interfering for the relief of His people. But if we remember

that, when it is said that our life is hid, and that we must re-
semble the dead, this is not a doctrine for any particular time,
but for all times, we shall not think it strange that afflictions
should continue. While it pleases God to give His enemies the
rein, our duty is to be quiet, although the time of our redemption tarries. Moreover, if He has promised to be the judge of
those who have brought His people under thraldom, we need
not doubt that He has a horrible punishment prepared for
such as have despised His majesty with such enormous pride,
and have cruelly persecuted those who call purely upon His
name. Put in practice, then, my brethren, that precept of
David's, and forget not the law of God, although your life
may be in your hands to be parted with at any hour. And
seeing that he employs your life in so worthy a cause as is the
witness of the Gospel, doubt not that it must be precious to
Him. The time draws nigh when the earth shall disclose the
blood which has been hid, and we, after having been disen-
cumbered of these fading bodies, shall be completely restored.
However, be the Son of God glorified by our shame, and let
us be content with this sure testimony, that though we are
persecuted and blamed we trust in the living God. In this we
have wherewith to despise the whole world with its pride,
till we be gathered into that everlasting kingdom, where we
shall fully enjoy those blessings which we now only possess
in hope.

My brethren, after having humbly besought your remembrance of me in your prayers, I pray our good Lord to have
you in His holy protection, to strengthen you more and more
by His power, to make you feel what care He takes of your
salvation, to increase in you the gifts of His Spirit, and to make
them subserve His glory unto the end.

I do not make my special remembrances to each of our
brethren because I believe that this letter will be common to
them all.[1] Hitherto I have deferred writing on account of the

1 Calvin refers here to other prisoners of Lyons, Mathieu Dimonet and

uncertainty of your state, fearing lest I might disquiet you to no purpose. I pray anew our good Lord to stretch out his arm for your confirmation.

39/TO THE PRISONERS OF LYONS[1]

He impresses on them the duty of maintaining their confession of the truth quietly and modestly.

This 7th of July 1553

My Brethren:

I believe you have been informed that I was absent from town when the tidings from your prison arrived, and did not return for eight days after. I need not, therefore, to excuse myself for having so long delayed writing to you. Now, although these tidings have proved sorrowful to the flesh, even in consequence of the love we justly bear you in God, as we are

---

Denis Peloquin, who kept up in prison a pious correspondence by letter with the scholars of Lausanne.

1 The dungeons in which Mathieu Dimonet still pined away, contained several other prisoners, Denis Peloquin of Blois, Louis de Marsac, gentleman of the Bourbonnais, and one of his cousins. It is to the last two, recently arrived at Lyons, that the letter of the Reformer is addressed. The prisoners maintained a correspondence with those outside their prison. Peloquin wrote to his relations, – '. . . My dear brothers and sisters, . . . do not stay yourselves, I beseech you, upon the judgment of the world, which is so blinded, that it cannot find life in death, nor blessing in cursing. Let us know that the means of being confirmed in Jesus Christ . . . is that we should carry our cross with him, for the servant is not greater than the master . . .' Louis de Marsac wrote to Calvin: – 'Sir and brother, . . . I cannot express to you the great comfort I have received . . . from the letter which you have sent to my brother Denis Peloquin, who found means to deliver it to one of our brethren who was in a vaulted cell above me, and read it to me aloud, as I could not read it myself, being unable to see anything in my dungeon. I entreat of you, therefore, to persevere in helping us with similar consolation, for it invites us to weep and to pray.'

bound to do, yet we submit ourselves to the will of this kind Father and sovereign Lord, and not only consider His way of disposing of us just and reasonable, but also accept it with a gentle and loving heart as altogether right and profitable for our salvation, patiently waiting until He palpably shows it to be so. Besides, we have whereof to rejoice even in the midst of our sorrow, in that he has so powerfully aided you, for need was that you should be strengthened by His Spirit, so that the confession of His sacred truth should be more precious to you than your own lives. We all know too well how difficult it is for men to forget self.

Therefore it must needs be that our gracious God put forth His strong arm; then, for the sake of glorifying Him, we do not fear torments, nor shame, nor death itself. Now, since He has girded you with His power, so as to sustain the first assault, it remains to entreat Him to strengthen you more and more according to your further conflict. And seeing that He has promised us victory in the end, do not doubt, that as He has imparted a measure of His strength, so you will have more ample evidence in future that He does not make a beginning only to leave His work imperfect, as it is said in the Psalm. Especially when He puts such honour upon His people, as to employ them in maintaining His truth, and leads them, as it were by the hand to martyrdom, He never leaves them unprovided with the needful weapons. Yet, meanwhile, remember to lift up your eyes to that everlasting kingdom of Jesus Christ, and to think of whose cause it is in which you fight; for that glance will not only make you overcome all temptations which may spring from the infirmity of your flesh, but will also render you invincible by all the wiles of Satan, whatever he may devise to darken God's truth,—for I am well assured, that it is by His grace you are so settled and grounded, that you do not walk at a venture, but that you can say with that valiant champion of Jesus Christ, I know in whom I have believed.

This is why I have not sent you such a confession of faith as our good brother Peloquin asked me for, for God will render that which He will enable you to make, according to the measure of mind which He has allotted you, far more profitable than any that might be suggested to you by others. Indeed, having been requested by some of our brethren who have lately shed their blood for the glory of God, to revise and correct the confession they had prepared, I have felt very glad to have a sight of it for my own edification, but I would neither add, nor take away, a single word; believing that any change would but lessen the authority and efficacy which the wisdom and constancy we clearly see to have proceeded from the Spirit of God deserved. Be then assured, that God who manifests himself in time of need, and perfects His strength in our weakness, will not leave you unprovided with that which will powerfully magnify His name. Only proceed therein with soberness and reverence, knowing that God will no less accept the sacrifice which you offer Him, according to the measure of ability which you have received from Him, than if you comprehended all the revelations of angels, and that He will make effectual that which He puts into your mouth, as well to confirm His own, as to confound the adversaries. And as you know that we have steadfastly to withstand the abominations of the Papacy, unless we would renounce the Son of God, who has purchased us to Himself at so dear a rate, meditate, likewise, on that celestial glory and immortality to which we are invited, and are certain of reaching through the Cross – through ignominy and death. It is strange, indeed, to human reason, that the children of God should be so surfeited with afflictions, while the wicked disport themselves in delights; but even more so, that the slaves of Satan should tread us under foot, as we say, and triumph over us. However, we have wherewith to comfort ourselves in all our miseries, looking for that happy issue which is promised to us, that He will not only deliver us by His angels, but will Himself wipe away the tears from our eyes. And thus we have good right to despise the pride of these poor blinded men, who to their own ruin lift up their rage against heaven; and although we are not at present in your condition, yet we do not on that account leave off fighting together with you by prayer, by anxiety and tender compassion, as fellow-members, seeing that it has pleased our heavenly Father, of his infinite goodness, to unite us into one body, under His Son, our Head. Whereupon I shall beseech Him, that He would vouchsafe you this grace, that being stayed upon Him, you may in no wise waver, but rather grow in strength; that He would keep you under His protection, and give you such assurance of it, that you may be able to despise all that is of the world. My brethren greet you very affectionately, and so do many others.

As this letter will, I hope, be in common to you both, I shall merely add, that there is no need whatever for a long exhortation from me; it is enough that I pray God that it may please Him to impress still better and better upon your heart, what I see by your letter, that you already enjoy. However grievous it may be to pine so long, if you got no other benefit by it than God's showing you that He has not reserved you until now without cause, you have good reason not to grow faint nor wearied out thereby. And as for the sickness, it is well for you to consider, that God in this way wishes to prepare you better for a greater conflict, so that the flesh being entirely subdued, may be more able to resign itself. Thus we ought to turn to profitable improvement everything that the heavenly Father sends us. If you can communicate with the other brethren, I pray you to salute them also from me. May God uphold you all by His strong hand, preserve and guide you, and make His own glory to shine forth in you more and more.

40/TO BULLINGER

Expression of regret for the death of the King of England
Sad condition of the German Churches.

Geneva, 3rd August 1553

Paulus an Italian, and a man of tried integrity, on writing lately to our friend Count Celso, stated, among other things, that he had brought a letter for me from the very honourable the Duchess of Ferrara, which he left with you. Seeing that I received a letter from Gualter not long since, in which he makes no mention of such a thing; and seeing, moreover, that John Liner, a merchant of Saint Gall, on passing through this place a short while before, alleged that you had written me through a certain Jew, I am really suspicious that you have been deceived by him. He was not seen by any one here; and indeed I have no doubt but that he has betaken himself to one who is likely to bring him greater gain. If it should turn out accordingly that this letter has been lost, I am anxious that the Duchess should be informed of it. Inasmuch, therefore, as this nobleman, whom she has now employed for many years as a messenger to the French king, was about to make a journey thither, I have requested him to ask you whether anything was done with the packet which Paulus left with you, in order that he may inform his mistress of it.

The messengers regarding the death of the English king are more numerous than I could wish.[1] We are therefore mourning him just as if we were already certain of his death, or

1 King Edward VI died on the 6th of July preceding. Bullinger verified this mournful event to Calvin in the following words: 'I have received intelligence from England of a very sad occurrence. That most pious king departed to the Lord on the 6th of July; and he departed very happily indeed with a holy confession. The book which I here send you was written by him, and published in the month of May. You will see from it how great a treasure the Church of Christ has lost.' Bullinger to Calvin, August 1553.

rather mourning over the fate of the Church, which has met with an incalculable loss in the person of a single individual. We are held at present in anxious suspense as to whether matters are to go to confusion. It is meanwhile very greatly to be lamented that Germany is being torn by intestine strife, by wounds inflicted by each on the other. But it is nothing wonderful that the Lord should employ violent remedies for such hopeless diseases. All we can do is to pray earnestly and unceasingly that He may not permit His Church to be utterly overwhelmed, but rather that He may guide her safe through the general wreck.

Adieu, most distinguished Sir, and most revered brother in Christ. Salute courteously your fellow-ministers, your wife, your sons-in-law, and your daughters. May the Lord shield you all by His protection and guide you by His Spirit. My colleagues salute you earnestly.

41/TO FAREL[1]

Arrest of Servetus, and institution of the process against him.

Geneva, 20th August 1553

It is as you say, my dear Farel. Although we may be severely buffeted hither and thither by many tempests, yet, seeing that a pilot steers the ship in which we sail, who will never allow us to perish even in the midst of shipwrecks, there is no reason

1 Wandering by turns in France, Germany, and Italy, Servetus had taken up his residence at Vienna in Dauphiné, where he at once exercised the profession of a doctor, and persisted in his daring attacks on Christianity, for which he aspired to substitute a rational philosophy. Such is the drift of his book entitled *Christianismi Restitutio, The Re-onstruction of Christianity* which he published anonymously in 1553, after having before directed his bold attacks against the doctrine of the Trinity, in his book *De Trinitatis Erroribus, On the Errors of the Trinity*, published at Haguenau in 1531. Accused by a

why our minds should be overwhelmed with fear and overcome with weariness. We have now new business in hand with Servetus. He intended perhaps passing through this city; for it is not yet known with what design he came. But after he had been recognized, I thought that he should be detained. My friend Nicolas summoned him on a capital charge, offering himself as security according to the *lex talionis*.[1] On the following day he adduced against him forty written charges. He at first sought to evade them. Accordingly we were summoned. He impudently reviled me, just as if he regarded me as obnoxious to him. I answered him as he deserved. At length the Senate pronounced all the charges proven. Nicolas was released from prison on the third day, having given up my brother as his surety; on the fourth day he was set free. Of the man's effrontery I will say nothing; but such was his madness that he did not hesitate to say that devils possessed divinity; yea, that many gods were in individual devils, inas-

Genevan refugee before the Inquisition of Lyons, as the author of these writings, Servetus was arrested, cast into the dungeons of Vienne, and condemned by Catholic judges to be burnt, from which he only escaped by flight. Theodore Beza recounts in a letter to Bullinger, the preparations for the trial of Servetus, of his escape from prison, and of his arrival and arrest at Geneva: 'You have heard doubtless of that impious blasphemer Servetus. He caused a book, or rather volume of his blasphemies to be secretly printed at Lyons. Certain good brethren at Lyons informed the magistrate of this deceitful action. Persons were despatched to Vienne, where he was practising as a physician, to bring him bound [to Lyons]. He was seized, but soon after effected his escape by deceit. At length he came to Geneva, where he went skulking about. He was forthwith recognised, however, by a certain person, and cast into prison. Calvin also, whom he treated very unhandsomely by name in thirty printed letters, pleaded the cause of the Church against him in the Council, in the presence of a great assembly of the pious. He continued in his impiety. What will come of it I know not. Let us pray the Lord to purge His Church of these monsters.' Letter of the 27th August 1553. Such was the opening of the process which terminated so fatally for Servetus. Born in an age not disposed to show mercy to errors of faith, he seems, says a historian, to have fled from Spain—the native country of the auto-da-fé – only to see his effigy burnt in a strange land by the torch of a Catholic executioner, and to come afterwards to expire amid flames kindled by Calvinistic justice.

1 Nicolas de la Fontaine, a servant of Calvin's, was made, in conformity to the judicial practice then in operation at Geneva, criminal prosecutor against Servetus.—*Registers of the Council*, 14th August 1553.

much as deity had been substantially communicated to those equally with wood and stone. I hope that sentence of death will at least be passed upon him; but I desire that the severity of the punishment may be mitigated.[1] Adieu. My colleagues again salute you. Budé does the same, and Normandie, who has now recovered. Present my regards to my brother Claude.

42/TO MELANCHTHON[2]

He deplores the silence of Melanchthon, and urges him to apply himself to the controverted questions of Election and the Lord's Supper.

Geneva, 27th August 1554

Though I am sorry and much surprised, that you did not answer my last letter, yet I can by no means bring myself to suspect that this occurred from any haughtiness or contempt

---

1 It is curious to read on this point the reply of Farel to Calvin: 'In desiring to mitigate the severity of his punishment, you act the part of a friend to a man who is most hostile to you. But I beseech you so to manage the matter that no one whatever may rashly dare to publish new dogmas, and throw all things into confusion with impunity for such a length of time as he has done.' In his relentless rigour against heresy, Farel did not hesitate to pronounce himself even to be worthy of death if he should teach any dogma opposed to the faith. His words deserve to be recorded: 'When I read Paul's statement that he did not refuse to suffer death if he had in any way deserved it, I saw clearly that I must be prepared to suffer death if I should teach anything contrary to the doctrine of piety. And I added, that I should be most worthy of any punishment whatever if I should seduce any one from the faith and doctrine of Christ,' 8th Sept. 1553.

2 In a letter dated the 14th October 1554, Melanchthon, replying to the reproaches which were addressed to him by Calvin, thus justified his attitude in the Sacramentarian dispute: 'In regard to the exhortation contained in your last letter to me, to repress the ignorant clamours of those who are renewing the contest about the adoration of the bread, know that certain persons are raising this dispute principally from hatred to me, that they may have a plausible reason for oppressing me. I have had many conferences with learned and good men on many contested points ... On these matters so highly important, I should like exceedingly to converse with you, whom I know to be a lover of truth, and to have a mind exempt from hatred and other foolish

on your part, feelings which I know to be most alien to your temper and manners. For that reason, having chanced on this messenger, who has offered me his services in conveying a letter to you, I have thought that I should make a second attempt to see whether I might not be able to draw something from you. I do not express myself thus, as doubting of your friendship towards me, which indeed has always been unbounded, but because your silence, as I deem it to be detrimental to the Church of God, cannot for that reason but be painful and annoying to me. I wrote to you lately respecting that article of doctrine in which you rather dissemble your own opinion than dissent from us. For what else can I suppose of a man of the most penetrating judgment, and profoundly learned in heavenly doctrine, when what you conceal as a thing unknown to you, cannot but force itself on the observation of every one, who is, however superficially, versed in the sacred Scriptures? And yet the doctrine of the gratuitous mercy of God is entirely destroyed, unless we hold that the faithful, whom God has thought fit to choose out for salvation, are distinguished from the reprobate by the mere good pleasure of God; unless this also be clearly established as a consequence, that faith flows from the secret election of God, because he enlightens, by his Spirit, those whom it seemed good to him to elect before they were born, and by the grace of adoption grafts them into his family. Weigh well in your wisdom, how absurd it is that this doctrine should be impugned by the greatest of theologians. You see that the manifest discordance which is certainly remarked between our writings has a pernicious tendency. Nor do I prescribe this law for the removal of our discrepancy that you should assent

---

affections . . . I do not despair of our having a conference before my soul departs from its earthly prison. For though, by reason of my advanced age, I am not far from the goal of this career, yet am I in daily expectation of being anew exiled.' This touching complaint, without disarming Calvin, no doubt moderated the free-spoken exhortations which he addressed to the German Reformer.

to me, but at least let us not be ashamed to subscribe to the sacred oracles of God. And, indeed, whatever method of reconciling our differences it shall please you to adopt, *that* I will gladly embrace. Behold how illiterate and turbulent men are renewing the Sacramentarian quarrel from your quarter. All good men lament and complain, that these same individuals are encouraged by your silence. For however audacious ignorance is, still nobody doubts, if you could bring your mind to speak out openly what you think, but that it would be an easy task for you to appease, at least in part, their violence. Nor indeed am I so forgetful of what is due to human feelings, as not to revolve in my own mind, and also to point out to others, with what sort of men you will have to deal; in what anxiety and perplexity the troubled state of affairs must keep you; and how necessary it will be for you to have an eye in all directions, to discover what obstacles impede and retard your course. But no consideration should have such weight with you, as to induce you by your dissimulation, to give a loose to frantic men to trouble and disperse the churches. Not to mention, moreover, how precious a thing we should deem an undisguised profession of sound doctrine. You know that, for upward of thirty years, the eyes of an innumerable multitude of men have been fixed upon you, who desire nothing more than to prove their docility to you. What! are you ignorant to-day what numbers are held floating in doubts in consequence of the ambiguous manner of teaching to which you too timidly adhere? But if you are not at liberty to declare, candidly and fully, what it would be advantageous to have made known, at least you should make an effort to bridle the fury of those who brawl unseasonably about nothing. For what, I would fain ask, do they aim at? Luther, during his whole life, loudly proclaimed that all he contended for, was but to assert the efficacy inherent in the sacraments. It is admitted that they are not empty figures, but that what they typify is in reality imparted to us—that there is present in baptism an efficacy of the Spirit which cleanses and regenerates us – that the Lord's Supper is truly a spiritual banquet, in which we feed on the flesh and blood of Christ.[1] In calming then the tumults which these absurd men have stirred up anew, the cause seems too favourable to permit you from fear of odium to hang back, and in the distinguished position which you occupy, you cannot moreover, if you would, escape from its various fluctuations. Endeavour only that the brazen wall of a good conscience may enable you to stand up courageously against these, and whatever violent attacks the whole world may bring against you. For when, by the partisans of Osiander, I hear you described both as versatile and more devoted to profane philosophy than heavenly wisdom, the reproach wounds me more deeply than if malevolent or wanton men upbraided you with what it would be not only honourable to avow, but glorious to exult in. Farewell, my very dear sir, and highly respected brother. May the Lord continue to shield you with his protection, and govern you by his Spirit, even unto the end.

---

1 Calvin often returns to this emphasis in his writings, e.g. in *The True Partaking of the Flesh and Blood of Christ*: 'When I say that the flesh and blood of Christ are substantially offered and exhibited to us in the Supper, I at the same time explain the mode, namely, that the flesh of Christ becomes vivifying to us, inasmuch as Christ, by the incomprehensible agency of his Spirit, transfuses his own proper life into us from the substance of his flesh, so that he himself lives in us, and his life is common to us . . . Christ by his boundless and wondrous power unites us into the same life with himself, and not only applies the fruit of his passion to us, but becomes truly ours by communicating his blessings to us, and accordingly conjoins us to himself in the same way in which head and members unite to form one body. I do not restrict this union to the divine essence, but affirm that it belongs to the flesh and blood, inasmuch as it was not simply said, My Spirit, but, My flesh is meat indeed; nor was it simply said, My Divinity, but, My blood is drink indeed.'

43/TO THE ENGLISH AT FRANKFORT[1]

He exhorts them to make in their liturgy all the changes compatible with the maintenance of union and the peace of their Church.

Geneva, 13th January 1555

This indeed grievously afflicts me and is highly absurd, that discord is springing up among brethren who are for the same faith exiles and fugitives from their country; and for a cause indeed which in your dispersion should like a sacred bond have held you closely united. For in this sad and wretched calamity, what could you do better, torn as you were from the bosom of your country, than adopt a church which received into its maternal bosom, those who were connected with you in minds and language? Now, on the contrary, that some of you should be stirring up contentions about forms of prayer and ceremonies, as if you were at ease and in a season of tranquillity and, thus throwing an obstacle in the way of your coalescing in one body of worshippers, this is really too unreasonable. Nor do I blame the firmness of those who, even to fight in a just cause, are unwillingly dragged into the contest, but I condemn, and with justice, that stubbornness which clogs and retards holy efforts to form a church. Though in

1 Numerous English refugees had spread themselves over the continent in order to profess freely there their faith persecuted with extreme rigour by the Catholic Mary. Some of them arrived at Frankfort, and having found in this city a French Church regularly established, they obtained from the magistrates the same privilege, and were permitted to celebrate their worship in the building granted to the French, on condition, however, that they should not innovate too much in the ceremonies. United by a common aversion for the doctrines of the Roman Church, they unfortunately differed on some particular points concerning public worship and ceremonies. Thence arose discussions, related at great length in a curious work published for the first time in 1575 *A brief discourse of the troubles begun at Frankfort in the year 1554.* The author of this work was William Whittingham, one of the pastors of the English Church of Frankfort, and a rigid Presbyterian, as well as his colleague the celebrated John Knox, the Scottish Reformer.

indifferent matters, such as are external rites, I shew myself indulgent and pliable, at the same time I do not deem it expedient always to comply with the foolish captiousness of those who will not give up a single point of their usual routine. In the Anglican liturgy, such as you describe it to me, I see that there were many silly things that might be tolerated. By this phrase I mean that it did not possess that purity which was to be desired. The faults, however, which could not straightway be corrected on the first day, if there lurked under them no manifest impiety, were to be endured for a time. Thus then it was lawful to begin from such rudiments, but still so that it might be proper for learned, grave, and virtuous ministers of Christ to proceed farther, and prune away unsightly excrescences, and aim at something purer. If undefiled religion had flourished up to this moment in England, there would have been a necessity for having many things corrected for the better, and many others lopped off. Now that, these first beginnings having been destroyed, a church is to be built up by you elsewhere, and you are at liberty to compose anew the form which will seem best adapted for the use and edification of that church, I really know not what those persons would be at, who take such delight in the scum and dregs of Papistry. But they are attached to those things to which they had been accustomed. This in the first place, is both nugatory and childish; next, this new institution differs greatly from a total change. For my part, if I would not have you to be unduly rigorous towards those whose weakness cannot scale the highest steps of the ladder, so again I would have the others admonished not to have too much complacency in their own ignorance; next, not to retard by their stubbornness the progress of this holy edifice: thirdly, not to be led astray by foolish jealousy. For what motive have they for wrangling, unless it be that they are ashamed of giving way to their betters? But it is idle to address my discourse to persons who, perhaps, do not think me of sufficient importance to deign to listen to advice coming from such a quarter. If they dread unfavourable rumours in England, as if they had fallen away from the religion which was the cause of their exile, they are greatly mistaken. For this more candid and sincere confession will compel the faithful that are still remaining in that country, to ponder deeply on the depth of the abyss into which they have fallen. For their own headlong fall will wound them more deeply when they shall see you advancing far beyond the middle of the course from which they themselves have been violently dragged back. Farewell, most excellent brethren, and faithful servants of Christ. May the Lord continue to protect and govern you.[1]

44/TO THE DUCHESS OF FERRARA[2]

He exhorts her to make a courageous display of her faith under persecution.

2nd February 1555

Madam:

As I have had no news of you except by flying rumours, since it has pleased God to make trial of your faith, I am quite at a loss what to write to you. I would not, however, let slip the

1 The answer of the English exiles of Frankfort to Calvin has been preserved: 'For we are not so entirely wedded to our country, as not to be able to tolerate the usages of others, nor do we set so high a value on the fathers and martyrs of Christ, that it is a point of religion with us not to think or decide any thing contrary to them.' They ask only to be permitted to retain their liturgy and some form in the administration of the sacraments. Among those who signed the letter is Edmund Grindal, who became, at a later period, Bishop of London, and remained attached by ties of fraternal affection to Calvin.

2 Persecution was raging at Ferrara. Neither age, sex, nor rank, escaped its fury. On the 7th of September, 1554, at the instigation of the king of France,

excellent opportunity offered me by the bearer. I was even extremely sorry to learn that a short time ago a person passed by here without letting me know, who most assuredly would have taken charge of my letters for you. For since the afflictions with which you have been visited, I know not whom to trust to, and however much in doubt I was concerning the issue of your distress, having no such certain information as I could have desired, I was indeed deeply grieved to have no means of writing to you. And as even up to this moment, I am far from having satisfactory accounts of your state, I only send you word for the present, that I shrewdly suspect you have been obliged to swerve from the strait path, in order to comply with the world; for it is an evil sign when those who have waged with you so relentless a war to turn you aside from God's service, now leave you at peace. And indeed the devil has so triumphed over us, that we have been constrained to groan over it, hold down our heads, and make no further enquiries. For the rest, Madam, as our heavenly Father is ever ready to admit us to his mercy, and when we have fallen holds out a hand to us that our falls prove not mortal, I entreat you to take courage, and if the enemy on one occasion has had some advantage over you, because of your infirmities, let him not boast as of a victory completely won, but feel that those whom God has raised up, have a two-fold strength to stand against all assaults. When you reflect, Madam, that God, in humbling his children, has no wish to cover them with shame for ever, that consideration will make you hope

---

Henry II, and Pope Julius III, the Duchess of Ferrara, declared guilty of the crime of heresy, was carried off from her palace, separated from her children, and subjected to a rigorous confinement in the old castle of Este. She owed the recovery of her liberty to an act of weakness, which Calvin deplored, and which was speedily followed by one of repentance. Under the impression of this melancholy event, the Reformer wrote to Farel: 'Of the Duchess of Ferrara a sad report, but better confirmed than I could wish, says that, overcome by threats and reproaches, she has fallen off from her profession. What can I say but that an example of constancy is a rare thing among princes?' Nov. 1, 1554.

in him, to the end that you may quit yourself more courageously in time to come. Indeed I am convinced that the same attacks which caused you to backslide, will be again ere long renewed, but I pray you to think how much you owe to Him, who has ransomed you at such cost, and daily invites you to His heavenly inheritance. He is not a master in whose service we should be niggardly, and especially when we consider the issue of all the opprobrium or affliction we have to suffer for His name. Call upon Him, trusting that He is sufficient to help our infirmities, and meditate on those noble promises which are to exalt us by the hope of glory in the heavens. For the foretaste alone should make us forget the world, and trample it under our feet. And to prove that the desire of glorifying God is increased in you, or at least is no wise deadened, bethink yourself, Madam, in God's name, not only how to bear testimony to Him in your person, but also so to order your household, that the mouths of evil speakers be closed. I trust you have not forgotten what I wrote to you some time ago, to my great regret, but from the respect I bear you, and the zeal I have for your salvation; though at the same time I must put you in mind, that I never enjoined any one to breathe a syllable about it to you. What is more, I took special care not to give any tokens of having lent the least credit to so many reports that I was obliged to listen to. And that the person who has so impertinently vexed you, might have no longer an opportunity of scattering his firebrands, I inform you I have taken great pains to moderate his folly, without however having been able to succeed. What is more, he broke out into invectives against me for wishing to restrain him. The individual is an Italian, named Mark. For the rest, Madam, I entreat you to be on the watch not to give a handle to such calumnies. Madam, having commended myself to your gracious favour I implore our merciful Father to have you in his keeping, to strengthen your hands, to increase in you the gifts of his Spirit, and cause them to redound to his honour.

45/TO MELANCHTHON[1]

Thanks for his approval of the condemnation of Servetus
Urgent entreaties to determine Melanchthon to pronounce with more
firmness in the question of the sacraments

Geneva, 5th March 1555

Your letter, most renowned sir, was grateful to me, not only because whatever comes from you is dear to me, and because it let me know that the affection, which you entertained for me in the commencement of our intercourse, still remains unaltered; but above all because in it I find a magnificent eulogium, in which you commend my zeal in crushing the impiety of Servetus. Whence also I conjecture that you have not been offended with the honest freedom of my admonitions. In this they were defective, that I could have wished them to have been more ample. And yet I do not urge them too importunately; still, as much as with your permission I may venture to do, I would again and again entreat you at least to weigh well, silently in your own mind, the points on which I have written. For so I am confident, you will endeavour, that respecting the gratuitous election of the pious, a more orthodox manner of teaching may be mutually agreed upon between us. About the worship of the bread, your most

1 Without laying aside the reserve which he had till then maintained in the midst of the theological quarrels, Melanchthon had just expressed to Calvin his entire approval of the trial and condemnation of Servetus. 'Reverend sir, and dearest brother, I have read your writing in which you have clearly refuted the horrid blasphemies of Servetus. . . . I maintain that your magistrates have acted with justice, in having put to death a blasphemer, after having regularly judged the affair.' In another letter of the 12th May, 1555, he showed himself disposed to refute the suggestions of Westphal, of which the parties made him bear a part of the responsibility; 'I have determined to reply simply and without ambiguity, and I judge that I owe that work to God and the church, nor at the age to which I have arrived do I fear either exile or any other dangers.' This language was the best answer to the wishes that had so long been expressed by Calvin.

intimate opinion has long been known to me, which you do not even dissemble in your letter. But your too great slowness displeases me, by which not only is kept up, but from day to day increased, the madness of those whom you see rushing on to the destruction of the church. And though it should not be easy for you to bridle such wild beasts, which however I think is a groundless fear, would you only set boldly about it, you know however that our duties by no means depend on our hopes of success, but that it behoves us to accomplish what God requires of us, even when we are in the greatest despair respecting the results. Nor indeed does that excuse satisfy me that malevolent men, who wish to crush you, may hence find a feasible pretext. For what are we to expect from the servants of Christ, unless, in despite of illwill, and contemning malicious rumours, they overcome by their victorious constancy whatever obstacles Satan may raise up against them? Certainly, however madly they may rage against you, nothing more cruel threatens you on their part than to be forced to abandon that part of the world where you are now; which thing in my judgment is what for many reasons you should spontaneously desire. But should you have to fear the worst extremes, still it is necessary that you should determine once for all what you owe to Christ, lest, by suppressing a candid confession of the truth, you should lend to wicked men a kind of implied patronage to oppress the church. That I might restrain their tumults, I have again comprised the summary of our doctrine in a short compendium. All the Swiss churches have subscribed to it. Those of Zurich gave it their unqualified approbation. Now I long to have your opinion; what also the rest of your countrymen think and say I am very desirous to know. But if those cease not to breed disturbances, who defame us so hostilely, we shall endeavour to make the whole world hear our complaints. Farewell, most renowned and my ever honoured sir. May the Lord govern you by his Spirit, defend you with his protection, sustain you by his power, and may he always keep us in holy union, till at length he gather us into his heavenly kingdom.

46/TO BULLINGER[1]

Defeat of the party of the Libertines at Geneva
Answer of the Swiss churches to the defence of the Consensus.

Geneva, about 9 o'clock, 5th June 1555

Of our disturbances many rumours have no doubt already reached you, nor are they without a foundation this time, for a single night had very nearly brought ruin on us all, and on the city along with us. But by the marvellous counsels of God it turned out that the remedy preceded the danger to which, without being aware of it, we had all been exposed. When the whole of that faction which has been continually hostile to us for the last three years, saw themselves defeated in every manner, they formed a resolution such as desperate men are wont to adopt. Slaves it is true were not let loose from their prison houses, as of old, when slaves existed, but worthless vagabonds were convoked in the taverns to sell their mercenary services. When in two places, as is established by unquestionable evidence, a supper had been given gratis to a band of scoundrels, all of a sudden a tumultuous attack was made on the city watch; as there was not one honest man among them, they all began to bawl out frequently to arms. The French, whom they designated by name, were continu-

1 It was not long before the anticipations of Calvin were realized. In the night of the 18th May the Libertines rioted and endeavoured to seize the power which escaped them in the Councils of the republic. This riot turned out unfavourably to the party which had attempted it, and brought on the final victory of the French party and the triumph of the Calvinistic institutions at Geneva.

ally in their mouths, by whom they said, the city had been betrayed. Of the French, not an individual made his appearance. A few of the citizens followed the syndics who had been roused from their beds. The syndics were exposed to so much violence, that nothing like it had ever been witnessed within the memory of men. The result, however, was very different from what these rioters had anticipated. They had settled, if any one of the French people had stirred out, to dispatch him, sing out victory, and immediately after to butcher the four syndics and the leaders of the Council. But the Lord exposed them, stripped of their false colours, to derision. As for the rest, proceedings against them were conducted with so much moderation, that their chief more than once took his seat among the judges, and heard even the evidence that was brought against himself, which he was at liberty to contradict. But when a tumult began to arise, ordered to quit the court, he took to flight with four of his accomplices. The others are kept in fetters and will probably be examined in a few days. A capital punishment was pronounced against the fugitives, after their culpability had been sufficiently demonstrated. Since that time there has been a certain degree of trepidation in the city, but public order has nevertheless been strictly preserved. If you desire to have a more ample account of the whole affair, I shall feel no reluctance to make it my business to give it you. Just now however I am afraid you would think me silly were I to go on collecting all the petty details of vulgar gossip. [We are still in ignorance of what has been decided at Berne respecting our cause. As I am so great an object of hatred among some, I perceive that they will scarcely make an end of raising disturbances, unless I shall have to give way perhaps to their profligate fury.[1]]

For our defence the inhabitants of Coire have thanked us some time ago in the name of all the churches of the Grisons.

1 These words were effaced, but whether by Calvin or some other is uncertain.

Of the people of Schaffhausen I say nothing, whose letter you yourself sent to me. The men of St Gall have also let us know that they have most willingly subscribed. What our friend Sulzer replied, as I am ashamed to tell it in my own words, I prefer that you should learn from his own letter. I have always feared his lukewarmness, while he wishes to appear the healer of strife. I expected something better or at least less insipid. But since he does not dissent from us, we must welcome him. Since the time I refuted his objections, I know not whether he has yielded a little from his former opinions, at least he has kept silence. From Germany we have no news of a peaceable state of things. You know that between France and the Emperor certain treaties were on foot, but nothing is more certain than war. The Turkish fleet moreover it is said is advancing, which would derange ten treaties of peace. I was informed too late of the departure of the messenger, when I had to study after supper the subject of to-morrow's sermon. Farewell, then, most accomplished sir, and most respected brother; salute in my name your fellow pastors and your family. I add also M. Lismannini. May God continually protect and govern you all. Amen.

47/TO JOHN KNOX[1]

Criticism of the Anglican Liturgy
Prudent counsels addressed to the parties which divide the foreign
church of Frankfort.

Geneva, 12th June 1555

I answer your letter, most worthy sirs, and truly honoured brethren, a little later perhaps than your thoughts and hopes led you to expect. But when you come to know that the roads for some time back have been so beset by robbers that very few messengers could go from here to your city, I hope you will have no difficulty in excusing me. Respecting that contention which had unhappily sprung up among you, I expressed my opinion freely to our excellent brother, Thomas Sampson, as far as I had been made acquainted with the circumstances of the case by the letters of certain persons. For some friends had complained to me that you insisted so peremptorily on the Anglican ceremonies, that it was evident you were more wedded to the usages of your country than is fitting. I confess indeed that I heard you had publicly produced the reasons which did not permit you to deviate from a received form. The refutation of these reasons, however, was

1 See the letter to the English at Frankfort, 13 Jan. 1555. Banished from Scotland, his native country, at the end of the year 1553, John Knox, after having for some time exercised the ministry of the gospel at Dieppe, in Normandy, had resided in Geneva and afterwards in Frankfort, where he resided during the last months of the year 1554. A declared enemy of the practices and ceremonies which brought to mind the Church of Rome, he soon became in the English congregation of Frankfort, the leader of that party which wished to bring back public worship to the strictest simplicity, in opposition to those who, like Richard Coxe, Baleus, and Sampson, wished to retain some of the forms in use in their country. The representatives of the two parties addressed themselves equally to Calvin, who, though he pronounced an opinion unfavourable to the latter, gave to both counsels dictated by a spirit of conciliation and meekness. These counsels unfortunately were not listened to, and Knox and Whittingham, denounced to the magistrates of Frankfort as dangerous innovators, thought of removing to Geneva.

both obvious and easy. And as I exhorted those who differed from you to give way a little with what moderation they could, so I own it displeased me, that in your turn you neither gave up nor conceded anything of your opinions. But as the name of no one was specially mentioned to me, I did not venture to interfere, lest my confidence should incur the blame of rashness. At present I rejoice that, in the management of the dispute, you have been more courteous and tractable, and that the whole business has been amicably arranged. Certainly no one, I think, who is possessed of a sound judgment, will deny that lighted tapers, and crucifixes, and other trumpery of the same description, flow from superstition. Whence I lay it down for certain, that those who from free choice retain these things, are but too eager to drink from polluted dregs. Nor do I see for what reason a church should be burdened with these frivolous and useless, not to call them by their real name, pernicious ceremonies, when a pure and simple order of worship is in our power. But I check myself, lest I should seem to stir up a new strife, respecting a matter which, as I hear from you, is happily set at rest. This indeed I do not dissemble, that in my opinion N. was neither piously nor fraternally dealt with, if it is true, that at the clandestine suggestions of certain persons, he had criminal charges brought against him. For it was better to remain in one's country than to carry into distant regions the brands of unjust cruelty, to inflame even those who were averse to discord. But as I am loth to allude even slightly to faults of which I would have the recollection buried in perpetual forgetfulness, I shall only exhort you, venerable brethren, if you shall find the minds of any still sore from rankling feelings, that you will do your best to appease their resentment. When I heard that a part of you intended to quit your present residence, I carefully admonished them, as was my duty, that if it was not convenient for all to inhabit the same place, yet that separation to a distance should not break up your fraternal union. For I was afraid that some lurking grudge arising from former contentions might still subsist, and nothing would be more grateful to me than to be relieved from this apprehension. For if by chance any of you should retire to this place, the very suspicion of secret discord among yourselves would be afflicting to me. Therefore I greatly desire that what I hear of your return to feelings of mutual good will is solid and stable, that if any of you chance to wander elsewhere, though separated by place you can cultivate a holy friendship. For though your discord should spread no farther, already more than sufficient mischief has been done. It will then belong to your wisdom and equity, in order that kindly affections be kept up, sedulously to disperse whatever remains there may be of estrangement. Farewell, respected brethren. May the Lord have you in his keeping, govern you by his Spirit, accompany you with his blessing, and mitigate the affliction of your exile. My colleagues affectionately salute you.

48/TO BULLINGER[1]

*Account of the nocturnal riot excited by the Libertines at Geneva
Defeat and total dispersion of that party.*

Geneva, 15th June 1555

With the request contained in your last letter that I should give you a more distinct and detailed account of our recent riot, I comply the more willingly, because it is very much our own interest that the affair should be put in a proper light

1 Vanquished in a last struggle, the party of the Libertines sought to stir up against Geneva the enmity of the Cantons in spreading calumnies against the Reformed party, and misrepresenting the character of the events which had brought about the definitive triumph of Calvin. At Berne as at Zurich these false accounts threw men's minds into trouble. The Council of Geneva took

among you and your neighbours. For it is perfectly well known that unfavourable reports are spread about concerning us, and that too by the artifices of those who for their own advantage wish to render us everywhere an object of detestation. You will therefore do us a very acceptable service, if you will take the trouble to have read over to your illustrious senate the substance of what I am about to write to you. Besides, if it is not tasking your patience too much, I should wish a part of my letter to be copied and sent to our brethren the ministers of Schaffhausen, that they too may acquit our city of the defamatory charges brought against it. Here is an exact statement of the whole affair. There were in the senate two unprincipled men and audacious to the highest pitch of impudence, both also in the most abject poverty. The one was named Perrin, the other Vandel. The former being Captain of the city has attached to his person a rabble of profligate fellows, by holding out to them the prospect of impunity for their crimes. For whatever knavish, riotous, or dissolute act was committed throughout the city, to screen the offender from the punishment of the laws, he was ever ready to undertake his defence. The other was his trusty abetter in all these enterprises. A part of the senate, whom they gained by their flatteries, was at their disposal. They forced, through their fears, certain mean creatures to obsequiousness – creatures who were unable to maintain their rank, if not countenanced by these men. Their kinsmen bound to them by the tie of relationship chimed in with them. By all these means their power had been so firmly established in the lesser council, that scarcely any one dared to resist their humour. Certainly all judicial proceedings had for several years been directed at

alarm: 'It is related that there are people at Zurich and elsewhere who give an account of the things which took place during the tumult, quite different from the real state of the transactions and to the disadvantage of our city.' Organ of the Seigneury in these grave circumstances, Calvin addressed to Bullinger, at the request of the latter, a circumstantial account of the whole affair, which was to be transmitted also to the ministers of Basle and Schaffhausen.

their pleasure, and this sale of justice was a secret to nobody. Not only the city saw this, but even among our neighbours and foreigners, through their fault, we were very ill-spoken of. And loud were the complaints of a great many, because they were frequently molested and outraged by the most atrocious acts of villainy. If any one of an inferior condition exposed their misdeeds, their vengeance was prompt. The reproaches of their equals they devoured in silence. In the mean time however many had become callous to servitude; all edicts were regarded as so much waste paper. Finally, provided only people were favoured by them, all fear of the laws, all respect for decency was set aside. For the judges, together with the prefect of the town, were annually appointed but as they signified their wishes; and to such a pitch did their insolence proceed, that the people themselves, after having elected by their votes I know not what ragamuffins, or rather the basest scum of the populace, were horrified at their own disgrace. This last year indeed all avowed, that if the elections had been entrusted to the enemies of the city, it was not possible for more worthless men, and with more contempt for decency, to be raised to honours. And when formerly if the lesser council had committed any fault, the two hundred were accustomed to afford some remedy for its errors and defects, now they have obtruded on the latter body many of the dregs of the population, partly noisy and turbulent young men, partly individuals of flagitious and dissolute lives. And lest they should fail in having a majority, without paying any attention to the established number, they have thrust into the crowd whomsoever they think will be most fit for their purposes. In a word their licence was so disorderly, that certain broke forcibly into the council who were not even elected by themselves. That was the faction, which, seeing the judgment of the church alone opposed a barrier to them and checked the unlimited impunity granted to all kinds of vices, in order that every vestige of discipline should disappear, stirred up a contest with us about the right of excommunication, nor ceased to turn everything upside down, till after much contention we obtained that they should at least consult the Churches of Switzerland. But as your answer defeated the hopes and wishes of those profligate men, we afterwards enjoyed a little more tranquillity; not however that from that time, ever on the watch for an opportunity, and shaking off all sense of shame, they did not attempt to break through every restraint. Moreover, tired of being kept in continual agitation, at length we plucked up courage to attack them in our turn, and so force them to take some decisive step. And here in a wonderful manner God disappointed their expectations. For in that promiscuous rabble we gained the majority of votes. Soon after followed the elections for the syndics in which an unexpected revolution showed itself. Here indeed these depraved men began to vent their fury openly, because they saw themselves forcibly reduced to order. They began then insolently to attempt many things in order to undermine the existing order. Our party always held it sufficient to quash, without any disturbance, or at least to impair their attempts. But because it was perfectly evident that they were gaping after innovations, the council resolved to oppose an excellent remedy to their licence. Of the French sojourners who have long lived here, and whose probity was well known, some were adopted into the rank of citizens, to the number of fifty perhaps. The worthless felt how much more secure the party of the good would be rendered by this succour. They therefore thought that they should leave no stone unturned in order to defeat this design. The affair was discussed among them everywhere in the cross ways, about the taverns, and clandestinely in private houses. When they had drawn over certain persons to their project, they began to make head against us, not only with murmurings but open threats. The prefect of the city was suborned, who, accompanied by a numerous but vile and disreputable crew, going up to the town house, signified to the council the danger of its persisting in its scheme. This escort was principally composed of watermen, fishermen, cooks, and confectioners, and such like gentry. Mixed up with them were many foreigners. As if without the aid of such champions, the city could not protect its rights! The council replied with dignity that they were introducing no new precedents, but such as had been sanctioned by the immemorial practice of the city; that it was shameful indeed that now both an ancient usage of the city should be abrogated, and those expelled from the rank of citizens who had been so long and so honourably settled in the city; and finally, that from themselves should be wrested a privilege which had been transmitted from the remotest period. But because the council conceived that they should not proceed against them by any rigorous exercise of power, they for the present accorded a pardon to their open conspiracy. The prefect was sharply reprimanded for having lent his aid to insolent men, in so unjust a cause. At the same time, a decree was voted for convoking the two hundred, and when the affair was carried before them, the decision of the lesser council was ratified, and permission granted them, that henceforth at their good pleasure they might select from the French sojourners those on whom they wished to confer the rights of citizenship. But before the two hundred had passed this last decree, the fury of those suddenly broke out more violently, who, as is generally the case in desperate situations, had determined to hazard the most perilous extremities. For from a nocturnal riot the state was brought almost to the brink of ruin. The day preceding this event, a dinner scot-free had been given to a number of scoundrels. The ringleaders feasted elsewhere, of whom one whom I have named Vandel, took on himself the expenses of the dinner, Perrin those of the supper. In the meantime rumours flew about, many suspicious symptoms were remarked, so that it was not without reason that honest men entertained fears for themselves. Now it is the custom, when the sentries for the night have been stationed at the gates, for the captain of the watch to go his rounds and inspect the posts. This duty each of the senators takes in his turn. When the sentries of that night were posted in the middle of the city, they hear a shout at no great distance. For in the quarter situated behind the booths of the market place, an individual hit by a stone cried out that he was killed. The guards in the discharge of their functions run up to him. Against them rush out two brothers, boon companions of Perrin and Vandel, men indeed of the lowest class, confectioners by trade, but who had supped gratis at the same table. It was then evident that the affair had been got up on purpose, since two men alone had ventured to attack several who were armed; and this both of them confessed to the judges and several others, and to myself in private. Nevertheless when they were led to trial, they denied that they had excited a tumult by any concerted signal, but they were convicted by so many proofs, that their impudence was of no service to them. This indeed they did not at all deny, that the same day between dinner and supper they had accompanied Perrin, who had gone for his recreation to a country house in the neighbourhood, and on the road there had been a talk of five hundred men to be called from some other place for the protection of the city. When during their afternoon's collation the conversation had been renewed on that subject, Perrin disconcerted by the arrival of some workmen had enjoined silence, repeating in German, Schwik, Schwik.[1] But as that country house was situated beyond the limits of the Genevese jurisdiction, he had said, that there a shelter and entertainment had been prepared for those who should perpetrate any capital crime in the city. The tumult still increasing, one of the syndics who chanced to be at no great distance, with the rod which is the badge of his office, and lighted torches, came among them. And so great is the respect which this people

1 Schwik in the dialect of Switzerland for silence.

has always entertained for this sacred rod, that at the sight of it, not only have the greatest disturbances been appeased, but even when they have come to bloodshed, their fury is checked. One of those brothers with drawn sword rushes against the syndic. The syndic, relying on the badge of his authority, lays hands upon him, that he may be led away to prison. Several of the faction fly to the aid of their confederate. The lights are put out in the scuffle, and they declare that they will not suffer an excellent comrade to be dragged to prison. Immediately Perrin presents himself, and at first, feigning a desire for pacification, wrenches away the syndic's rod, whispering in his ear, It is mine, not yours. The syndic, though a man of diminutive stature, was not however inclined to yield it, and struggled manfully and stoutly against this violence. In the meantime a cry was everywhere raised along the streets and spread about almost in a moment, that the Frenchmen were in arms, and the city betrayed by treachery; the house of the senator who was that night captain of the watch, was crowded with armed men. Emissaries shouted out tumultuously for those whom they knew to be favourable to their party. Perrin, when he was fully persuaded that his band was sufficiently strong, began to vociferate, 'We are in possession of the syndic's rod, for it is in my hands.' To this cry no mark of approbation was returned, and nevertheless he was surrounded by conspirators, so that it was very evident that they were held back by some mysterious suggestion from God. Then, troubled with shame and at the same time terrified, he gave ground a little. But falling in with the other syndic, a relation of his, he wrested from him by force and with great violence his rod of office. The latter called out for help – that his person was assaulted, that the rights of the city were violated. But as the profligate party was much superior in force of arms, on the complaint of the syndic, no one moved a foot to come to his aid. But again a kind of religious scruple held back some of the very worst from chiming in with Perrin.

Thus compelled by fear, he privately gave back the rod of office. There was now in arms a numerous body of villains. One cry was everywhere heard, 'The Frenchmen must be massacred: the city has been betrayed by them!' But the Lord in a wonderful manner watching over his wretched exiles, partly threw them into so deep a sleep, that during these horrid outcries, they were tranquilly reposing in their beds; partly strengthened their hearts so that they were not dismayed by the threats nor fears of danger. What is certain none of them stirred out of the house. And by this single miraculous interference of God, the rage of the ungodly was defeated because no one presented himself to the conflict. For they had resolved, as was afterwards clearly discovered, if any should essay to defend themselves, after having dispatched a few, they should fall on the others, as if the sedition had originated with us. Nor were the sojourners alone threatened, but some cried out that their protectors should be put to death, and punishment inflicted on the senate. And here remark the clemency of our senate; for though the authors of so atrocious a cry were arrested and convicted, not only were their lives spared, but even a moderate chastisement was not inflicted upon them, so that they were not even beaten with rods. The syndics, while they give orders for the council to be assembled, hurry up and down the city. But these wicked men, relying on their numbers, not only elude and despise their commands, but pursue them with outrageous hootings, so that there was small hope of any remedy. Nevertheless, contrary to our expectations, through divine interposition this tempest gradually blew over. Two days after, it was decreed, that an enquiry should be set on foot respecting this public outrage. The council having spent three days in summoning witnesses, that no one might say that he was crushed under false pretences, call together the two hundred. While the evidence is being taken, among the other judges were seated even those who had conspired. According as any of these appeared chargeable with guilt, or violently suspected of doubtful conduct, they were ordered to leave the court, as it was impossible they could be sufficiently impartial to pronounce a proper sentence. But Perrin, seeing his crime detected, made his escape with three others. The general council, of which the just indignation had been kindled by the atrocity of the thing, decreed that the crime of conspiracy should be severely punished, and exhorted the lesser council, whose prerogative it is to exercise judicial functions, to exact an exemplary penalty. The runaways are cited to appear by the first pursuivant, then by the public crier, according to the usual forms, that is by sound of trumpet during fifteen days. They having sent letters under their own hand declare that they will not present themselves unless the public faith be pledged for their safety. But it would have been the height of absurdity, that culprits who were held to plead their cause in bonds should, like privileged persons, be excused from complying with the formalities of the laws. On the day appointed them, five were condemned. But before the judges gave their sentence, in the presence of the whole people the charges were read over, of which it was necessary that the persons should be fully convicted, who, being called to take their trial, did not establish their innocence. The confession of those on whom punishment was inflicted, followed soon after, and they are still in prison. Whence it is evident that they are too criminal and mischievous to find any loophole for escape. And yet as they are men of the most unabashed effrontery, they do not cease to spread odious reports: that they had been borne down by unmerited odium, because they had defended the cause of the citizens against the French and the council devoted to the French. As if, forsooth, the two hundred to whose prejudices they have fallen a sacrifice were not of the citizens. As if they had been expelled by a hostile army. As if the common people, if they saw the defenders of their liberties cruelly oppressed, would suffer so great an injustice. But on the contrary, all disturbances have been appeased since their departure. The mist which they had spread over affairs has been dissipated; the laws have recovered their vigour; tranquillity has been restored to the city. Those who at their request came here to intercede for them, saw that the city was not torn by opposite factions, was not inflamed by any contentions, but with the tranquil consent of all, the sentence passed on them was approved of. As they are gifted with the most consummate impudence, they not only extenuate the crime they have committed, but by futile cavils they give out that a charge has been got up against them out of nothing. Their assertions however it is not difficult to refute. They assert, for example, that it is not probable that when they could dispose of a numerous band of men, they would by themselves without a strong guard have rushed to arms. As if indeed it were a rare thing, or of unfrequent occurrence, that wicked men blinded by fury, rush headlong to their own ruin. Certainly whatever they pretend, an evident madness urged on one of the band to knock down a man by throwing a stone, whence the outcry arose. The same blindness of mind impelled the two brothers, when with drawn swords they made an attack upon armed guards. And then insolently and with mockery to make light of the commands of the syndics, whom to disobey has always been judged a capital offence, is not only a sign by no means ambiguous of sudden fury, but of audacity meditated beforehand and long meditated between themselves. Moreover the cry so unanimously uttered by all of them respecting the city betrayed to the Frenchmen, could only have proceeded from a preconcerted plan. For unless by a mutual compact they had given each other this war cry, how was it possible that an expression produced by chance, should have been so uniform, and uttered almost instantaneously in places so distant from each other? For the wife of that Vandel whom I have spoken of, going from door to door, summoned those whom she believed would be for their faction, accusing the French of treason. But this indeed is what was avowed by a creature of Perrin's, one of those with whom he was on the most intimate footing. For he confessed that those two ringleaders of the sedition, four or five days before, had in an interview exchanged with one another words to this effect: 'Wherefore do we not shake off inertness, if in so short time we are sure to pay dearly for our cowardliness? It is now three years since our enemies have conspired to massacre us.' (In the list of these enemies moreover he assigned to me the first place.) 'It is then absolutely necessary to anticipate their projects. And now we are furnished with an excellent pretext. We will say that it is not the interest of the commonwealth, that so many persons should have the rights of citizenship conferred on them. We shall obtain nothing either in the lesser council or among the two hundred. We will appeal to the people. The multitude will flock to us even in despite of the opposition of the syndics. We will bribe some men of our own party to get up a tumult. It will be no very difficult thing to destroy our enemies. Let us only show boldness, we are certain of the victory.' This is what that bosom friend, who followed Perrin like his shadow, four distinct times repeated. Let them deny that they have been justly condemned, they who in the midst of a popular assembly, in a sacred place, had formed the resolution of murdering two of the syndics, several senators, the most virtuous of the citizens, all innocent men. Of myself I say nothing, whom they have gratuitously assumed to be their personal enemy. For what their effrontery invented to colour their own proceedings, viz: that I was plotting assassination, is too foul a calumny to need to be refuted. And yet the council has not up to this moment brought Vandel to a trial. But he has quitted the city, self-banished by his own evil conscience. Thus it will be abundantly evident, that after so great a tumult the moderation which is wont to be observed in a tranquil state of things, has not been departed from, and that no measure was craftily or precipitately adopted against these profligate men. On the contrary, had you been here, you would have been apt to say that our council had proceeded slackly and with remissness. But it is preferable to have erred on this side, lest anyone should preposterously complain, that they had been treated, as sometimes happens in the first burst of resentment, with vindictive severity. May the Lord grant that the remembrance of so great a deliverance may continually stir us up to gratitude and bind us to our duty. When I began to dictate this letter, I had no idea that it would be conveyed to you by our friend Othman. For though he had spoken to me of his journey, yet as he seemed uncertain whether he should go straight to your city, I had determined to employ another messenger. Now, as circumstances have turned out, I am not a little pleased at being able to profit by this opportunity, because if any thing from the brevity of my account be rather obscure, he will be able in conversation to repeat and explain it more fully. As you have twice exhorted me to patience, I may remark, that it seems to me I have calmly endured, and as it were swallowed so many indignities, that in keeping down my resentment, my courage also has failed me. I wish that by my silence and dissimulation, I could at least appease those who, from hatred to me, cease not to rage against all good men. But though the madness which has already spread but too widely be still more inflamed by this reserve, still it is my firm resolution not to interfere. I am glad that N. has obtained an office in which he may usefully exercise himself. May the Lord enable him faithfully to discharge its duties. I wish him and N. all prosperity. You will present my most affectionate respects to all your fellow pastors, as well as to your wife and family. Farewell, most accomplished sir, and ever respected brother. May the Lord continue to direct you by his Spirit, and accompany you with his blessing.

49/TO PETER MARTYR[1]

Fall of the French Church of Strassburg
Grief of Calvin.

Geneva, 8th August 1555

The misfortune of your poor French Church afflicts me not a little. We will look after Garnier's prospects indeed when he comes, but the re-establishment of the ruined church is the first thing to be cared for; if you direct all your energies to that object, I have hopes you will do much good. From Bocquin[2] I have always feared what has happened, and I wish Baudouin had stayed at Bourges, for then he would not have contaminated the flock of Christ, with the stench of this he-goat.[3] But strive assiduously, as you are now doing, to remedy this evil. You will have for faithful fellow workmen, I imagine, in this task, M. Sturm and Sleidan. Of the state of our affairs, this brother will be able to give you a better account than I can possibly do in a letter. Wherefore, that I may not tire you with a twice-told tale, I abstain from all further narration. Farewell, most accomplished sir, whom I honour in the Lord. Carefully salute our friends, M. Sturm, Zanchi, and the rest. Unwillingly I pass over M. Peter Alexander, to whom I shall make no allusion till I learn something

1 The position of the French Church of Strassburg became daily more and more difficult. The minister Garnier, having wished to maintain the rights of ecclesiastical discipline, which had numerous adversaries among the Lutheran clergy, was dismissed by the authority of the magistrate. Calvin complained bitterly of that in a letter to Locquet: 'And certainly I have received the deepest wound from the news that a magistrate, by his own good pleasure, not to say anything more, has overturned the legitimate o. der of the church and oppressed its liberty.'

2 Pastor of the French Church.

3 This pun is in allusion to the name of Bocquin, (a he-goat). Baudouin had just quit the chair of law at the university of Bourges to go to Strassburg, where his extreme fickleness of character was destined to draw on him the criticisms of the Reformer.

more certain. I have just this moment, before sealing up my letter, learned from one written by Garnier, that the disturbances have been in a great measure appeased by his arrival. I wish my services could be of any use in assisting him, but if he has been elected by the votes of the little church, he will immediately, unless I am very much deceived, restore it to tranquillity by his moderation. May the Lord always protect and govern you by his Spirit, and accompany you with his blessing.

50/TO RICHARD VAUVILLE[1]

Christian consolations on the occasion of his wife's death.

[November, 1555]

How deep a wound the death of your wife must have inflicted on your heart, I judge from my own feelings. For I recollect how difficult it was for me seven years ago to get over a similar sorrow. But as you know perfectly well what are the suitable remedies for alleviating an excessive sorrow, I have nothing else to do than to remind you to summon them to your aid. Among other things, this is no mean source of consolation, which nevertheless the flesh seizes upon to aggravate our sorrow, that you lived with a wife of such a disposition that you will willingly renew your fellowship

---

1 To Richard Vauville, pastor of the French Church of Frankfort.
A letter printed with an incorrect date, 1556. Vauville, falling a victim in this town to the plague which had carried off his wife, died in the latter months of the preceding year, as is testified by a letter of Calvin to the Church of Frankfort of the 24th December 1555; 'As to the death of our good brother, Master Richard Vauville, it was very sorrowful news for us. For God had provided for you in him a good and faithful pastor, which is a thing not always easily to be found.' The letter of consolation addressed to Vauville on the occasion of his wife's death, should be placed, we think, in November 1555.

with her when you shall be called out of this world. Then an example of dying piously was offered to you by the companion of your life. If it were my task to exhort a private person, I should order him to weigh in his own mind what he owes to his Creator. For we unjustly defraud God of his right, unless each of us lives and dies in dependence on his sovereign pleasure. But it is your duty to reflect what part you sustain in the church of God. As, however, our principal motive of consolation consists in this, that by the admirable providence of God, the things which we consider adverse, contribute to our salvation, and that we are separated in the world only that we may be once more reunited in his celestial kingdom, in this you will from your piety acquiesce. As I hear that the heat of contentions in your church is a little abated, you will do your endeavour that no secret grudges remain in people's minds. That cannot be accomplished all at once, I know. Therefore by degrees you will study to mollify the tempers which have been exasperated, till offences be completely softened down. Farewell, my most worthy and dearest brother. May the Lord alleviate the sorrow of your widowerhood, by the grace of his Spirit, and bless all your labours.

51/TO THE KING OF POLAND[1]

He exhorts him to undertake courageously the reform of his states in proposing to him the example of David, Hezekiah, and Josiah.

Geneva, 24th December 1555

Most excellent king, though I neither wonder nor doubt that at the time in which your majesty held a convention of your estates, distracted as you were by a load of business, and a

1 This prince always inclined towards the religious reformation of his states, in which he flattered himself to associate the Pope himself; but the nobility of

multiplicity of weighty cares, you had no leisure to peruse my exhortation; nevertheless I am confident, that since the pressure of affairs is a little diminished, you have found a vacant hour to give to it, so that my labour may not have been altogether unprofitable. For from the letter which your majesty condescended to send, I understand that my earnestness was not displeasing, that neither from haughtiness nor contempt was that writing of mine rejected, in which I had briefly attempted to point out the true method of reforming the church, and what were the most suitable measures to begin with. What is more, as your majesty has signified that you had graciously received and willingly inspected it, and that, when a more perfect leisure would permit, it was your intention to meditate more attentively on each of the points to which it referred, I have thence naturally concluded, that greater encouragement was held out to me to renew my task of writing. If now therefore I am emboldened to exhort a second time your majesty, I deem it superfluous to demand further permission or trouble you with any laboured apology. I am not ignorant indeed nor forgetful of the vast distance which separates a person of my humble and abject condition from the exalted rank in which God has placed so great a king. But as your majesty perfectly comprehends the imports of that heavenly edict by which all kings are commanded to embrace the Son of God, and knows at the same time that by the external rite of embracing is denoted that obedience of faith which reverently accepts the holy admonitions proceeding from the mouth of Christ and the Spirit, it seems to me

---

the kingdom did not share his illusions, as is attested by the following fragment of a letter of Laski to Calvin: 'The king and the order of the nobles now seem to differ a little respecting the cause of religion; the difference is not so great as to prevent the progress of the cause. The king wishes to determine nothing without having first consulted the Pope, whom he entreats to send deputies to the first Diet, in which, in preference to every other thing, the question of religion is to be handled. The nobles demand that whether the Pope send or do not send his representatives, the true religion be restored.' Calvin in his turn addressed frank advice to the king.

that all fear and hesitation are put an end to. Since then in Poland true religion has already begun to dawn on the darkness of Popery; since many pious and wise men having cast aside impious superstitions, voluntarily aspire after the pure worship of God, I whom the King of kings has appointed a preacher of his gospel, and a minister of his church, call upon your majesty in his name, to make this work above all others your especial care. And assuredly as much as the eternal glory of God surpasses the obscure and perishable state of this world, so much does it become us, giving a subordinate place to every other consideration, to put forth all our endeavours to defend and assert the doctrine of piety. That Poland up to this time, defiled by the corruptions of Popery and a polluted and perverted worship of God, has gone astray after human devices; that, in fine, sunk in the slough of errors, it has been deprived of the view of the heavenly light – was a sad and wretched spectacle. But now, when the Lord begins to deliver it from that foolishness and infatuation with which the whole world has been struck, it is necessary that all – the highest like the humblest – should awake from their lethargy. Ought kings then to loiter whom God has set on high for this very purpose, that from their elevation they might send forth their light to all people? Besides, of what importance we should deem undefiled religion through which a tribunal is erected among us to Christ – of what importance the legitimate worship of God, in which the symbol and lively image of his presence shines forth – your majesty knows too well to require to be reminded of it by me. And indeed if the example of David alone does not animate us on this subject, our sluggishness is altogether inexcusable. For when in his days the fathers worshipped God only under obscure figures in an earthly tabernacle, it is nevertheless related, that he had solemnly sworn, that he would neither give sleep to his eyes, nor slumber to his eyelids, nor enter the threshold of his house, till he had found out a place for the Lord, a tabernacle for the God of Jacob. If a pious solicitude for a legal worship did not suffer that prince to rest, but that day and night he was not less anxiously than assiduously intent on seeking out a fixed abode for the ark of the covenant, how much more at present should the spiritual worship of God absorb all the zeal of a christian sovereign, and all his endavours be more keenly directed to the discharge of this office so distinguished and honourable, by which Christ should be exalted above all! Add to these considerations that David, though he was deprived of the honour of building the temple, did not cease however during the whole course of his life to amass stones, materials, gold and silver, in order that Solomon, his successor, furnished with all the means, might forthwith, without any delay, set about the work with greater alacrity. Wherefore it becomes a christian king so much the more courageously to bring together all his means for the reconstruction of God's temple, and strive with all his might, that the worship of God lie no longer defaced amid unseemly ruins. And though obstacles are never wanting to retard this pious zeal, yet your majesty has far less difficulty to struggle with, than of old the pious princes Hezekiah and Josiah, who had an arduous and severe contest with the contumacy of their people; whereas in our days the greater part of the Polish nobility shows a prompt and cheerful disposition to embrace the faith of Christ. With such aid it becomes a wise prince to rouse himself, and in his turn put his hand not less actively to the work. Nor indeed should you give ear in this matter to those flattering reasons by which, through the instrumentality of profane men, Satan, spreading a mortal coldness, plunges in an ignoble lethargy the senses of many. On the contrary, shaking off all torpor, you should bestir every member to proceed in so excellent a work, and especially since things now seem ripe for action; for if the opportunity offered by God is neglected, you may afterwards have to stand in vain before a door that is closed. Meanwhile we will put up continual prayers, that the Lord of his incredible power may happily perfect the work he has begun, may arm your majesty with an heroic spirit, and preserve you safe in a prosperous condition.

52/TO FAREL

Complaints about the bad proceedings of the Seigneurs of Berne Domestic griefs.

Geneva, 3rd February 1557

Besides open contentions, you can have no idea, my dear Farel, with how many ambushes and clandestine machinations Satan daily assails us. So then, though the state of public affairs be tranquil, it is not allowed, for all that, to every body to enjoy repose. When we had already, at home, many concealed enemies, of whom, however, some are delighted to throw off the mask, our neighbours also threaten us in the most outrageous manner. And I wish their fury confined itself to threats, but when an opportunity presents itself they spit out their venom. My brother and Normandie had lately a proof of that. For when they proceeded against Perrin in virtue of an edict of the Bernese, the latter did not content themselves with requiring them to abdicate their rights, but wished the pursuers to incur the whole costs of the trial. Moreover it is past belief how insultingly they exasperate our citizens. And in addition to that we are weighed down by a load of domestic affliction. Of the city I say nothing, for our private calamity almost completely absorbs us. The judges find no way of disengaging my brother.[1] I interpret their

1 The divorce was pronounced a short time afterwards, as the Registers of the Council of the 15*th* *February* 1557 testify: 'Anthony Calvin obtained his divorce on account of the adultery of his wife, who is banished on pain of

blindness as a just punishment for our own, because for up-wards of two years though I was pillaged by a thief, I saw nothing. My brother perceived neither the thief nor the adulterer. But if no results can be obtained judicially, we are determined to have recourse to some other method, to break through the difficulty. I warn you, however, not to let a word escape you on this subject, for I should be loth to resort to this measure unless compelled by an urgent necessity.

Of the departure of our brother Gaspar, I have heard no reports. I now rejoice at what I had always apprehended. As to pass by us will make the journey longer, I would willingly have spared him that trouble. Let him decide himself according to his convenience, whether he will have the letter sent to him or receive it here as he passes through. Unless I am mistaken in my opinion, a man admirably fitted for your school has been chosen. He writes elegantly and neatly, and is possessed of that dexterity which suits your countrymen. He is endowed besides with other accomplishments fitted to procure him authority. The messengers will be better able to tell you the rest.

Farewell, best and worthiest brother. Salute in my name your prefect and other friends. Towards your colleagues the messengers will perform this duty. May the Lord always govern and strengthen you even to the end. I commend me to your prayers in my grave inquietudes.

All our friends whom you begged me to salute, salute you affectionately in their turn.

being publicly whipped.' Anthony Calvin married again on the 14*th January* 1560, Antoinette Commelin, the widow of the minister John de Saint-André, by whom he had several children, mentioned, as well as those of the former marriage, in the Testament of the Reformer.

53/TO MONSIEUR D'ANDELOT[1]

*He blames him for his weakness
and exhorts him to repair the scandal caused by his fall.*

July 1558

Monseigneur:

I should not have delayed so long in writing to you after we received the sad tidings of what had fallen out, contrary to our expectations, but that I feared for want of proper information I might adopt a style of writing unsuitable to the circumstances. Thus I preferred to allow those to act who were at a shorter distance. I would have answered your letter sooner, however, if the bearer of it had not told me that he was not to return to you, and because he was the most eligible person to charge with such a commission. I am well aware that, in respect of the act which you have committed, the excuses which you adduce have a certain plausibility to ex-

1 Brother of Admiral Coligny and Captain General of the French Infantry he had recanted his Protestant profession after an imprisonment of several months. This sad news, immediately known all over the church of Paris, was announced by the minister, Macar, to Calvin: 'Alas! shall he in whom we triumphed fall off, that God may humble us in every manner?' Here are the contents of that letter, which D'Andelot wrote to the king: 'Sire, I have received singular pleasure from the company of Dr Ruslé, whom I have detained two days, as well for the satisfaction I felt in being instructed by so good a personage, as in order to have time and means to give him some slight explanation of my faith and religion, which I should be sorry were such as some have perhaps been inclined to believe. I beg, very humbly, your Majesty to deign to do me so much favour and kindness as to consent to give him a patient hearing, and I trust in God, that after his report you will not remain dissatisfied with me; for some part of it will give you satisfaction. Having the happiness of being able to hear him, I shall inform your Majesty that I will obey you, as God commands me, and the duty of your very humble and obliged servant requires.' 7th July 1558.

After his first act of weakness, D'Andelot committed a second. He consented to hear mass: 'which, however,' says Beza, 'he acknowledged to have done from great infirmity; and which act he always condemned even till death, and amended by all the means which it is possible to desire.'

tenuate its culpability in part. But when you shall have duly considered the matter with a closer scrutiny, you will scarcely find anything in it to hold you excusable before God. For you know how many poor weak souls have been troubled by such a scandal, and how many people will be able to confirm their wavering by your example. And even if the evil of having ruined what you yourself built up should not follow, yet in itself is it no small or slight offence to have preferred men to God, and, to gratify a mortal creature, to have forgotten Him who made and supports us, who has redeemed us by the death of his only Son, and made us partakers of his kingdom. In a word, God has been defrauded by your too great deference for men, whether from their favour, from fear, or from respect. The capital point is that the enemies of truth have had occasion to triumph not only in having shaken your faith, but in having had their abominations approved of. In your person, they have even imagined that they have vanquished our Lord Jesus Christ, having brought his doctrine into disgrace, for you well know that they have not failed to scoff and disgorge their blasphemies. It appears to you, since one easily sees that you have yielded to force, that the fault was not so very great; but I beg you to think of the numerous martyrs, who during the shadows of the law, chose rather to die than merely to eat the flesh of swine; no doubt in consideration of the consequence, because such an act was an implied testimony that they polluted themselves with the heathen in quitting the God of Israel. You are not ignorant of what those persons pretend, who have wrung from you your consent to be present at their idolatries. It is to make you renounce the confession by which they felt themselves endangered, and efface the praise of courage and constancy which God had conferred on you, or to present it in quite an opposite light as if it had been a puff of empty wind. And in that you should have better practised the exhortation of St Paul not to give a handle to those who seek it, and not to open their mouths to despite God. Your fall has thus been very grievous, and you ought to remember it with bitterness of heart.

I have no doubt but what I tell you will at first sight appear harsh to you, but I will say with St Paul, that I shall not repent of having afflicted you, provided it be for your salvation. Nay, if you desire to be spared of God, it is good and salutary for you not to be spared of those to whom he has given in charge to bring you to repentance. For since those who seek to absolve themselves are the most severely condemned by him, he shows you singular favour in chiding you by his word, in order to render you your own judge. Nevertheless, it is not my intention to grieve you beyond measure, so that you should lose all heart for the future. Only I entreat you to be so offended with yourself for what has been already done amiss, as that to repair it you shall return into that course which you had so well begun, striving to glorify God in purity, and shewing by deeds that if you have once stumbled, you have not strayed entirely from the right path. In a worldly point of view, it is a very hard condition to quit unreservedly things which have so much power to allure and detain us; but there is nothing which should be put in the balance with the honour of God. Nay, if we reflect properly on the shortness of life, it ought not to cost us much to follow our Lord Jesus in his death and burial in order to be partakers of his glory. And this is the end which the remarks I offered you in my letters had in view – that not only we must patiently endure to die with our Head, but also to be buried with him until he fully restore us against his coming. For I made use of this simile, comparing your affliction to a death; but because your trials were not yet over, that you might be better disposed to perseverance, I reminded you of the saying of St Paul, that we must be buried along with him – not to faint though the evil should be prolonged, and we should be obliged to languish longer than we might wish, as he expresses himself in another passage, that we must continually bear about the dying of Jesus Christ, in order that his life may be manifested in us. In short, this burial consists in our daily more and more forgetting the world. When we shall do this, just as we shall have put off our earthly affections, so much the nearer shall we draw to God to enjoy his presence after our death, as St Paul says in another passage, Now we walk by faith not by sight, but when we have left this perishing tabernacle we shall be with God, expecting to receive a crown of glory when Jesus Christ shall appear in his majesty. Wherefore, with this confident hope, we have to combat valiantly and not faint, knowing that He who hath promised is faithful. And because experience must have taught you to fear, you cannot follow a better counsel than that which you have taken, to fly the temptations which might again cause to fall, seeing that you cannot seek them nor approach them without manifestly tempting God. Since also the constancy in question is that which overcometh the world, have recourse to God, praying him to strengthen you and not to permit . . .

54/TO THE EARL OF ARRAN[1]

Eulogiums on his attachment to the gospel, and on his zeal to spread it.

1st August 1558

Monseigneur:

First of all I have to make my excuses for answering your letters so long after the time in which you were pleased to write them. Had I received them a month after their date, I

---

1 James Hamilton, Duke of Chatelherault, Earl of Arran, eldest son of the nobleman of that name, who was regent of Scotland during the minority of

should have been ashamed to have received so much honour without acquitting myself earlier of my duty. But I know not how it happened that they came to hand only six weeks ago. Since then till to-day I have not had an opportunity of a trustworthy messenger, to thank you for the trouble which you have kindly taken, in letting me know such good news, which has furnished me an occasion of abundant rejoicing and magnifying the name of God, because of his infinite goodness he has gathered you into his flock. True it is that this privilege is not much prized by the great ones of this world, whose eyes are dazzled by the honours to which they have been raised. But I doubt not, Monseigneur, but you put in practice what has been said by St James, that the most noble and the most excellent have to glory in their littleness in order to be classed among the subjects of Jesus Christ who are rejected and despised. And in fact, if we consider well this life so frail and perishing, the riches, pomps, and dignities which are but its accessories will not fix us here below. It is then highly proper that we should prefer the inheritance of the kingdom of heaven to everything which might turn us aside from it, and that with such constancy as to choose rather to be partakers of the reproach of Jesus Christ and his church, than to be absorbed in the delights of Egypt. All protest indeed that they wish to be Christians, and yet they profane the holy name which they have continually in their mouths. But since God has enlightened you by the pure knowledge of

---

Mary Stuart. The young Earl of Arran passed several years in France as Captain of the Scots Guards, and contributed by his credit to the formation of the Reformed Church of Chatelherault. Imprisoned in the Castle of Vincennes for having spoken too freely on religious matters, he succeeded in absconding in 1559, and thus escaped the vengeance of the Guises, resolved to strike in him an illustrious victim, in order to arrest the progress of schism. The Earl of Arran immediately after his return to Scotland, joined the Prior of St Andrews, favoured the preaching of Knox, and while he aspired to the hand of Mary Stuart, he constantly opposed the free exercise of the Catholic religion at the court. He became insane a short time after the second marriage of Mary, but lived long enough to see in 1579 the disgrace and ruin of the noble family of Hamilton, of which he had become the chief by the death of his father.

his truth, you can easily judge, Monseigneur, by comparing white with black, how few find the right path. That ought to make you prize still more that inestimable treasure of the gospel, since it is the true key to give us an entrance into the eternal kingdom from which all unbelievers are far removed and shut out. Nay, inasmuch as but few of us are called, we are the more strictly bound to the Father of mercies, who has looked upon us with compassion to confer on us this special privilege, which no more belonged to us than to the vast number of persons who are denied any part in it, except that by his gratuitous bounty he has been pleased to adopt and elect us. Thus, Monseigneur, let the poor blinded persons whom you see wandering in darkness be to you a mirror, in which to contemplate the inestimable blessing which has been bestowed on you, of being enlightened by the Sun of righteousness, which is our Lord Jesus Christ, to the end that you might arrive at the life which is in heaven. And let this contemplation rouse you to give to him your whole heart as to your alone treasure, and strengthen you in true perseverance, according to the solemn obligation into which you have entered in receiving the holy supper of the Lord, in which our Saviour Jesus Christ bestows himself upon us in such a manner that he desires we should belong to him, body and soul, as indeed he is the Redeemer of both. I am very glad, Monseigneur, that you have Captain Bourdick with you, who, from the fervent zeal which I have ascertained to be in him for advancing the kingdom of God, will serve you as a good example. I am disposed to think also that you have retained him for that end, especially desiring to have about you people who may aid you to serve God, in such sort that he may rule and be honoured both by your followers, and by yourself who are their chief.

I praise God, likewise, Monseigneur, for the care and holy desire which you manifest that the pure doctrine of the gospel should be preached in your nation. To which duty I doubt

not but our brother, Master Knox,[1] will willingly dedicate
his services, as indeed he has already shewn. But as he has
such a charge here, he is not quite at liberty; some means must
be skilfully devised to disengage him, when I am confident he
will make no difficulty about undertaking the journey. However that may be, we must not, if possible, allow the good
beginnings which God has bestowed to fall to the ground,
without striving to advance them still further.

55/TO THE MINISTERS OF NEUCHATEL[2]

*He deplores the marriage of Farel, in recalling to their minds the
glorious services which he has rendered to the cause of truth.*

Geneva, 26th September 1558

Beloved Brethren:

I am in such perplexity that I do not know how to begin my
letter to you. It is certain that poor Master William has been
for once so ill-advised that we cannot but blush for his weak-

1 He discharged at this time the duties of minister of the English Church at
Geneva, and returned to Scotland in the end of this same year.

2 To my well beloved brethren, the pastors and ministers of the Church of
Neuchâtel. – Farel, after having lived in a state of celibacy to a very advanced
age, was on the point of marrying Mary Torel, daughter of a refugee of
Rouen. – 'This marriage,' says the author of the unpublished life of Farel,
'was deemed very strange and unseasonable by most people, and it seemed to
them that since Farel had attained the age of sixty-nine years without having
thought of marriage, he might easily have dispensed with it now that he was
on the brink of the tomb. Farel was a good deal molested by the censures of
his friends and the different rumours of the public. It was the opinion of all
that his intention was to provide against the infirmities of old age, by the
means which God himself has ordained.' The bans of this marriage, which
the friends of the old Reformer disapproved of so greatly, were written by
his own hand: 'May God bless the promise of marriage between William
Farel and Mary, daughter of the late Alexander Torel, of the town of Rouen.
Published the 11th September, the 25th September, and the 2nd October.
Married on Tuesday 20th December (before Christmas) 1558.'

ness. But as the matter stands, I do not see the possibility of applying to the evil such a remedy as, by what I hear, has been contemplated. For since there is no law which forbids such a marriage, to break it off when it is contracted is, I am afraid, beyond our power. Unquestionably, we should thus increase the scandal. Were it a private person, I should be less at a loss for means. As it is, what will the sneerers say, and what will the simple think, but that the preachers wish to have a law for themselves; and that, in favour of their profession, they violate the most indissoluble tie in the world? For though you have another object in view, yet men will believe that you assume a privilege above others, as if you were not subject to the law and the common rule. If people had been informed in time of the fact, it would have been their duty to prevent this foolish enterprise, as they would that of a man who had lost his wits; but to make matters worse, he was so very precipitate that we can by no means obviate the consequences of his fall. Examine deliberately whether it be a suitable remedy to break off a marriage which is already contracted. If it be alleged that such a promise, being contrary to the order and seemliness of nature, ought not to be kept, reflect whether this defect is not to be tolerated like many others which cannot be remedied. Half a year ago our poor brother would have declared that they should have bound like a madman the person who at so advanced an age desired to marry so young a woman. But the deed being accomplished, it is by no means so easy to annul it. For my own part, as I did not see how he could be freed from his engagement, nor any means that we could employ for that purpose, I told him that it was better to terminate the affair promptly, than by delaying it to occasion a great deal more of foolish gossip. If there had been fraud or circumvention on either side, your remedy for it would have been good and suitable; but since the only objection that can be raised is the inequality of their years, I consider this fact as an evil that cannot be cured. It is for that reason that, after having made him sufficiently sharp reproaches, I forbore to say anything more to him on the subject, for fear of reducing him to despair altogether. And, in fact, I have always feared and conjectured that the consequences which I had anticipated from this affair would occasion his death. If at least he had followed my advice not to quit the spot, a milder and more moderate course might have been adopted towards him. Now his absence is the cause why they have proceeded against him with greater severity and violence; for which I feel a double compassion for him. But I blush at the same time, inasmuch as it would seem to have been his wish to shut himself out from all remedy. Nevertheless, I cannot help entreating you to remember how he has employed himself, during the space of thirty-six years and more, in serving God and edifying his church, how profitable his labours have been, with what zeal he laboured, and even what advantages you have derived from him. Let that dispose you to some indulgence, not to approve of the evil, but at least not to proceed with extreme rigour. Meanwhile, as it does not belong to me to point out to you your line of conduct, I shall only pray God to conduct you in the matter with such prudence and discretion that the scandal may be hushed up and produce as little evil as possible, and that our poor brother be not overwhelmed with sorrow.

I beg to be humbly commended to the superiors of your city, to whom I have abstained from writing, because I am dumb with astonishment. Meanwhile, I will again pray our God and Father, that he may have you in his keeping, increase you in every good, strengthen you in every virtue, to the end that his name may be always glorified in you.

56/TO FAREL[1]

He makes an excuse for not being able to be present at the marriage of his friend.

GENEVA, September 1558

When I told you to your face that I would come neither to your espousals nor your marriage, both because it was a thing not possible, and because I judged it inexpedient, I am surprised what your new invitation can mean. Had I the greatest desire to comply with your wishes, I am nevertheless prevented by several causes. You know that Macaire is absent. Raymond and another of my colleagues still keep their beds. The rest of us can scarcely meet the additional burden imposed on us. Certainly I cannot absent myself without causing interruption to our meetings for public worship. In such a perturbation of affairs the senate would never permit me to withdraw to any distance from the city. You see clearly then if I could readily, and without serious losses, undertake a journey. But, should no obstacle stand in my way, yet as my coming would afford an admirable handle for the ungodly and the badly disposed to vent their malice in evil speaking, you neither seem to do prudently in inviting me, nor should I act with due consideration if I complied with your wishes. I wish you had rather followed the plan which you had approved of, which was to hasten your espousals, so that they might have taken place at least immediately after your return. Now, by putting them off, I do not doubt but you have occasioned much clandestine talking, which will break out

1 By a letter of the 5th September, Farel had invited Calvin to come to his marriage. This matrimonial missive, of which the terms betrayed a slight embarrassment, concluded with these words: 'Farewell, and aid us with your prayers that God may look upon us with a propitious eye, by whose hand it behoves us to be supported lest we stumble before we reach the mark.'

more freely afterwards. For you are much mistaken in thinking that the affair is quite a secret. When De Collonge lately passed through your neighbourhood, the minister of Bonneville knew it. Know, then, that many who pretend to be ignorant of it are privately whispering about it. I myself, when I thought that the matter was fairly brought to a conclusion, admonished my colleagues to check the scandal as much as lay in their power by their temperate conversation. At the same time I besought them not to give publicity to the fact; and lately, when at my request Jonvillers made enquiries of Cherpon, how people had been affected by what had taken place, I wished to be relieved of a part of my anxiety. He who held the pen for me did not know the drift of my question. But I was under the impression that all the business had been completely gone through. That you should openly busy yourself with the cause of Metz would not be, in my judgment, a very prudent deliberation. I explained to you in a letter my reasons, which I am confident were more fully communicated to you by the Council. I confess that though I did not think Peter Alexandre a very suitable person, I was obliged to name him. I do not know if the time will be very seasonable now, because the new emperor is said to threaten the Protestants because they do not contribute supplies to aid him in carrying on his war with the Turks. It will be necessary, however, to attempt something, for they will perhaps be excited by his threats to collect their forces.

57/TO WILLIAM CECIL[1]

Hopes connected with the accession of Elizabeth.
Wishes for the establishment of the pure gospel in England.

GENEVA, 29th January, 1559

I shall make no tedious apology, most distinguished sir, for now writing to you familiarly, though personally I am unknown to you; for, relying on the information of some pious individuals, who have extolled your courtesy, I trust that you will be naturally disposed to give a favourable reception to my letter, and especially when, after having perused it, you shall be aware of the motives which dictated it. Since the time when, dispersing the fearful cloud of darkness that had well nigh reduced to despair all pious minds, a new light has miraculously shone forth, the fame is rife that you are strenuously engaged in directing the no common influence which you possess over the queen, to scatter the superstitions of popery which have over-shadowed your land for the last four years, and to cause the uncorrupted doctrine of the gospel and the pure worship of God again to flourish among you. One thing, however, I may suggest, that what you are now doing you should go on to do with increased activity and a constancy which is not to be overcome; and that no vexatious difficulties, struggles, or terrors, should ever, I do not say, defeat, but even for one moment retard your holy endeavours. I doubt not indeed but obstacles are every now and then occurring, or that even dangers openly menace you,

1 William Cecil, Baron Burghley, secretary of state under Edward VI., and one of the ablest ministers of Queen Elizabeth. He took a leading part in the convocation of the Parliament, the promulgation of the thirty-nine articles, and the adoption of the different measures which re-established the Reformation in England. He died in 1598. Informed by Peter Martyr of the death of Mary, and the accession of a princess known for her attachment to the Protestant faith, Calvin hastened to offer to Cecil his wishes and counsels.

which would damp the resolution of the most courageous, did not God sustain them by the marvellous efficacy of his Spirit. But this is a cause above all others for the defence of which we are not permitted to shrink from any kind of labour. As long as the children of God were exposed to open and avowed slaughter, you yourself held your place along with the others. Now at last when by the recent and unlooked for blessing of God greater liberty has been restored to them, it behoves you to take heart, so that if hitherto you have been timid, you may now make up for your deficiency by the ardour of your zeal. Not that I am ignorant how much mischief is sometimes produced by undue precipitation, and how many persons retard, by an inconsiderate and headlong zeal, what they strive to drag all at once to an issue. But on the other hand you are bound gravely to ponder that we are doing God's work when we assert the uncorrupted truth of his gospel and all-holiness, and that so it should not be set about with slackness. From your position you can better ascertain how much of progress it will be expedient to make, and where it may be fitting to adopt a prudent moderation; still, however, remember that all delay, coloured by whatever specious pretexts, ought to be regarded by you with suspicion.

One thing, which, as I conjecture, you have to fear, is a popular tumult, since among the nobles of the kingdom are not wanting many sowers of sedition, and should the English be torn by domestic broils, their neighbours are there, ever on the watch to improve and aggravate every opportunity. Nevertheless as her most excellent majesty, the queen, has been raised to the throne in a wonderful manner by the hand of God, she cannot otherwise testify her gratitude than by a prompt alacrity in shaking off all obstacles and overcoming by her magnanimity all impediments. But since it is scarcely possible that in so disturbed and confused a state of affairs, she should not, in the beginning of her reign, be distracted, held in suspense by perplexities, and often forced to hold a vacillating course, I have taken the liberty of advising her that having once entered upon the right path, she should unflinchingly persevere therein. Whether I have acted prudently in so doing, let others judge. If by your co-operation my admonitions shall bring forth fruit, I shall not repent of my advice.

And do you also, most illustrious sir, continually keep in mind that you have been exalted by providence to the rank of dignity and favour which you now occupy, in order that you should give yourself entirely up to this task, and strain every nerve for the promotion of this great work. And lest you should feel any supineness stealing upon you, let the momentousness of these two things be ever and anon presenting themselves to your mind: first, that religion which has fallen into such wretched abasement, the doctrine of salvation which has been corrupted by such execrable errors, the worship of God which has been so foully polluted, should recover their primitive lustre, and the church should be cleansed from her defilements; next, that the children of God should be at liberty to invoke his name in purity, and those who have been scattered again assembled together.

Farewell, most illustrious and most respected sir. May the Lord govern you by his Spirit, protect you, and enrich you with every blessing.

58/TO JEROME ZANCHI[1]

Call to the ministry in the Church of Geneva

GENEVA, 14th March, 1559

I suppose the tidings of the death of our most excellent brother have already reached you, and I am convinced they have produced the same feelings of regret as among us. Assuredly the Italian church has sustained no ordinary loss, towards which he strove to perform all the duties which can be desired of a faithful and active pastor. And now that you have been elected his successor by the suffrages of the people, see that you do not disappoint the wishes of your countrymen, and abandon an unhappy flock in its utmost need. I know and remember the numerous objections which you formerly represented to me when at the request of all I tendered you a call. At that time I was unwilling to press you too earnestly, lest in forcing your inclinations I should consult neither your own private interests nor the public advantages of the church. At present, in my judgment, the case is altogether different.

A flock bereaved of its pastor and unable to find elsewhere a person fitted for the discharge of the pastoral functions, makes an appeal to your fidelity. Unless they be speedily succoured, it is to be feared that a dispersion will take place, which would be to us a matter of the deepest distress. Satan is watching his opportunity, and unless there be some extraordinary authority to restrain certain individuals, their perverseness will speedily break out. How fruitful your present

1 Jerome Zanchi of Bergamo, one of the most distinguished disciples of Peter Martyr, left Italy in 1543, in order to retire to Switzerland, and merited by his learned writings to be classed in the first rank among the theologians of the Italian emigration. Appointed in 1553 professor in the school of Theology at Strassburg, from which the ultra-Lutheran intolerance represented by the theologians of Marbach was to drive him ten years later, he became successively professor at Chiavenna and at Heidelberg. He died in the latter city in 1590.

labours are I have no means of knowing, except that with great sorrow I have heard that your auditory is thin and almost deserted. If this is the case, it is not the consideration of public utility which will make you hesitate, and we are thoroughly convinced that you are swayed by no regard to private interest or your own ease and indulgence. So much more urgent are the motives and binding the obligation, which should decide you on taking such steps as may correspond to the high confidence reposed in you by your countrymen.

I am aware that you are not at liberty to abandon your present position till you be relieved from the tie which binds you to it, but the whole deliberation turns on this point: if your labours, where you now are, are sterile, and if here an abundant harvest awaits them, which is the most forcible tie, the one by which God draws you hither, or the one that detains you there? When once you shall have yielded to this consideration, you will have no difficulty in obtaining your discharge, nor is the necessity of soliciting it imposed on you, for our senate will petition yours to grant you permission to establish yourself here. If then your intention be to bring succour to an afflicted church, remember the old proverb: He gives twice who gives speedily.

Farewell, most distinguished sir and respected brother. May the Lord govern you in this deliberation by his Spirit, stand always by you, keep you in safety and bless you.

59/TO WILLIAM CECIL[1]

He exculpates himself to this minister of state of the imputations
brought against him on account of a writing of Knox's

GENEVA, May, 1559

The messenger to whom I had given my commentaries on Isaiah to be offered to the queen, brought me back word, that my homage was rather distasteful to her majesty, because she had been offended with me on account of certain writings that had been published in this city. He also repeated to me, most illustrious sir, the substance of a conversation he had with you, in which you appeared more harsh towards me than your usual urbanity led me to suppose, especially when from my letter you were informed how much I promised myself from your affection towards me. Now though just causes prevent me from exculpating myself by a laboured refutation, lest, however, I should seem by my silence to confess that to a certain extent my conscience blames me, I have thought proper to put you in possession of the main facts of the case.

Two years ago, John Knox in a private conversation, asked

1 Letter without a date – written no doubt in May, 1559, as seems to be indicated by Cecil's answer to Calvin of the 22nd June following. Public opinion had been warmly excited by Knox's pamphlet against the government of women. Directed against Queen Mary, this book was appealed to by ardent sectaries against the authority of Elizabeth herself, and Calvin's name was associated with that of Knox in the controversies to which the writing gave rise. The Reformer judged it necessary then to offer to Cecil explanations indirectly addressed to the queen herself. Cecil showed himself satisfied with them, if we may judge by his answer to Calvin: 'In what concerns you, I know most certainly that, for many reasons, all writings of this kind are displeasing to you. And if some of our countrymen afflicted with this mania have affirmed that you had answered, "though in the ordinary course of things, as we say, and in virtue of the Divine word the right of governing is forbidden to a woman, nevertheless there are extraordinary occasions in which it may be permitted," this distinction, I venture to affirm, you by no means approve of.' Queen Elizabeth's secretary signed his letter to Calvin, 'Yours most affectionately, and with the warmest zeal for the evangelical profession. W. C.'

my opinion respecting female government. I frankly answered that because it was a deviation from the primitive and established order of nature, it ought to be held as a judgment on man for his dereliction of his rights, just like slavery; that nevertheless certain women had sometimes been so gifted that the singular blessing of God was conspicuous in them, and made it manifest that they had been raised up by the providence of God, either because he willed by such examples to condemn the supineness of men, or thus show more distinctly his own glory. I here instanced Huldah and Deborah. I added to the same effect that God promised by the mouth of Isaiah that queens should be the nursing mothers of the church, which clearly distinguished such persons from private women. Finally I added in conclusion, that since by custom, common consent, and long-established usage, it had been admitted that kingdoms and principalities might be by hereditary right transmitted to women, it did not seem proper to me that this question should be mooted, not only because the thing was odious in itself, but because in my judgment it is not permitted to unsettle governments that have been set up by the peculiar providence of God. Of the book I had not the slightest suspicion, and it had been published a whole year before I was aware of its existence.

Informed of the fact by some persons, I testified in the most unequivocal manner that the public was not to be familiarized with paradoxes of that kind. But because the remedy did not depend on me, I conceived that an evil which could not be redressed had better be hushed up than publicly canvassed. Ask of your father-in-law, when he reminded me of it through Beza, what answer I made. Mary being then still alive, I could not be suspected of an intention to flatter. Of the contents of the work I am ignorant; but that the tenor of the discourse I had with Knox is such as I have described it, he himself will confess. But though I was affected by the complaints of pious individuals, yet as I had not been informed in time, lest greater disturbances should arise out of it, I did not venture to make any loud outcry.

If my slackness offends any one, I think I had reason to fear, if the affair had been brought to a trial, that for the inconsiderate vanity of one man, an unfortunate crowd of exiles would be driven not only from this city, but from almost every part of the world, especially as the evil now admitted of no other remedy than the exercise of indulgence. Besides that I have been loaded with undeserved blame, for that very reason I still less merited to have my book rejected, as if a pretext had been sought to throw the follies of others upon me. Your queen, if the work did not please her, might with one word have refused to accept my proffered courtesy. That would have been more straightforward, and assuredly it would have been more agreeable to me than, besides the disgrace of a repulse, to be charged at the same time with false accusations. I shall nevertheless always cherish the most profound respect for your most excellent queen; and you too, renowned sir, I shall not cease to love and honour on account of your extraordinary talents and other virtues, though I have found you less friendly than I had expected, and though you may not in future reciprocate my feelings of affection. I am unwilling, however, to augur this last result.

Farewell, most beloved and honoured sir. May the Lord always stand by you, govern and protect you, and enrich you with his gifts.

P. S. Because I am in doubt whether you received my former letter, I have thought proper to send you a copy of it.

60/TO JOHN KNOX[1]

Answers to different ecclesiastical questions

GENEVA, 7th November, 1559

If I answer your letter, most excellent brother, later than you expected, your fellow countryman who brought it to me will be the best witness that laziness was not the cause of my delay. You yourself know also how seldom a suitable opportunity of writing to you occurs, because in the disturbed state of affairs all access to your country is difficult. It was a source of pleasure, not to me only but to all the pious persons to whom I communicated the agreeable tidings, to hear of the very great success which has crowned your labours.

But as we are astonished at such incredible progress in so brief a space of time, so we likewise give thanks to God whose singular blessing is signally displayed herein. This affords you ample matter for confidence for the future, and ought to animate you to overcome all opposition. As I am not ignorant how strenuous you are in stirring up others, and what abilities and energies God has endowed you with for going through with this task, I have deemed it superfluous to stimulate the brethren. Meanwhile we are not less anxious about your perils, than if we were engaged along with you in a common warfare; and what is alone in our power, we join our vows to yours, that our heavenly Father would strike all your furious adversaries with the spirit of folly and blindness,

---

1 By a letter of the 27th August of the same year, Knox had addressed to Calvin two questions relating to the administration of baptism and to ecclesiastical property. The message of the Scots Reformer terminated with these words: 'I am prevented from writing to you more amply by a fever which afflicts me, by the weight of labours which oppress me, and the cannon of the French which they have now brought over to crush us. He whose cause we defend, will come to the aid of his own. Be mindful of us in your prayers. Grace be with you.'

scatter all their counsels, and defeat all their attempts and preparations. Certainly they labour under great difficulties in arming their fleet; especially for want of money. So much the more obstinately will the old dragon essay to throw everything into confusion, rather than not attempt something.

Respecting the questions of which you ask for a solution, after I had laid them before my colleagues, here is the answer which we unanimously resolved to send. It is not without reason that you inquire whether it be lawful to admit to the sacrament of baptism the children of idolaters and excommunicated persons before their parents have testified their repentance. For we ought always to be carefully on our guard that the sanctity of this mystery be not profaned, which it certainly should be if it were promiscuously administered to aliens, or if any one received it without having such sponsors as may be counted among the legitimate members of the church. But as in the proper use of baptism the authority of God is to be considered, and his institution ought to derive its authority from certain conditions, one of the first things to be considered is who are the persons that God by his own voice invites to be baptized.

Now God's promise comprehends not only the offspring of every believer in the first line of descent, but extends to thousands of generations. Whence it has happened that the interruption of piety which has prevailed in Popery has not taken away from baptism its force and efficacy. For we must look to its origin, and the very reason and nature of baptism is to be esteemed as arising from the promise of God. To us then it is by no means doubtful that offspring descended from holy and pious ancestors, belong to the body of the church, though their fathers and grandfathers may have been apostates. For just as in Popery it was a pernicious and insane superstition, to steal or forcibly abduct their children from Jews or Turks, and forthwith to have them baptized; so likewise, wherever the profession of Christianity has not been altogether interrupted or destroyed, children are defrauded of their privileges if they are excluded from the common symbol; because it is unjust, when God, three hundred years ago or more, has thought them worthy of his adoption, that the subsequent impiety of some of their progenitors should interrupt the course of heavenly grace. In fine, as each person is not admitted to baptism from respect or regard to one of his parents alone, but on account of the perpetual covenant of God; so in like manner, no just reason suffers children to be debarred from their initiation into the church in consequence of the bad conduct of only one parent. In the meantime we confess that it is indispensable for them to have sponsors. For nothing is more preposterous than that persons should be incorporated with Christ, of whom we have no hopes of their ever becoming his disciples. Wherefore if none of its relations present himself to pledge his faith to the church that he will undertake the task of instructing the infant, the rite is a mockery and baptism is prostituted.

But we see no reason for rejecting any child for whom a due pledge has been given. Add to these considerations that the manner of proceeding adopted by a church now arising from its ruins, and that of one duly formed and established are two very different things. For whilst a church is being composed out of that horrible state of dispersion, since the form of baptism has prevailed through a long series of ages down to our times, it is to be retained, but with the progress of time the abuses which have crept in are to be corrected, and the parents forced to present their children themselves and become the first sponsors. For if in the first commencements an absolute perfection is severely exacted, it is greatly to be feared that many laying eagerly hold of this pretext will continue to wallow in their corruptions.

We confess indeed that we should not attach so much importance to anything as to swerve even a hair's breadth from the line prescribed to us by God; but we imagine we have demonstrated in a few words that if we exclude from baptism those whom we have had proofs of having been domesticated, as it were, in the church, the exclusion would be too rigorous. In the meantime, therefore, waiting till greater progress have been made, and discipline have gained strength, let children be admitted to baptism on the condition we have mentioned, viz: that their sponsors engage that they will make it their business to have them brought up in the principles of a pious and uncorrupted religion. Though in the meantime we do not deny, that idolaters, as often as children are born unto them, should be sharply admonished and stirred up to devote themselves truly to God, as also excommunicated persons to be reconciled to the church.

To monks and priests it is certain that maintenance is not due from the public that they may live uselessly in idleness. If any of them then are fitted for edifying the church, let them be called to take a part in that labour. But as most of them are ignorant and void of capacity, it seems proper that we should act towards them with humanity. For though they have no claim to receive public support, inasmuch as they contribute nothing to the service of the church, yet it would be cruel that those who have been inveigled by ignorance and error, and have spent a part of their life in idleness, should be reduced to destitution. They are to be admonished indeed rather to seek their livelihood from labour, than devour the substance destined for the ministers of the church and the poor. A middle course is also to be pursued, as for example from rich benefices a part might be set aside for pious uses. In the meantime, however, provided the church recover by their death the ecclesiastical property, it does not seem fitting to raise a strife about the annual revenue, except that its present possessors are to be reminded that they retain by indulgence and forbearance, not from approbation, what they had never had any right to possess. They are also to be exhorted not to pamper themselves, but contented with a frugal manner of living, to restore to the church what belongs to it, rather than suffer it to be deprived of faithful pastors, or the pastors themselves to be starved.

Farewell, most excellent sir and our very dear brother. The whole assembly of the pious in our name wish you prosperity; and we pray God that he may govern you all by his Spirit even to the end, sustain you by his power, and shield you with his protection.

61/TO THE BRETHREN OF FRANCE[1]

He exhorts them to redouble their faith to meet their redoubled persecutions, and to live and die for the confession of Jesus Christ

GENEVA, November, 1559

Dearly beloved Brethren:

I have no doubt but certain persons will think me importunate for writing to you at the present moment, while the cruelty of the ungodly rages with such fury against the Christians,

1 The death of Henry II (10th July, 1559) and the accession of the young king Francis II., who was ruled by the Guises, rendered the situation of the Protestants more cruel. Informers multiplied the number of suspected persons whom the *chambres ardentes*, instituted by the edict of Blois for that purpose, handed over to the executioner. 'From the month of August to the month of March of the following year,' says the historian of the martyrs, 'there was nothing but arrests, and imprisonments, pillage of houses, outlawing, and massacres of the servants of God. God, however, amid these storms and tempests, preserved the residue of his church, and the preaching of the gospel was not abandoned.' The language of Beza is no less expressive: 'We may say of this reign which lasted only seventeen months, what Jesus Christ says in St Matthew, viz: 'Except those days should be shortened there should no flesh be saved; but for the elect's sake those days shall be shortened.' Notwithstanding this, He who suffers not his own to be loaded beyond what they can bear, gave such assistance to his lambs, that were for the most part only newly born, and in like manner to the pastors who had just begun to arrange them in little flocks, that amid all those storms, they not only subsisted, but, what is more, assumed a regular order, and increased their numbers in many parts of the kingdom.' Disseminated from church to church, and multiplied by pious hands, the letters of the Reformer spread everywhere courage and self-denial.

and while it requires so little to exasperate it more and more. But those who think so are mistaken; for it is in times like these that you have most need of exhortations to give you courage. Persecutions are the true combats of Christians to try the constancy and firmness of their faith. Wherefore being assailed, what ought they to do but to fly to arms?

Now our arms to combat valiantly in this cause, and resist the enemy, are to fortify ourselves by what God shows us in his word. And just as each of us feels himself more timid, so ought he to seek for the remedy. And herein we see how much most men are apt to flatter themselves in their infirmities, for those who are from weakness most disposed to be thrown into consternation are those who most refuse to seek strength from God by the means which he has appointed. Learn then, my brethren, that this is the true season to write to you, when the fire of persecutions is lighted, and when the alarms of the poor church of God are carried to an extremity. We see that the worthy martyrs followed this practice – to be so much the more vigilant in stirring up one another by holy admonitions, as they saw their tyrants employing greater efforts to ruin Christianity. There then is an example for us to follow. And in fact we hear that our Lord Jesus Christ, after having warned the disciples of the great troubles which were to come, and of which we see a part, adds: *Rejoice, and lift up your heads, for your redemption is at hand.* If we do not rejoice, at least we ought to strive to correct the vice which prevents us from so doing.

I know the dangers to which you are exposed, and I would not from inconsiderate zeal put a new sword into the hands of these enraged enemies; but yet it is necessary to set bounds to our own fears, so that those who have need of being strengthened by the word of God be not deprived of such a blessing; I leave you to judge if you do not see much unbelief among you, inasmuch as many are downcast as if God were no longer a living God. Thence you may judge that it is the more necessary for me, as much as in me lies, to endeavour to correct this defect, in order that the grace of God be not altogether quenched in you. It is no new thing for you to be like sheep in the jaws of the wolf; but the rage of your foes is at present more than ever inflamed to destroy the poor flock of Jesus Christ. And it is not only in one place: reflect that your brethren who are members of the same body, have to suffer like you for the same cause in distant countries. It is therefore the time to show more than ever that we have not been taught in vain. We are bound to live and die for Him who died for us, for our faith is not styled a victory over the world merely to make us triumph in the shade and without a struggle: but much rather that we should be armed by it to overcome Satan with all that he can devise against us; and the doctrine of the gospel is not for us to speculate about at our ease, but to demonstrate, by its effects, that the world should be held cheap by us in comparison of the heavenly kingdom.

Wherefore those that are so terrified in the time of persecution that they know not how to act, have not profited much as yet in the school of God. If there is terror, that is nothing new; for as we are men, it is not possible that we should not be environed by human passions. And since God supports our infirmity, it is but reasonable that we should do the like. Even those who feel themselves shaken with astonishment ought not to lose heart, as if they were already vanquished. But the capital point is that instead of indulging this weakness we should seek to shake it off and be re-animated by the Spirit of God. I say then that nothing is more opposite to Christianity, of which we make a profession, than that when the Son of God our captain calls us to the combat, we should be not only cold and faint-hearted, but seized with such consternation as to desert his standard. Let us then strive against our flesh, seeing that it is our greatest enemy, and that we may obtain pardon of God let us not pardon ourselves, but rather let us be our own judges to condemn ourselves.

Let each as he finds himself tardy, push himself on, and let all of us collectively, knowing that we do not do our duty, be pleased to be stirred up by others, and may God let us feel the spur as often as he knows that our indolence requires it.

The thing most calculated to terrify us is the enormous cruelty practised against our poor brethren. In fact it is a frightful spectacle, and one which might well make the inconstant shudder. But we ought on the other hand to contemplate the invincible courage with which God has endowed them. For in some way or other they surmount all the torments which the ungodly can devise to cast down their courage. So then Satan, on the one hand, is contriving everything to trouble the poor brethren to make them swerve from the truth and turn aside from the path of salvation. With unbridled rage he vents against them all his spite. While on the other, God meanwhile assists them, and though they suffer extreme anguish according to the weakness of the flesh, yet still do they persevere in the confession of his name. In that you see they are victorious. Should then the cruelty of the adversaries, which in spite of all their efforts is vanquished, have more weight with you to deaden your hearts, than that power from on high, with which God aids his children, ought to have to increase in you the perseverance which you should maintain in his truth? You see the assistance of God which remains victorious and will you not repose your confidence in it? You see the faith which triumphs in the martyrs, who endure death, and shall it be the cause of annihilating yours? Wherefore, my brethren, when the tyrants exhaust all their fury, learn to turn your eyes to contemplate the succour which God affords his followers; and seeing that they are not forsaken by him, take new comfort and cease not to war against the temptations of your flesh, till you have attained the full conviction that we are happy in belonging to Christ whether it be to die or to live.

I am aware what reflections may here present themselves to

our minds; that in the meantime the servants of God do nevertheless suffer, and that the wicked from the impunity with which they commit their acts of cruelty, break out more and more into all sorts of excesses. But since it is our duty to suffer, we ought humbly to submit; as it is the will of God that his church be subjected to such conditions that even as the plough passes over the field, so should the ungodly have leave to pass their sword over us all from the least to the greatest. According then to what is said in the psalm, *we should prepare our back for stripes.* If that condition is hard and painful, let us be satisfied that our heavenly Father, in exposing us to death, turns it to our eternal welfare. And indeed it is better for us to suffer for his name, without flinching, than to possess his word without being visited by affliction. For in prosperity we do not experience the worth of his assistance and the power of his Spirit, as when we are oppressed by men. That seems strange to us; but he who sees more clearly than we, knows far better what is advantageous for us. Now when he permits his children to be afflicted, there is no doubt but that it is for their good. Thus we are forced to conclude that whatever he orders, is the best thing we could desire.

If we are not satisfied with that, he shows us that as much as our faith is more precious than gold or silver, so it is the more reasonable that it should be tried. Also it is by this means that we are mortified, in order not to be rooted in our love for this world; and more evil affections than we can imagine are thus corrected, were it but to teach us humility and bring down that pride which is always greater in us than it ought to be. By it he also wishes to put us in mind of the esteem in which we ought to hold his word; for if it cost us nothing we should not know its worth. He permits us then to be afflicted for it, in order to show us how very precious he considers it. But above all by sufferings he wishes us to be conformed to the image of his Son, as it is fitting that there should be conformity between the head and the members.

Let us not then suppose that we are forsaken of God when we suffer persecution for his truth, but rather that he so disposes matters for our greater good. If that is repugnant to our senses, it is so because we are always more inclined to seek for our rest here below than in the kingdom of heaven. Now since our triumph is in heaven, we must be prepared for the combat while we live here upon earth.

Moreover, my brethren, from the example that is now set before you, learn that God will strengthen you in proportion to your necessities. For he knows well how to adapt the measure of our temptations to the strength with which it is his will to endow us in order to endure them. We are sufficiently admonished, besides, by the Scriptures, that tyrants can do nothing more against us than what our merciful Father permits them. Now in permitting them, he knows who we are, and will thus provide for the issue. The cause then of our great consternation is that looking at our own weakness we do not turn our eyes to the succour which we ought to expect and demand of God. So it is but just that he come not to our aid since we do not seek for him. We must even hope, that when he shall have tried his church, he will bridle the fury of the tyrants and cause it to cease in despite of all their efforts. In waiting for such an issue it is our duty to possess our souls in patience. Most certainly he will accomplish what he has promised in the psalm, which I have already quoted, viz: *that he will break the cords of the plough which they drag over us to cut and destroy us,* and in another passage – *that the sceptre of the ungodly will not remain for ever in their inheritance, for fear the just stretch out their hands to do evil.* Whatever happen, do you profit by the constancy with which you see your brethren endure persecution to support the truth of God, that it may confirm you to persevere in the faith.

It has been said of old that the blood of the martyrs is the seed of the church. If it is a seed from which we derive our origin in Jesus Christ, it should also be a shower to water us that we may grow and make progress, even so as to die well. For if this blood is precious in the sight of God, it ought not to be unprofitable for us; thus we see that St Paul boasts that his bonds have contributed to the advancement of the gospel and expects that in his death the name of Jesus Christ will be exalted. The reason is that when we are persecuted we are called by God to maintain his cause, being, as it were, his attorneys; not that he has need of us or that we are proper for that, but since he does us the honour to employ us therein, it is not his will that we should lose our pains. Wherefore we ought to have in the utmost detestation that blasphemy of ancient hypocrites who murmur against those who glorify the name of God, even to the offering up of their own lives, just as if by the confession of their Christianity these martyrs created scandal. Such persons have never known what Jesus Christ is, but have forged to themselves an idol under his name, when they reckon for a scandal what ought to stand for a signature to ratify more and more to our consciences the truth of the gospel. And since they are not ashamed to despise the servants of God for their rashness, because the latter expose themselves to death to defend the cause of God's Son, they will feel one day to their sore confusion, how much more agreeable this temerity, as they style it, is to God than their wisdom, or rather the diabolical cunning which they display, in denying the truth in order to exempt themselves from all danger. It is horrible that those who call themselves Christians should be so stupid, or rather brutalized, as to renounce Jesus Christ as soon as he displays his cross. As for you, my brethren, hold in reverence the blood of the martyrs which is shed for a testimony to the truth, as being dedicated and consecrated to the glory of God; then apply it for your edification, stirring yourselves up to follow their example. But if you do not yet feel in yourselves such an inclination, pray God that he may give it you, groaning because of your infirmity, which holds you back from doing your duty; for, as I said in the beginning, it is far too dangerous a thing to flatter ourselves in our infirmities. For faith cannot be long lulled to sleep without being at last quenched, as the example of those worldly-wise dissemblers shows us, who, desiring with their false pretences to play fast and loose with God, come at last to lose all knowledge of the gospel, as if they had never heard of it. Meanwhile, since you see that the poor flock of God's Son is scattered by the wolves, repair to him, praying him to have compassion on you and strengthen your weakness, to stretch out his mighty arm to repel them, to shut their bloody mouths and break their claws, or finally to change them into harmless lambs. Above all, pray him to make manifest that he is seated on the right hand of God his Father to maintain both the honour of his majesty and the salvation of his children. It is in this way that you will derive relief from him, humbling yourselves with tears and prayers, and not in murmuring and gnashing your teeth against the tyrants, as some do who seek not the refuge to which persecutions ought to drive us. For my own part, I could wish that God had given me the means of being nearer at hand to assist you, but since that is not possible I will pray our merciful Father that since he has once confided you to the keeping of our Lord Jesus Christ, he would cause you to feel how safe you are under so good a protector, to the end that you may cast all your cares upon him; and that he would be pleased to have compassion on you and all those who are in affliction, delivering you from the hands of the ungodly. And as he has once made you partakers of the knowledge of the truth, that he would, from day to day, increase you therein, making it bring forth fruits to his glory. Amen.

62/TO THE BISHOP OF LONDON[1]

Recommendation of the French Church of London
Eulogium of Des Gallars
Wish for a complete Reform of the Anglican Church

GENEVA, May, 1560

Though you do not expect me to thank you for an office of piety performed by you to the Church of Christ, yet the case is different with regard to the protection which you have deigned to afford those of our countrymen who inhabit the principal city of your diocese. By your cares, they have had permission, through the indulgence of the queen, not only to invoke God in purity, but also to send over to us a demand for a faithful pastor; if then for these acts of kindness, I did not profess myself bound to you, I should be deservedly chargeable with folly and a want of common courtesy. And since you have not hesitated of your own free impulse to ask and entreat me to see that a fitting pastor should be selected for my countrymen, I have no need to recommend to your fidelity and protection the persons for whose salvation you

1 Without date – May 1560. We get the date of this letter from that of the letter from the French Church in London to Calvin asking for a pastor, in which they say: 'What a glory would be added, not only to the foreign churches, but also to the Anglican, if Viret or Th. Beza or Nicholas des Gallars should join himself to us!' March 28th, 1560. The Bishop of London had accompanied this request with the most urgent recommendations. A refugee on the continent during the reign of the intolerant Mary, Edmund Grindal had learned how to appreciate the Reformers of Switzerland, and professed for Calvin the most affectionate admiration. He wrote to him in 1563: 'Our church and nation are greatly indebted to you, illustrious brother, ... it is then with the deepest sorrow we have learned the deplorable state of your health. Most assuredly it is the excess of your labours that has occasioned this illness. Renounce then these prolonged vigils, otherwise the evil will increase, and you will no longer be of such utility to the church. Recall Gregory of Nazianzen, who, as he advanced in age, being unwilling to relax from the austerity of his youth, was forced almost always to keep his bed, and thereby became less useful. Since you and Bullinger remain almost alone among the pillars of the house of God, we desire to enjoy you, if the Lord shall think fit as long as possible.'

are so solicitous. And assuredly as, in assisting them so liberally up to this moment, you have given a rare and singular proof of your pious zeal, so now you will of your constancy in continuing your good offices to the end. In what concerns ourselves, both because the situation seemed to require a man furnished with eminent gifts, and because the foreigners among you particularly desired that one of our society should be accorded to them, we have preferred to despoil ourselves rather than not comply with so holy a desire. For that reason we have granted to their request our brother Nicholas des Gallars one of the three whom they themselves named in the beginning.[1] Now though it was painful for him to be torn away from us whom he knew to entertain no ordinary degree of affection for him, and though he quitted with reluctance a station in which he had long rendered services not less productive than faithfully performed, yet vanquished by our entreaties he has undertaken this office, because he hoped that he should thus contribute in no small degree to the spread of the kingdom of Christ.

Certainly nothing but necessity could have wrung from us our consent to be separated from him, but we feared that it was not possible otherwise than by his arrival among you to provide for the wants of a rising, and as yet but imperfectly organized church. For this place will incur no slight loss by his departure, where he was held in high esteem, and where he bore himself in a manner worthy of a servant of Christ. As far as my personal feelings are concerned, the greatest intimacy and affection having subsisted between us, I did not without the most poignant sorrow give my consent to this disruption of our familiar intercourse. But everything was to be endured rather than refuse the aid so anxiously implored by our destitute and distressed brethren.

1 Nicholas des Gallars was elected (26th April, 1560) minister of the French Church of London. On the 3rd of May he took leave of the Seigneurs of Geneva. 'The Lord,' say the Registers of Geneva, 'has seen fit to make use of him for his own glory and our joy and consolation.'

Wherefore I feel the greater solicitude, that he should at least find among you a welcome station to alleviate and solace his sorrow at quitting his country. When a closer connection, which your natural courtesy makes me confidently expect, shall have revealed to you his real character, you will be sufficiently convinced, Reverend Sir, without any foreign recommendation, how worthy he is of your affection. In the meantime if I hold any place in your esteem, I entreat you again and again to honour with your favour and kindness a man whom you see to be so cherished by me.

It is a matter of deep regret that the churches of your whole kingdom have not yet been organized as all good men could wish, and as in the beginning they had hoped.[1] But to overcome all difficulties there is need of unflagging efforts. Then indeed it is expedient and even absolutely necessary that the queen should discriminate, and you in your turn should lay aside, nay, cast from you entirely whatever savours of earthly domination, in order that for the exercise of a spiritual office you may have a legitimate authority and such as shall be bestowed on you by God. This indeed will be her supremacy and pre-eminence; then she will hold the highest rank of dignity under Christ our head, if she stretch forth a helping hand to legitimate pastors, for the execution of these functions that have been enjoined us. But as neither your wisdom stands in need of counsel, nor your magnanimity of incitements, I shall only have recourse to prayers, and supplicate God, my most excellent and honoured sir, to govern you by his Spirit, sustain you by his power, shield you with his protection and bless all your holy labours.

All my colleagues most respectfully salute your reverence.

---

1 This regret was shared in by Grindal himself. In his letter to Calvin of the 18th March, 1560, we read: 'I commend to your prayers, and those of the other brethren, the state of our churches, not yet settled sufficiently according to our mind.'

63/TO THE KING OF NAVARRE[1]

He exhorts him to pursue with ardour the restoration of the
gospel in France

GENEVA, 16th January, 1561

Sire:

If I thought that my letters were disagreeable to you I should
fear to importune or annoy you in writing them. But the
confidence I entertain emboldens me, because as I feel that
you are convinced of the respect I bear towards you, and of
my good intentions to strive to render you service, so I am
sure you will receive graciously the testimony which I endeavour to give of them. Wherefore, sire, though I am aware
that you have no need of my counsels, yet I do not cease to
entreat and even exhort you, in the name of God, to be pleased
to take courage, in order to do combat courageously and
more and more overcome all the difficulties with which I
know you to be surrounded. And, in truth, the re-establishment of such a kingdom is an object for which we should
spare nothing, and still more it is our most imperious duty to
strive that the reign of the Son of God, true religion and the
pure doctrine of salvation, which are things more precious
than the whole world, should be completely re-established.

1 The weakness and ignorance of the King of Navarre had deceived the
calculations of Calvin, and the just hopes of the Reformed party. 'For though,'
says Beza, 'both God and the laws called him to the government of the kingdom, and the consent of the states required it of him, in which he would
neither have found want of counsel nor of force to re-establish every thing, in
case of resistance, he was so far from supporting his rank that, on the contrary, he contented himself with the shadow of it, leaving willingly the body
and the substance to the queen mother, without her experiencing any difficulty.' Nevertheless, as lieutenant general of the kingdom, the King of Navarre
had it in his power to contribute greatly to the consolidation and progress of
the Reformed churches. Calvin spared this prince neither warnings nor admonitions.

The greatest obstacle that stands in your way seems to me easy to be overcome, whenever you shall be pleased, sire, to remonstrate frankly with the adverse party,[1] and let her feel keenly that she ought not to apply in thwarting you the power which she holds only by your favour. For the rest, sire, there is one subject of which I have thought it good and expedient to remind you, that your majesty may be pleased to provide for it according to your wisdom. It is not my natural disposition, nor my habit, to intrude and interfere. But it seemed to me to be my duty to recommend to you the bearer of this letter, that you may learn from him, by word of mouth, the matter in question, when your good pleasure shall decide upon giving him an audience.

Sire, having humbly commended myself to your indulgent favour, I will pray our heavenly Father to have you in his keeping, to sustain you by his power, and increase in you all good and prosperity.

---

[1] The regent Catharine de Medici.

64/TO THE QUEEN OF NAVARRE[1]

He congratulates her on her conversion, and lays before her her principal duties as a Christian princess

GENEVA, 16th January, 1561

Madame:

I cannot adequately express my joy at the letter you were pleased to write to my brother Monsieur de Chalonné,[2] seeing how powerfully God had wrought in you in a few hours. For though already long ago he had sown in you some good seed, you know at present that it was almost choked by the thorns of this world; as for want of daily exercising ourselves in the holy Scriptures, the truth which we had known little by little drops away, till at length it totally disappears, unless

1 Without date. Written no doubt at the same time as the preceding – 16th January, 1561.
Daughter of Henry d'Albret King of Navarre and Margaret de Valois, the sister of Francis I, Jeanne d'Albret joined to the talents of her mother, superior judgment and a heroic soul. Betrothed in her childhood to the Duke of Cleves, and married in 1548 to Antony de Bourbon, Duke of Vendôme, she inherited a few years afterwards the kingdom of Navarre. The Reform had already long before penetrated into this country, and the preachers of Geneva found support and favour at the court of Nérac. 'But the queen,' says Brantôme, 'who was a young, beautiful, and very virtuous princess, and who loved, moreover, quite as much a dance as a sermon, took no great pleasure in this innovation in religion.' It was only at a later period, during the process of the Prince of Condé and the captivity of the King of Navarre, that this princess, taught by misfortune, showed herself more attentive to evangelical exhortations: 'Seeing,' says Beza, 'that the trust she had reposed in men was deceived, and that all human succour failed her, being touched to the heart by the love of God, she had recourse to him with all humility, and in sorrow and tears ... so that in the time of her greatest tribulation she made a public profession of the pure doctrine, being fortified by Francis Le Guay, otherwise called Bois Normand, and Henry, faithful ministers of the word of God.'

2 A pseudonym of Theodore Beza. Sent on the 30th July, 1560, to Nérac, 'to instruct the King and Queen of Navarre in the word of God,' he acquitted himself successfully of this mission, and had commenced his journey back to Geneva in the month of November of the same year.

our compassionate Father provide a remedy. Now of his infinite goodness he has made provision to keep you from coming to that extremity. It is true that those who yield to indifference, take a pleasure in their inactivity, not perceiving that it is a mortal lethargy. But when it pleases God to rouse us up and draw us effectually to the fear of his holy name, and kindle in our hearts an ardent desire to serve his glory, that is an inquietude happier and more desirable than all the delights, pleasures, and enjoyments, in which poor worldlings lose themselves. I speak familiarly, Madame, believing that you will without hesitation give me leave to do so, as moreover, I have derived this advantage from your letter that it has given me an occasion and a liberal access to write to you.

Wherefore, Madame, I pray you to prize the mercy of God as it deserves, not only because it has brought you all at once out of the darkness of death to show you the light of life in his Son, who is the true Sun of righteousness, but also because he has deeply imprinted on your heart a faith in his gospel, giving to it a living root, that it may bring forth its due fruits. For you have felt by experience how the vanities of this world deaden the knowledge of the truth. We would fain swim between two currents, so that the word of God is made cold and of no effect, if the power of God be not conjoined therewith. And this is the true and perfect covenant which he promises to contract with his own children, namely, to impress and engrave his doctrine on their inward parts. Having then received so great and inestimable a benefit, you have reason to be so much the more zealous to dedicate yourself (as you do) entirely to Him, who has bound you so closely to himself. And whereas kings and princes would often wish to be exempted from subjection to Jesus Christ, and are accustomed to make a buckler of their privileges under pretence of their greatness, being ashamed even to belong to the fold of this great Shepherd, do you, Madame, bethink you that the dignity and grandeur in which this God of goodness has brought you up, should be in your esteem a double tie to bind you to obedience to him, seeing that it is from him that you hold everything, and that according to the measure which each one has received, he shall have to render a stricter account. But since I see how the Spirit of God governs you, I have more reason to render him thanks than to exhort you as if you had need to be goaded forward. When, besides, I doubt not but you apply all your zeal to that end, as is indeed very requisite, when we reflect on the coldness, weakness, and frailty that is in us.

Long ago we had already essayed to discharge our duty with respect of the king your husband, and even more than once, to the end that he might quit himself manfully. But you will see once more, Madame, by the copy of the letter which we have sent to him, what effects your admonition has produced.

Madame, having very humbly commended myself to your indulgent favour, I will pray our heavenly Father to have you always in his keeping, to govern and direct you by his Spirit, to strengthen you by his power, and increase you in all good.

65/TO THE ADMIRAL COLIGNY[1]

*Encomiums on the constancy of the Admiral
Recommendation of Geneva*

GENEVA, 16th January, 1561

Monseigneur:

We have indeed occasion to praise God for the singular courage which he has bestowed on us to serve his glory and the advancement of the kingdom of his Son. It were to be desired that you had many companions to aid you in your task, but though others are slow in acquitting themselves of their duty, nevertheless you ought to put in practice the saying of our Lord, that each should follow cheerfully without looking upon others. St Peter fearing to march by himself said to Jesus of John, And this man, what of him? The answer given to one man should be applied to all. Let every one go whither he shall be called, even if he should not have a single follower, though I trust that the magnanimity which God has hitherto

1 Restored to liberty after the conclusion of the peace between Spain and France, the Admiral had openly declared for the Reformation. Unshaken by the threats as well as by the seductions of the court, he had the courage to present to King Francis II. in the assembly of the Notables at Fontainebleau an address from the Protestants of Normandy demanding the free exercise of their worship, and added proudly in presence of the Guises, that in this single province fifty thousand persons were prepared to sign their names to this petition. Some months later (November 1561) he quitted Châtillon to repair at the peril of his life to the Estates of Orleans. 'On leaving his house,' says Beza, 'he was unwilling to dissemble from his wife (one of the most Christian and virtuous ladies of her times) the dangers by which he was going to be surrounded, and without expecting from them any prosperous issue, saying, however, that he had perfect confidence that God would have compassion on his poor church and on the kingdom; exhorting the lady as well as her family to remain constant in the doctrine of the gospel, in which they had been rightly instructed, since God had given them to know that it was the only true and heavenly food, and that it was their duty to think it the greatest happiness to suffer for his name.' The sudden death of King Francis II., having disappointed the hopes of the Guises, and brought on a change favourable to the Reformed, the Admiral did not hesitate to have the gospel preached in his own house at Paris.

caused to shine forth in you, will be a good lesson to draw out the lukewarm. Even if the whole world should be blind and ungrateful, and that it should seem to you that all your pains had been laid out in vain, let it satisfy you that God and the angels approve of your conduct. And in reality it ought to suffice you that you cannot miss the heavenly crown, after having courageously battled for the glory of the Son of God, in which consists our eternal salvation.

For the rest, Monseigneur, I have made bold to address to you the bearer of this letter in order that he may expose to you an affair of which you will have a more ample detail from his mouth, whenever you shall be pleased to grant him an audience. I believe that after having listened to him you will not find the advice amiss nor the execution of it importunate; at least you will in your wisdom conclude, that I have nothing at heart but the repose and prosperity of the kingdom. I do not dissemble the desire I feel that some measures should be adopted in favour of this poor city, in order that it may not be exposed to pillage.[1] But as I am convinced that the safety of this place needs not to be recommended to you, you will not blame the anxiety I feel respecting it, especially as that anxiety tends to the public good of France, and is intimately connected with it.

Whereupon, in conclusion, Monseigneur, after humbly commending myself to your indulgent favour. I will supplicate our heavenly Father to keep you under his protection, and increase in you the gifts of his Spirit, that his name may be more and more glorified in you.

---

1 After the peace of Cateau Cambrésis and the restoration of the Duke of Savoy to his states, Geneva was constantly threatened with an attack by this prince, supported by the Pope and Philip II. Emmanuel Philibert asked the Catholic powers to guarantee to him beforehand his conquest. But could France abandon Geneva without alienating the Swiss Cantons from which she drew precious succours? The independence of Geneva was necessary for the security of France. Such was the sense of Calvin's representations to the Admiral, and of the Admiral's to the court, of which the policy at this moment appeared more favourable to the Reformed party.

66/TO JOHN KNOX[1]

Explanations on the subject of a letter
Expression of satisfaction at the progress of the Reformation in
Scotland and of sympathy for a domestic affliction

GENEVA, 23rd April, 1561

About four months previous to the receipt of your last letter,
I had received from you another, in which you took great
pains to exculpate yourself, because I felt offended at being
consulted a second time by your friends and countrymen,
about certain questions respecting which I had already given
them an answer. Here is a correct statement of the case. If
they had not promised that my letter should arrive in safety
at its destination, I should at least have preserved a copy of it.
It was their fault, and in consequence of their pledging themselves rather inconsiderately, that I took no better pre-
cautions. When then, some time afterwards, they informed
me that the answer about which they had asserted I had
nothing to fear, had completely miscarried, and demanded
that I should a second time undertake a new labour, I confess
I was displeased, and I answered them that I had a suspicion,
that what they asked was only with the intention of insi-
diously sounding me. But lest you should be surprised that I
answered them so harshly, know that I had previously learned
from a sure source that the counsel which I had given them
was not to their liking. When I knew then that I had by no
means given them satisfaction, I not unnaturally conjectured
that they desired to suppress what displeased them, and returned to me to elicit something more in accordance with their

1 There exists only a small number of letters exchanged between Knox and
Calvin. Those of the Scots Reformer alluded to in Calvin's answer, have been
lost and the letters of the Reformer of Geneva have not had a better fate.

wishes; but that you acted with any degree of dissimulation in the matter, I never said nor even suspected. And even at the moment all offence dropped so entirely from my mind that there was not the least need of making any apology. But it grieves me that anything which has fallen from my lips should have made such an impression on your mind, as to lead you to suppose that you were taxed with craft or bad faith, things which I judge the most alien to your character. Banish then that apprehension or that inquietude.

I come now to your letter, which was lately brought to me by a pious brother who has come here to pursue his studies. I rejoice exceedingly, as you may easily suppose, that the gospel has made such rapid and happy progress among you. That they should have stirred up violent opposition against you is nothing new. But the power of God is the more conspicuously displayed in this, that no attacks either of Satan or of the ungodly have hitherto prevented you from advancing with triumphant constancy in the right course, though you could never have been equal to the task of resistance, unless He who is superior to all the world had held out to you from heaven a helping hand. With regard to ceremonies, I trust, even should you displease many, that you will moderate your rigour. Of course it is your duty to see that the church be purged of all defilements which flow from error and superstition. For it behoves us to strive sedulously that the mysteries of God be not polluted by the admixture of ludicrous or disgusting rites. But with this exception, you are well aware that certain things should be tolerated even if you do not quite approve of them. I am deeply afflicted, as you may well believe, that the nobles of your nation are split into factions,[1] and it is not without reason that you are

1 Among the noblemen the most devoted to the cause of the Reformation were the Earls of Arran and Murray who maintained a correspondence with Calvin: 'The Earl of Arran would have written to you but he was absent. ames the brother of the queen salutes you. The old man is the only one of those who frequent the court who sets himself against its impiety. And yet

more distressed and tormented, because Satan is now plotting in the bosom of your church, than you were formerly by the commotions stirred up by the French. But God is to be intreated that he may heal this evil also. Here we are exposed to many dangers. Nothing but our confidence in the divine protection exempts us from trepidation, though we are not free from fears.

Farewell, distinguished sir and honoured brother. May the Lord always stand by you, govern, protect, and sustain you by his power. Your distress for the loss of your wife justly commands my deepest sympathy.[1] Persons of her merit are not often to be met with. But as you have well learned from what source consolation for your sorrow is to be sought, I doubt not but you endure with patience this calamity. You will salute very courteously all your pious brethren. My colleagues also beg me to present to you their best respects.

---

even he is fascinated as well as the others, inasmuch as he fears to hurl down by violent means that idol.' Letter of Knox to Calvin, 24th October, 1561. In this same letter, Knox announced the re-establishment of the mass in the chapel of Mary Stuart at Holyrood, and asked if it was not the duty of the Reformed to abolish this last relic of superstition in Scotland.

1 Knox had just lost his first wife, Margery Bowes, who had been the companion of his exile on the Continent. This domestic grief was announced to Calvin by Goodman in a letter of the 13th February, 1561. 'Our brother Knox has just been bereaved of his wife. He himself, feeble in body but robust in mind, never flinches from labours. His arrival in Scotland was very seasonable, and his presence there just now is not less necessary. I pray that the course of his life may be prolonged for years, that his services may profit his country and the church.' Knox remained a widower for two years, and in 1564 married Margaret Stewart a daughter of Lord Ochiltree.

67/TO THE KING OF NAVARRE[1]

Warning on the subject of the Lutheran intrigues to introduce into France the Confession of Augsburg

GENEVA, August, 1561

Sire:

The sad news which we have of the state of the kingdom has forced us to write to you, and beg you to open your eyes and see what must be sufficiently notorious. For even the most blinded may perceive, as if they felt with their hands, the plottings and intrigues which have been set on foot, to break off whatever has been well commenced, and overturn from one day to another all good conclusions, and bring back things to such a point, that Jesus Christ with his gospel will ere long be banished from the kingdom.[2] Now he will not suffer himself to be thus mocked, and he will know well how to take the crafty in their own trap; but in the mean time, sire, it is your duty not to permit and suffer the truth of God to be thus betrayed in the sight of all. It is possible you may have thought to gain something by concessions, but the evil is springing up abundantly and gaining but too much strength; and if you be not on your guard disorders will arise

1 The end of this letter is missing. An intrigue ably contrived by the Duke of Guise and the Cardinal of Lorraine had engaged the Duke of Würtemberg to demand the adoption of the formulary of Augsburg, as the symbol of the Reformed churches of France. This step, provoked by the adversaries of French Protestantism, to bring on a conflict between the two grand communions of the Reformation, unhappily divided on the question of the sacraments, had already excited the concern of the theologians of both parties. Always feeble and irresolute, the King of Navarre seemed to be inclined to favour the project of the Guises. In a severe message Calvin warned him, in vain, to be on his guard against the intrigues of his enemies.

2 The edict of July (1561), promulgated at the demand of the Cardinal of Lorraine, had just interdicted, under pain of banishment, the religious meetings of the Reformed, before the assembling of a general council.

from it, in a moment of time much more serious than you imagine, and then it will no longer be time to remedy them, for God will take vengeance, in order to punish the indifference of those who shall have neglected their duty, according to the rank and degree in which he had established them. If we speak rather sharply, sire, believe me now is the time to do so, or never.

On the other hand, we have heard that the Duke of Würtemberg, suborned by those whom it is not necessary to mention, is soliciting you to employ your influence to have the Confession of Augsburg received in France.[1] Suppose, sire, that this man is playing on a stage his part just as it has been distributed to him.[2] But in God's name reflect how the Confession of Faith which the French churches have sworn to follow and maintain has been ratified, and even though it had not been signed by the blood of martyrs, yet since it has been extracted from the pure word of God and presented to the king and his council, you cannot reject it, nor so huddle up the matter but that God will oppose your designs, and show you by effects that he will be listened to and believed. With regard to the Confession of Augsburg, how dare the Duke of Würtemberg beg you to receive it, when we reflect that he and his like condemn the author of it, who is Melanchthon? However, we shall leave him out of the question, since they have forced him to play a part in speaking of a thing of which he is entirely ignorant. The fact is, that the most renowned persons of that party agree like dog and cat. We are much deceived if the person who brought you the letters be not the nephew of one Vergerio, a foreigner from Italy, and one of the most barefaced intriguers that ever

---

1 The Duke of Würtemberg, accompanied by two of his ministers, Brentz and André, had met the princes of Lorraine at Saverne. 'The Cardinal,' says Beza, 'having made a present of some silver plate to these two good preachers, he knew so well how to adapt himself to them, that this simple prince thought he had more than half converted him.'

2 There are here some words missing in the manuscript.

existed.[1] There is another clownish apostate, Baudouin,[2] who has already apostatized three or four times from Jesus Christ, and it is just possible he may have so insinuated himself into your favour, as to deceive you with regard to his character, if you were not apprized of it. We then entreat your majesty to be on your guard amid so many snares, and again we pray you in the name of God not to allow yourself to be shaken hither and thither, in order that the word of God may be maintained unimpaired, which it is impossible to be otherwise than by preserving to it its simplicity. There is a common saying among the people about crooked loaves in a batch, which might teach you to reject those who endeavour to persuade you by dissembling pretexts. For though at first they may make you believe this or that, we declare to you in virtue of Him who has given us authority to speak, that the issue will be unfortunate, and we warn you of it in good time, fearing lest you experience[3] ...

1 Paolo Vergerio, formerly Bishop of Capo d'Istria di Friuli, and Legate of Pope Paul III, at Ratisbon. Gained over to the Reform by Melanchthon, he gave up his bishopric, and took up his abode in the Grisons. Being an ardent Lutheran, he was accused of having devoted himself to the propagation of the formulary of Augsburg, from motives of personal interest.

2 A Calvinist at Geneva, a Catholic at Paris, a Lutheran at Heidelberg, Baudouin had but too well merited by his religious inconstancy, the stigmatizing epithets of triple apostate and outcast. A deserter from all communions, he had been favourably received by the King of Navarre, who counted on employing him usefully in effecting a reconciliation between the parties.

3 Without date. The end is missing. But the date is furnished us by a letter of Calvin to Bullinger of the 5th November, 1561, in which there is the following passage: 'Long ago I had discovered that the devil was plotting, by clandestine arts, a thing which is now very apparent, and three months before I had carefully reminded the King of Navarre to be on his guard against snares.' The letter to which he alludes in this passage is then of the month of August, 1561.

68/TO THE PHYSICIANS OF MONTPELLIER

Medical consultation

GENEVA, 8th February, 1564

When the physician Sarrazin, on whose directions I principally rely for the re-establishment of my health, presented me
not long ago some remedies which you prescribed for the
relief of my complaints, I asked him, who had without my
knowledge taken that task upon him. He replied that at the
request of one of my colleagues, who is at present resident
among you, he had drawn up a short abstract of matters
connected with my case, in order that you might give me the
benefit of your advice. On my part, I cannot but recognize
from the very minute answers you have transmitted, how
much interest you take in my life, about the prolongation of
which you have spontaneously shown yourselves so solicitous.
If to have given yourselves that trouble at my demand would
have been no small token of kindness on your part, how much
more must I feel indebted to you for thus anticipating my
desires by your unsolicited benevolence! Moreover, I have
no other means of testifying my gratitude to you, besides
that of recommending you to draw in your turn from my
writings what may afford you a spiritual medicine. Twenty
years ago I experienced the same courteous services from the
distinguished Parisian physicians, Acatus, Tagant, and Gallois.
But at that time I was not attacked by arthritic pains, knew
nothing of the stone or the gravel – I was not tormented with
the gripings of the cholic, nor afflicted with haemorrhoids,
nor threatened with expectoration of blood. At present all
these ailments as it were in troops assail me. As soon as I
recovered from a quartan ague, I was seized with severe and
acute pains in the calves of my legs, which after being

partially relieved returned a second and a third time. At last they degenerated into a disease in my articulations, which spread from my feet to my knees. An ulcer in the haemorrhoid veins long caused me excruciating sufferings, and intestinal ascarides subjected me to painful titillations, though I am now relieved from this vermicular disease, but immediately after in the course of last summer I had an attack of nephritis. As I could not endure the jolting motion of horseback, I was conveyed into the country in a litter. On my return I wished to accomplish a part of the journey on foot. I had scarcely proceeded a mile when I was obliged to repose myself, in consequence of lassitude in the reins. And then to my surprise I discovered that I discharged blood instead of urine. As soon as I got home I took to bed. The nephritis gave me exquisite pain, from which I only obtained a partial relief by the application of remedies. At length not without the most painful strainings I ejected a calculus which in some degree mitigated my sufferings, but such was its size, that it lacerated the urinary canal and a copious discharge of blood followed. This haemorrhage could only be arrested by an injection of milk through a syringe. After that I ejected several others, and the oppressive numbness of the reins is a sufficient symptom that there still exist there some remains of uric calculus. It is a fortunate thing, however, that minute or at least moderately sized particles still continue to be emitted. My sedentary way of life to which I am condemned by the gout in my feet precludes all hopes of a cure. I am also prevented from taking exercise on horseback by my haemorrhoids. Add to my other complaints that whatever nourishment I take imperfectly digested turns into phlegm, which by its density sticks like paste to my stomach. But I am thoughtlessly tasking your patience, giving you double labour as the reward of your previous kindness, not indeed in consulting you, but in giving you the trouble to read over my vain complaints.

Farewell, most accomplished sirs whom I sincerely honour. May the Lord always direct you by his Spirit, sustain you by his power, and enrich you more and more with his gifts.

69/TO BULLINGER

Sufferings of Calvin and the inefficacy of the healing art to relieve them
News of France and Germany

GENEVA, 6th April, 1564

I do not claim your indulgence for my long silence, respected brother, because you must have learned from others how just an excuse I have had for my delay, and which excuse I may in a great measure still allege.[1] For though the pain in my side is abated, my lungs are nevertheless so charged with phlegmatic humours that my respiration is difficult and interrupted. A calculus in my bladder also gives me very exquisite pain for the last twelve days. Add to that the anxious doubts we entertain about the possibility of curing it, for all remedies have hitherto proved ineffectual; exercise on horseback would have been the best and most expeditious method of getting rid of it, but an ulcer in my abdomen gives me excruciating pain even when seated or lying in bed, so that

1 Already the preceding year Calvin had been repeatedly forced to interrupt his correspondence because of the multiplied sufferings of his illness. His secretary Charles de Jonvillers wrote on this occasion to Bullinger: 'These few words I have thought proper to add hurriedly, that you may know that M. Calvin is such a martyr to sufferings, that far from being able to write, he cannot even dictate anything to be sent to you, in consequence of the pressure of his disease. I know the high esteem in which he holds you, as you deserve, and I can scarcely write without tears. I entreat of you then that in your prayers and those of your whole church, you in the meantime commend to God both him and all of us.' Letter of 11th June, 1563. The days of the Reformer were already numbered, and before a year had elapsed, that great light was withdrawn from the church and the world.

the agitation of riding is out of the question. Within the last three days the gout has also been troublesome. You will not be surprised then if so many united sufferings make me lazy. It is with much ado I can be brought to take any food. The taste of wine is bitter. But while I wish to discharge my duty in writing to you, I am only tiring out your patience with my insipid details.

Respecting the affairs of France, Beza has promised to write[1] to you. I dispense then with saying anything, not to repeat a twice-told tale. I shall only allude to one subject however. You have heard long ago that the king has gone to Lorraine. The cause of his journey was a secret to the courtiers themselves, but it was revealed to me lately by the person who was charged to convey instructions backwards and forwards. The envoy of the king to the emperor, and who formerly was among you at the time he was Abbot of St Laurence, is holding out to the queen-mother great and dazzling prospects from King Maximilian. But in the mean time he stipulates that the queen should not openly declare that she entertains any hopes. I make no doubt, therefore, but he will sell himself to the cardinal of Lorraine. For after having failed in all his projects, he conceives that his only remaining resource is to gain time by giving out these ambiguous intimations. I see no other fraud or treachery concealed in this mission, except to amuse the queen with false expectations, and bring himself forward by his insinuations, to undertake affairs which he will never bring to any conclusion. For it is evident that Roschetelle has made a false use of King Maximilian's name, since he childishly advises the queen to dis-

---

[1] In a letter of Beza's to Bullinger of the 4th May, 1564, there are some details respecting the illness of Calvin: 'But what gives us the most poignant distress is the uninterrupted sufferings of that most excellent man, our father and the faithful servant of God. Of his life, humanly speaking, we now utterly despair. He is alive, however, and thus indeed, as he had afforded us a rare example of an upright life, so now he furnishes us with one of a courageous and truly Christian death. But ah wretched me!, what shall I do upon whom so overwhelming a charge devolves?'

semble and keep everything a profound secret. But my cough and a difficulty of breathing leave me no voice to dictate any more. Farewell, then, venerable brother, along with Mr Gualter, your other colleagues, and your whole family. May the Lord protect you all, enrich you more and more with his benefits, and sustain you by his power. I am unwilling to lose my pains in writing to you about the state of our city.

70/TO FAREL

Last adieus

GENEVA, 2nd May, 1564

Farewell, my most excellent and upright brother; and since it is the will of God that you should survive me in the world, live mindful of our intimacy, which, as it was useful to the church of God, so the fruits of it await us in heaven.[1] I am unwilling that you should fatigue yourself for my sake.[2] I draw my breath with difficulty, and every moment I am in expectation of breathing my last. It is enough that I live and die for Christ, who is to all his followers a gain both in life and death. Again I bid you and your brethren Farewell.

1 It cannot fail to be interesting to produce along with this moving farewell the noble testimony rendered by Farel to Calvin in a letter to Fabri of the 6th June, 1564: 'Oh why was I not taken away in his stead, and he preserved to the church which he has so well served, and in combats harder than death? He has done more and with greater promptitude than any one, surpassing not only the others but himself. Oh, how happily he has run a noble race! May the Lord grant that we run like him, and according to the measure of grace that has been dealt out to us.'

2 In spite of his great age Farel took a journey to see again once more his friend, his fellow labourer now on his death-bed. 'And nevertheless, that excellent old man came to Geneva, and after they had an interview together, the following day he returned to Neuchâtel.' Beza, *Life of Calvin*.

LAST DISCOURSES OF CALVIN

CALVIN'S TESTAMENT.

LAST WILL AND TESTAMENT OF MASTER JOHN CALVIN

In the name of God, be it known to all men by these presents that in the year 1564, and the 25th day of the month of April, I Peter Chenelat, citizen and sworn Notary of Geneva, have been sent for by *spectable*[1] John Calvin, minister of the word of God in the Church of Geneva, and burgess of the said Geneva, who, being sick and indisposed in body alone, has declared to me his intention to make his testament and declaration of his last will, begging me to write it according as it should be by him dictated and pronounced, which, at his said request, I have done, and have written it under him, and according as he hath dictated and pronounced it, word for word, without omitting or adding anything – in form as follows:

In the name of God, I John Calvin, minister of the word of God in the Church of Geneva, feeling myself reduced so low by diverse maladies, that I cannot but think that it is the will of God to withdraw me shortly from this world, have advised to make and set down in writing my testament and declaration of my last will in form, as follows:

In the first place, I render thanks to God, not only because he has had compassion on me, his poor creature, to draw me out of the abyss of idolatry in which I was plunged, in order to bring me to the light of his gospel and make me a partaker of the doctrine of salvation, of which I was altogether unworthy, and continuing his mercy he has supported me amid so many sins and short-comings, which were such that I well deserved

---

1 Epithet marking respect, used in title deeds, etc.

to be rejected by him a hundred thousand times – but what is more, he has so far extended his mercy towards me as to make use of me and of my labour, to convey and announce the truth of his gospel; protesting that it is my wish to live and die in this faith which he has bestowed on me, having no other hope nor refuge except in his gratuitous adoption, upon which all my salvation is founded; embracing the grace which he has given me in our Lord Jesus Christ, and accepting the merits of his death and passion, in order that by this means all my sins may be buried; and praying him so to wash and cleanse me by the blood of this great Redeemer, which has been shed for us poor sinners, that I may appear before his face, bearing as it were his image.

I protest also that I have endeavoured, according to the measure of grace he has given me, to teach his word in purity, both in my sermons and writings, and to expound faithfully the Holy Scriptures; and moreover, that in all the disputes I have had with the enemies of the truth, I have never made use of subtle craft nor sophistry, but have gone to work straight-forwardly in maintaining his quarrel. But alas! the desire which I have had, and the zeal, if so it must be called, has been so cold and so sluggish that I feel myself a debtor in everything and everywhere, and that, were it not for his infinite goodness, all the affection I have had would be but as smoke, nay, that even the favours which he has accorded me would but render me so much the more guilty; so that my only recourse is this, that being the Father of mercies he will show himself the Father of so miserable a sinner.

Moreover, I desire that my body after my decease be interred in the usual manner, to wait for the day of the blessed resurrection.

Touching the little earthly goods which God has given me here to dispose of, I name and appoint for my sole heir, my well-beloved brother Antony Calvin, but only as honorary heir however, leaving to him the right of possessing nothing save the cup which I have had from Monsieur de Varennes,[1] and begging him to be satisfied with that, as I am well assured he will be, because he knows that I do this for no other reason but that the little which I leave may remain to his children. I next bequeath to the college ten crowns, and to the treasure of poor foreigners the same sum. Item, to Jane, daughter of Charles Costan and my half-sister,[2] that is to say, by the father's side, the sum of ten crowns; and afterwards to each of my nephews, Samuel and John, sons of my aforesaid brother,[3] forty crowns; and to each of my nieces, Anne, Susannah, and Dorothy, thirty crowns. As for my nephew David their brother, because he has been thoughtless and unsettled, I leave to him but twenty-five crowns as a chastisement.[4] This is the total of all the property which God has given me, according as I have been able to value and estimate it, whether in books,[5] furniture,[6] plate, or anything else. However, should

1 Guillaume de Trie, Seigneur de Varennes. He died in 1562, leaving the guardianship of his children to Calvin.

2 Mary, daughter by a second marriage of Gérard Calvin. She had left Noyon in 1536, to follow her brothers John and Antony to Switzerland.

3 Antony Calvin had by his first wife two sons, Samuel and David, and two daughters, Anne and Susannah; by the second, a son, John, who died without posterity in 1601. and three daughters, Dorothy, Judith, and Mary, who died of the plague in 1574.

4 This David, as well as Samuel his brother, were disinherited by Antony Calvin, because of their 'disobedience.'

5 Calvin's books were purchased after his death by the Seigneury, as we see by the registers of the council, 8th July, 1564: 'Resolved to buy for the republic such of the books of Mr Calvin as Mr Beza shall judge proper.'

6 A part of Calvin's furniture belonged to the republic of Geneva, as is proved by the inventory preserved in the archives. (No. 1426.) We extract from it the list of articles lent to the Reformer, 27th December, 1548, and restored to the Seigneury after his death:

1st. A bedstead of walnut-tree wood, rough and unplaned; Item. A walnut-tree table of a square form jointed with iron; A bench turned on the lathe to correspond to this table; A buffet of walnut-tree jointed with iron; A walnut-tree wash hand stand; Another bedstead, planed by the joiner; A walnut wood chest, consolidated with iron; A high-backed chair of polished walnut tree; A square wooden table; A polished walnut-tree buffet (has not been found); A coffer buffet; A long bench turned on the lathe; Another square walnut wood table; A walnut wood bedstead; Four long tables with their trestles of fir, and another long table of walnut wood; A dozen forms good and bad (new ones given back in their stead); A desk for books.

The present furniture given back this 25th September, 1564.

the result of the sale amount to anything more, I mean that it should be distributed among my said nephews and nieces, not excluding David, if God shall have given him grace to be more moderate and staid. But I believe that on this subject there will be no difficulty, especially when my debts shall be paid, as I have given charge to my brother on whom I rely, naming him executor of this testament along with the *spectable* Laurence de Normandie, giving them all power and authority to make an inventory without any judicial forms, and sell my furniture to raise money from it in order to accomplish the directions of this testament as it is here set down in writing, this 25th April, 1564.

Witness my hand,

JOHN CALVIN.

After being written as above, at the same instant the said *spectable* Calvin undersigned with his usual signature the minute of the said testament. And the following day, which was the 26th of the month of April, the said *spectable* Calvin sent for me a second time together with *spectable* Theodore Beza, Raymond Chauvet, Michael Cop, Louis Enoch, Nicholas Coladon, Jacques Desbordes, ministers of the word of God in this church, and *spectable* Henry Seringer, professor of letters, all burgesses of Geneva, in presence of whom he declared that he had caused me to write under him, and at his dictation, the said testament in the form, and with the same words as here above, praying me to read it aloud in the presence of the said witnesses sent for and required for that purpose, which I did with an audible voice, and word for word. After which reading he declared that such was his will and last disposition, desiring that it might be observed. And for still greater confirmation of the same, begged and requested the above-mentioned persons to subscribe it along with me, which was also done on the year and day above written, at Geneva in the street called *Des chanoines*, and the dwelling house of the said testator. In faith of which, and to serve for sufficient proof, I have drawn up in the form as here above presented, the present testament, in order to expedite it to whom it may concern, under the common seal of our most honourable seigneurs and superiors and my own usual sign-manual.

Witness my hand,

P. CHENELAT.

CALVIN'S FAREWELL TO THE SEIGNEURS OF GENEVA

Taken down by the Secretary of the Republic

[Follow the words and exhortations of *spectable* John Calvin, minister of the word of God in this church spoken this day, 27th April, 1564, to our most honourable seigneurs the Syndics and Council].

First, after having thanked Messeigneurs for the trouble they had taken in coming to his house, though his wish was to have had himself carried to the town house, he declared that he has always had the desire to address them once more; and though heretofore he has been very low, nevertheless he was unwilling to hurry, inasmuch as God had not given him so precise an advertisement as he does at present.

Then after he had thanked them, because they had been pleased to do him more honour than was due to him, and to bear with him in many circumstances in which he stood in great need of their indulgence, he still considers himself so much the more obliged to the said seigneurs that they have always shown him such marks of affection, that it was impossible for them to show more. True it is that while he has resided here, he has had many combats and subjects of vexation, as no doubt all good men must be tried, yet none of these were owing to Messeigneurs. He prays them then, if he has not done what he ought to have done, that Messeigneurs will be pleased to take the will for the deed, for he has desired the good of this city, and has contributed to it, but he is far from having accomplished all his duty in respect to it. It is true he does not deny that God has made use of him as an instrument for the little he has done, and if he said otherwise he should be a hypocrite; he begs then again to be excused for having done so little in proportion to what he was bound to do, both in public and private, and he feels persuaded that Messeigneurs have borne with his natural disposition, too vehement by far, and with which he is offended, and with his other vices as God also has been.

Moreover, he protests before God and before Messeigneurs, that he has made it his endeavour to speak in purity the word which God has confided to him, making sure not to walk at random nor in error. Otherwise he should expect a condemnation on his head, not doubting, as we see, but that the devil, whose only aim is to pervert, stirs up wicked people, having the spirit of madness to aim at the same end.

For the rest, it is necessary that Messeigneurs should have a short word of exhortation. For they see in what position they are placed, and whether they fancy they shall stand in surety or shall be threatened, it behoves them always to keep in mind that God wishes to be honoured, and that he reserves to himself the right of maintaining both public states and private conditions, and wills that we do him homage, by recognizing that we are wholly dependent on him. We have an example in David, who confesses that when he was quietly settled in his kingdom, he forgot himself so far as to have stumbled mortally, if God had not had compassion upon him.

And if a man who was so excellent a . . .[1] both trembles and stumbles, what should we who are nothing feel? We shall have much occasion to humble ourselves, keeping ourselves

[1] A word is here left in blank in the registers.

concealed under the wings of God on whom should repose all our confidence. And though we are, as it were, suspended by a thread, we should trust that he will continue to protect us as in times past, since we have experienced already that he has saved us in divers ways.

If our Lord gives us prosperity, we rejoice. But when we are assailed on all sides, and it seems that there is a host of evils encompassing us, we ought not for all that to cease to have confidence in him, and how often soever, and in what manner soever we may be taken by surprise, let us know that it is God who wills to awaken us, to the end, that we may humble ourselves and take shelter under his wings.

And if we desire to be maintained in our present condition, we must beware that the seat in which we have been placed be not dishonoured; for he says he will honour those who shall honour him, and on the contrary will bring to disgrace those who shall despise him.

There is no superiority but from God, who is King of kings, and Lord of lords.

This is said in order that we may serve him in purity according to his word, and think of him more than ever. For we are very far indeed from acquitting ourselves fully of that duty, and with such integrity as we ought to do.

For the rest, he has said that all our conduct and whatever we do is open to his eyes; we stand then in great need of being exhorted.

Every one has his imperfections. It is our duty to examine them. Wherefore let each one look to himself and combat them.

Some are indifferent, absorbed by their own affairs, and but little concerned about the public good; others are given up to their passions.

Others, when God has bestowed on them a spirit of prudence, do not make use of it.

Others are wedded to their opinions, wishing to be held for

oracles, to seem something, to be in credit and reputation.

Let the old not bear envy towards the young, for the grace they may have received, but let them rejoice and bless God for having bestowed it on them.

Let the young continue to be modest, without wishing to put themselves forward too much; for there is always a boastful character in young folks, who cannot bridle themselves, and who push on in despising others.

Do not discourage one another, be not an obstacle to one another, do not make yourselves odious to one another. For when animosities are kindled, people fall off from their duty. And to avoid inconveniences, let every one walk according to his rank, and busy himself according as God has given him means to support this republic.

As to civil or criminal processes – cast from you all favour, hatred, crooked means, recommendations, and renounce all self-interest, holding by integrity and equity; and if ever you are tempted to swerve from them, resist and be firm, looking unto Him who hath established us, and praying him to conduct us by his Holy Spirit, and he will not fail us.

Finally, after having again begged to be excused and supported in his infirmities, which he will not deny (for since God and the angels know them, he will not deny them before men), and to accept with good will his small labours, he prayed God to conduct and govern us, continually increasing his grace in us, and causing it to turn to our own salvation and that of all this poor people.[1]

---

1 Whereupon, says Beza, having prayed [Messeigneurs] to forgive him all his faults which no one thought greater than himself, he held out his hand to them. I do not know if there could have happened to these seigneurs a more sad spectacle, who all with great justice considered him, in respect of his office, as the mouth of the Lord, and in respect of his affection as their father. Indeed he had known and instructed a part of them from their youth.

CALVIN'S FAREWELL TO THE MINISTERS OF GENEVA

Taken down by the minister Pinant

[On Friday, 28th April, 1564, taken down by (Pinant) and written as pronounced as nearly as the memory could preserve it word for word, though in a slightly different order with respect to some words and phrases.]

Brethren, inasmuch as I have had something to say to you, which concerns not only this church, but also several others, which in a certain manner depend on it, it will be good to begin with prayer, in order that God may give me grace to say every thing without ambition, always having a respect to his glory, and also that every one may retain and profit by what shall be said.

It may be thought that I am too precipitate in concluding my end to be drawing near, and that I am not so ill as I persuade myself; but I assure you, that though I have often felt myself very ill, yet I have never found myself in such a state, nor so weak as I am. When they take me to put me in bed, my head fails me and I swoon away forthwith. There is also this shortness of breathing, which oppresses me more and more. I am altogether different from other sick persons, for when their end is approaching their senses fail them and they become delirious. With respect to myself, true it is that I feel stupefied, but it seems to me that God wills to concentrate all my senses within me, and I believe indeed that I shall have much difficulty and that it will cost me a great effort to die. I may perhaps lose the faculty of speech, and yet preserve my sound sense; but I have also advertised my friends of that and told them what I wished them to do for me, and it is for this very reason I have desired to speak with you before God call me away; not that God may not indeed do otherwise than I think; it would be temerity on my part to wish to enter into his counsel.

When I first came to this church, I found almost nothing in it. There was preaching and that was all. They would look out for idols it is true, and they burned them. But there was no reformation. Everything was in disorder. There was no doubt the good man Master William,[1] and then blind Courant (not born blind, but he became so at Bâle). There was besides Master Antony Saulnier, [2]and that fine preacher Froment, who having laid aside his apron got up into the pulpit, then went back to his shop where he prated, and thus gave a double sermon.[3]

I have lived here amid continual bickerings. I have been from derision saluted of an evening before my door with forty of fifty shots of an arquebuse. How think you must that have astonished a poor scholar timid as I am, and as I have always been, I confess?[4]

Then afterwards I was expelled from this town and went away to Strasbourg, and when I had lived there some time I was called back hither, but I had no less trouble when I wished to discharge my duty than heretofore. They set the dogs at my heels, crying, Hère! hère![5] and these snapped at my gown and my legs. I went my way to the council of the two hundred when they were fighting, and I kept back the others who wanted to go, and who had nothing to do there; and

1 Farel.

2 Banished from Geneva in 1538, Saulnier became the minister of the Church of Morges. The date of his death is not known.

3 It is known that Froment first presented himself at Geneva as a school-master. Of a vain and inconstant spirit, he was incapable of maintaining his dignity in the glorious part of a missionary of the Reformation. In 1553 he abandoned the office of the ministry, bought the charge of a notary, and merited on more than one occasion for his inconsiderate conduct the censures of the seigneury.

4 . . . 'and repeated twice or thrice these words: I assure you I am naturally timid and fearful.' Beza, *Life of Calvin*. The same confession is several times expressed in the preface of the Commentary on the Psalms, a real autobio-graphy of the Reformer.

5 A term borrowed from hunting – a young fawn of a year old.

though they boast that it was they who did everything, like M. de Saulx,[1] yet I was there, and as I entered, people said to me, 'Withdraw, sir, we have nothing to say to you.' I replied, 'I will do no such thing – come, come, wicked men that you are; kill me, and my blood will rise up against you, and these very benches will require it.' Thus I have been amid combats, and you will experience that there will be others not less but greater. For you are a perverse and unhappy nation, and though there are good men in it the nation is perverse and wicked, and you will have troubles when God shall have called me away; for though I am nothing, yet know I well that I have prevented three thousand tumults that would have broken out in Geneva. But take courage and fortify yourselves, for God will make use of this church and will maintain it, and assures you that he will protect it.

I have had many infirmities which you have been obliged to bear with, and what is more, all I have done has been worth nothing. The ungodly will greedily seize upon this word, but I say it again that all I have done has been worth nothing, and that I am a miserable creature. But certainly I can say this, that I have willed what is good, that my vices have always displeased me, and that the root of the fear of God has been in my heart; and you may say that the disposition was good; and I pray you, that the evil be forgiven me, and if there was any good, that you conform yourselves to it and make it an example.

As to my doctrine, I have taught faithfully, and God has given me grace to write what I have written as faithfully as it was in my power. I have not falsified a single passage of the Scriptures, nor given it a wrong interpretation, to the best of my knowledge; and though I might have introduced subtle senses, had I studied subtlety, I cast that temptation under my feet and always aimed at simplicity.

1 Is it the minister Nicholas des Gallars, otherwise called M. de Saules? He was pastor in 1564 o. the church of Orleans.

I have written nothing out of hatred to any one, but I have always faithfully propounded what I esteemed to be for the glory of God.

As to our internal state, you have elected M. Beza to hold my place. Advise how to relieve him, for the charge is great, and so weighty that he might well sink under the load. But advise how to support him. Of him I know that he has a good will and will do what he can.

Let every one consider the obligation which he has not only to this church but also to the city, which you have promised to serve in adversity as well as in prosperity; thus let each keep by his vocation and not endeavour to retire from it nor enter into cabals. For when people go under ground to seek for shifts, they may say indeed that they did not reflect, and that they did aim at this or that. But let them consider the obligation that they have here contracted before God.

And study too that that there be no bickerings or sharp words among you, as sometimes biting gibes will be bandied about. This will take place, it is true, in laughing, but there will be bitterness in the heart. All that is good for nothing, and is even contrary to a Christian disposition. You should then guard against it, and live in good accord and all friendship and sincerity.

I had forgotten this point: I pray you make no change, no innovation. People often ask for novelties. Not that I desire for my own sake out of ambition that what I have established should remain, and that people should retain it without wishing for something better, but because all changes are dangerous and sometimes hurtful.

On my return from Strassburg, I composed the catechism and in haste, for I would never accept the ministry till they had taken an oath respecting these two points: namely, to preserve the catechism and discipline; and while I was writing it, they came to fetch bits of paper as big as my hand and carry them to the printing office. Though Master Peter Viret was then in this town, do you think I ever showed him a word of it? I never had leisure; I have sometimes indeed thought of putting a finishing hand to it if I had had leisure.

As to the prayers for the Sabbath I adopted the form of Strassburg, and borrowed the greater part of it. Of the other prayers, I could not take any part from that formulary, for it contained nothing of the kind; but I took the whole from the Holy Scriptures.

I was also obliged to compose a formulary of baptism when I was at Strasbourg, where people brought me the children of Anabaptists from five or six leagues off to have them baptized. I then composed this unpolished formulary, which I would not advise you, notwithstanding, to change.

The Church of (Berne)[1] has betrayed this one, and they have always feared me more than they loved me. I am desirous they should know that I died in the opinion that they feared rather than loved me, and even now they fear me more than they love me, and have always been afraid lest I should disturb them about their eucharisty.

This remark ought to have been introduced before in some place of which I have not a distinct recollection.

He made use of the aforesaid words. I have not set them down in doubt or uncertainty. I doubt not but he himself would have set them down better, and would have said more. But what I did not recollect with the most perfect distinctness I have left out. He took a courteous leave of all the brethren who shook him by the hand, one after the other, all melting into tears.

Written the 1st day of May, 1564, on the 27th day of which month he died.[2]

---

1 There is a blank space left for a word in the two narratives.

2 In the Minutes o. the Consistory of Geneva, we read these words with a simple cross † opposite to the name of Calvin: 'Gone to God, May 27th of the present year, between 8 and 9 o'clock. P. M.'